Russia's new fin de siècle

Russia's new fin de siècle
Contemporary culture between past and present

Edited by Birgit Beumers

intellect Bristol, UK / Chicago, USA

First published in the UK in 2013 by
Intellect, The Mill, Parnall Road, Fishponds, Bristol, BS16 3JG, UK

First published in the USA in 2013 by
Intellect, The University of Chicago Press, 1427 E. 60th Street,
Chicago, IL 60637, USA

A catalogue record for this book is available from the
British Library.

Cover designer: Ellen Thomas
Copy-editor: MPS Technologies
Production manager: Melanie Marshall/Tom Newman
Typesetting: Contentra Technologies

Print ISBN: 978-1-84150-730-9
ePDF ISBN: 978-1-78320-085-6
ePub ISBN: 978-1-78320-086-3

Printed and bound by Hobbs the Printers Ltd, UK

Contents

Acknowledgements   vii

Contributors' Notes   ix

Introduction: Russia's New fin de siècle: Contemporary Culture between Past and Present   1

PART I: Written Discourse   **11**

Chapter 1:   The Function of the Soviet Experience in Post-Soviet Discourse   13
Maria Litovskaya

Chapter 2:   Cycles, Continuity and Change in Contemporary Russian Culture   29
Mark Lipovetsky

Chapter 3:   Victor Pelevin and the Void   47
Meghan Vicks

Chapter 4:   From Homo Zapiens to Media Sapiens: Post-Soviet Television in Russian Fiction   65
Andrei Rogatchevski

PART II: Visual and Popular Culture   **79**

Chapter 5:   Afrika and Monroe – Post-Soviet Appropriation, East and West   81
Amy Bryzgel

Chapter 6:   Military Dandyism, Cosmism and Eurasian Imper-Art   99
Maria Engström

Chapter 7:   Sweet Dreams: Retro Imagery on Chocolate Packaging
             in Post-Soviet Russia   119
Bettina Jungen

Chapter 8:   Victory Day: Rituals and Practices of War
             Commemoration in Russia   131
Nataliya Danilova

PART III: Cinematic Culture   **153**

Chapter 9:   A Kiss for the KGB: Putin as Cinematic Hero   155
Stephen M. Norris

Chapter 10: 'Address Your Questions to Dostoevsky': Privatizing
             Punishment in Russian Cinema   175
Serguei Alex. Oushakine

Chapter 11: Freedom and Uncertainty: The Cinema of Slava Tsukerman   195
Peter Rollberg

Chapter 12: Muratova's Cinema before and after Perestroika:
             Deconstructing and Rebuilding Film Aesthetics   215
Eugénie Zvonkine

Chapter 13: The Place of Action Must Not be Changed:
             Aleksei Balabanov's St Petersburg   231
Birgit Beumers

Index   245

Acknowledgements

This book is largely the result of discussions at the International Congress of Slavists (ICCEES) in Stockholm in 2010, organized by Irina Sandomirskaya, who is the godmother of this volume.

I would like to thank all the contributors for their patience and commitment, but especially Mark Lipovetsky for his unwavering support. I would also like to thank Melanie Marshall at Intellect for her patience, competence and commitment, and especially the designers Holly Rose and Ellen Thomas who have shown again an exquisite sense of style! And a huge thank you to Tom Newman, who has competently seen through the final production process.

A Note on Transliteration: We have used Library of Congress transliteration, except where a particular spelling is widely accepted (Yeltsin, Dostoevsky) and where otherwise indicated (i.e. where a particular translation of a novel has been used for references).

Contributors' Notes

Birgit Beumers is Professor in Film Studies at Aberystwyth University. She completed her D.Phil at St Antony's College, Oxford, and taught at Bristol University's Russian Department from 1994–2012. She specializes in contemporary Russian culture and has published widely on cinema and theatre. Her most recent publications include *A History of Russian Cinema* (2009) and, with Mark Lipovetsky, *Performing Violence* (2009), as well as *Nikita Mikhalkov* (2005), *PopCulture Russia!* (2005); she has edited *24 Frames: Russia* (2007); *The Post-Soviet Russian Media* (2009, with S. Hutchings and N. Rulyova), *Alexander Shiryaev, Master of Movement* (2009, with D. Robinson and V. Bocharov), *Directory of World Cinema: Russia* (2010) and (with Nancy Condee) *The Cinema of Alexander Sokurov* (2011). She is currently working on Russian animation. She is editor of the online quarterly *KinoKultura* and of the scholarly journal *Studies in Russian and Soviet Cinema* that appears thrice a year.

Amy Bryzgel received her PhD in Art History from Rutgers University in 2008, and has been a Lecturer in History of Art at the University of Aberdeen since 2009. Her research is focused on performance art from East-Central Europe and Russia. She has published a book titled *Performing the East: Performance Art in Russia, Latvia and Poland since 1980* (2013), which presents case studies of performance artists working both before and after the dissolution of the Soviet Union. Her work aims to nuance current understandings of contemporary performance art, by considering the genre as it developed within Eastern Europe. She has also just completed a monograph of the Latvian painter and performance artist, Miervaldis Polis.

Nataliya Danilova holds a PhD in Politics and International Relations from the University of Nottingham. Her academic interests include civil-military relations, politics of war memory and commemoration in Britain, Russia and in the United States. She is currently working on the international politics of commemoration in post-conflict societies. She also holds a degree in Sociology and served as Lecturer in Sociology at the National Research University Higher School of Economics (St Petersburg Campus). She currently holds a postdoctoral fellowship at the Centre for Advanced Studies at the University of Nottingham. She has published on veterans' politics in Russia, civil-military relations and war memory of post-Soviet conflicts.

Maria Engström has studied Russian philology at the Moscow State University in 1988–91 and gained a PhD in Slavic languages at Stockholm University in 2004. She held a research fellowship from Swedish Research Council in 2005–07. Her research has also been supported by grants from Helge Ax:son Johnson Foundation, Birgit and Gad Rausing Foundation for Humanistic Research and Magnus Bergvall Foundation. She has taught Russian language, literature and cultural history at Stockholm University, Uppsala University, Dalarna University, Södertörn University College and Stockholm School of Economics. Since 2012 she is Head of Russian at the School of Languages and Media at Dalarna University. Engström's current research examines the post-Soviet conservative intellectual milieu and explores cultural manifestation of identity in contemporary Russia.

Bettina Jungen earned her doctoral degree in 2005 at Zurich University with a dissertation about Soviet sculptor Vera Mukhina. She taught courses on European, American and Russian art at the universities of Zurich and Basel and schools for continued education. Bettina published about Russian and Soviet art. Her research interests include sculpture, Russian art of the nineteenth, twentieth and twenty-first centuries and popular visual culture. Since 2009 she is the curator of Russian art at the Mead Art Museum at Amherst College, Massachusetts.

Mark Lipovetsky is a literary critic and culture historian. He is Professor of Russian Studies at the University of Colorado-Boulder (USA). In 1996 he defended one of the first doctoral dissertations on the topic of post-modernism. Lipovetsky is the author of eight books and co-editor of seven volumes on Russian literature and culture. Among his monographs are *Russian Postmodernist Fiction: Dialogue with Chaos* (1999), *Modern Russian Literature: 1950s–1990s* (in Russian, co-authored with his father Naum Leiderman, 2001), *Paralogies: Transformation of (Post)modernist Discourse in Russian Culture of the 1920s–2000s* (in Russian, 2008), *Performing Violence: Literary and Theatrical Experiments of New Russian Drama* (2009, with Birgit Beumers; in Russian, 2012) and *Charms of Cynical Reason: The Transformations of the Trickster Trope in Soviet and Post-Soviet Culture* (2011). Co-edited volumes include *Dictionary of Literary Biography: Russian Writers Since 1980* (2003), an anthology of Russian and Soviet wonder-tales (2005) and Russian twentieth-century short stories (2011), *Jolly Little Characters: Cult Heroes of the Soviet Childhood* (in Russian, 2008), and *Non-Canonical Classic: Dmitri A. Prigov* (in Russian, 2010). His works have been nominated for Russian Little Booker Prize (1997) and shortlisted for the Andrey Bely Prize (2008). From 2009–12, Lipovetsky served on the jury for Russian Literary Prize NOS (2011–12 as chair).

Maria Litovskaya is professor of Russian literature of the twentieth and twenty-first centuries at the Ural Federal University. She is the author of books on Valentin Kataev (*Feniks poet pered solntsem: Fenomen Valentina Kataeva*, 1999), on contemporary mass literature (co-authored, 2009), and has written numerous articles on the history of Russian literature of the twentieth century. She has edited volumes of articles on Russian women (*Russkaia zhenshchina*, 1998, 1999, 2000, 2001); on 'Boys and Girls: realities of socialisation' (2004), as well as an almanac on children's literature (*Detskie chteniia*, 2012) and textbooks on literature.

Stephen M. Norris is professor of History at Miami University (OH), where he is also a faculty associate at the Havighurst Center for Russian and Post-Soviet Studies. His teaching and research interests are in modern Russian history, with a focus on visual culture since 1800. His first book, *A War of Images: Russian Popular Prints, Wartime Culture, and National Identity, 1812–1945* (2006), examines the *lubok* and how it served as an important medium for articulating Russian nationhood. His second book, *Blockbuster History in the New Russia: Movies, Memory, and Patriotism* (2012), traces a similar story after communism, arguing that recent Russian historical films sparked a revival of nationalist and patriotic sentiments. Norris is also the co-editor of three books: *Preserving Petersburg: History, Memory, Nostalgia* (with Helena Goscilo, 2008); *Insiders and Outsiders in Russian Cinema* (with Zara Torlone, 2008); and *Russia's People of Empire: Life Stories from Eurasia, 1500–Present* (with Willard Sunderland, 2012). He is presently working on a biography of the Soviet caricaturist Boris Efimov (1900–2008).

Serguei Alex. Oushakine teaches Anthropology and Slavic Studies at Princeton University. His research interests lie in several areas and disciplines. As an anthropologist, he works in Eurasia, where he explores how the collapse of state socialism has simultaneously undermined already existing communities and precipitated the emergence of new ones. In his award-winning book, *The Patriotism of Despair: Nation, War, and Loss in Russia*, Oushakine traces the importance of experienced or imagined traumas for creating post-socialist identities and meanings. He also studies cultural representations of identities that emerge at the intersection of gender, nation and law by writing about male bandits in Russian cinema and female detectives in Russian prose. His new areas of research focus on postcolonial authoritarianism in Belarus and Kyrgyzstan, the practices of late Soviet consumption, the political mobilization of popular culture in Soviet Russia and the history of Russian formalism and constructivism.

Andrei Rogatchevski is a graduate of Moscow State University (1988) and in 1998 completed his PhD at the University of Glasgow, where he is currently the Russian Programme Director. He also studied at the Charles University in Prague and the University of West Bohemia in Pilsen. He has taught at the University of Helsinki, Masaryk University in Brno, University of Ostrava, University of Mainz/Germersheim, University of Ghent, and held a research post at Uppsala University. Among the publications he has (co-)authored or (co-)edited are: *Bribery and Blat in Russia: Negotiating Reciprocity from the Middle Ages to the 1990s* (2000), *A Biographical and Critical Study of the Russian Writer Eduard Limonov* (2003), *Filming the Unfilmable: Casper Wrede's 'One Day in the Life of Ivan Denisovich'* (2010) and a special issue of *Canadian-American Slavic Studies* (2–4, 1999) titled 'East and Central European Émigré Literatures: Past, Present – and Future?'

Peter Rollberg is professor of Slavic Languages, Film Studies, and International Affairs at George Washington University in Washington D.C. In 1988, he earned his PhD in Russian Literature from the University of Leipzig. In 1990–91, he taught at Duke University in Durham, North Carolina. Among his English, German and Russian publications are articles on Pushkin, Dostoevskii, Nabokov, Bulgakov, Prishvin, Makanin and Anatolii Kim. In 2009, he published *Historical Dictionary of Russian and Soviet Cinema*, which appeared in paperback as *The A to Z of Russian and Soviet Cinema* (2010). He was Director of the GW Film Studies Program in 2000–10, and currently is Director of the Institute for European, Russian, and Eurasian Studies (IERES).

Meghan Vicks holds her PhD in Comparative Literature from the University of Colorado in Boulder. Her dissertation, *Narratives of Nothing in Twentieth-Century Literature*, analyses the relationship between nothingness and narrative in the works of Samuel Beckett, Nikolai Gogol, Herman Melville, Vladimir Nabokov and Victor Pelevin. She has previously published on Vladimir Nabokov, and is a lecturer of Russian literature in the Department of Germanic and Slavic Languages and Literatures at CU Boulder.

Eugénie Zvonkine is senior lecturer in cinema at the University of Paris 8. She has programmed Central Asian films for various festivals for many years: she has curated Kazakh Retrospectives at AsiaticaFilmMediale in 2005 and, covering films from 1938–2011, for the Asian Film Festival in Vesoul, France. She regularly presents papers on Central Asian cinema at national and international conferences and has written articles and reviews for *KinoKultura*. Her PhD thesis on Kira Muratova led to article publications (among others, in *Studies in Russian and Soviet Cinema*) and has appeared as monograph with the title *Kira Mouratova un Cinema de la Dissonance* (2012).

Introduction

Russia's New fin de siècle: Contemporary Culture between Past and Present

Birgit Beumers

The term fin de siècle is usually applied to the period of the turn of the nineteenth century, a period doomed by a sense of the end of an era and of crisis before a new age. For artists of Russia's Silver Age[1] it was also a time of looking towards the East for inspiration.

The end of the twentieth century caused a sense of worry mainly for computer scientists, concerned with the Y2K issue, which did not lead to the expected meltdown of technology; nor did the world come to an end on 21 December 2012, the last day accounted for in the Mayan calendar. However, the reorganization of the geopolitical landscape after the demise of communism led to a collapse of one set of political beliefs that would be replaced by a completely different value system. This, along with the global economic crisis, created a sense of insecurity about political, social, economic and cultural strategies that bore some resemblance to the concerns that prevailed at the turn of the nineteenth century.

For Russian culture, the collapse of the Soviet state brought with it the loss of the 'Soviet' identity and the search for a new identity, often looking back at the imperial past. The return to the Soviet and imperial past speaks also of the inability to create a brand new identity without reflecting on tradition and heritage, echoed in the label for the historical period as 'post-Soviet', which expresses anxiety about the past and about tradition: a desire to be other than Soviet but to show simultaneously a sense of belonging to that past, a dichotomy between what is 'ours' and what is 'other' that Lev Gudkov (2004) has defined as a typical marker for Russian culture. It is this paradoxical and ambivalent relationship to the Soviet past that stands at the centre of this collection: the consideration of the past with a sense of pride for the power and authority of the Soviet Empire, which seems decadent and vulgar in the face of the atrocities of Stalinism and the violence exercised by the Soviet state; and the search for an imperial rather than national identity, as has been observed in Nancy Condee's work on Russian cinema (2009).

The cover image for this volume shows the collapse of key architectural symbols of both imperial periods, the Russian and the Soviet one: the bas-reliefs of the Triumphal Arch in Moscow,[2] built to commemorate imperial Russia's victory over Napoleon, lay dismantled in the courtyard of the Museum of Architecture, while the hotel Moscow,[3] the pride of Stalinist architecture was being pulled down, only to be rebuilt according to the old design but with a new interior. Great history had been demoted to back-street culture, its symbols relegated to museums and cemeteries of monuments, like the park of sculptures behind the new building of the Tretyakov Gallery by the Moscow River. At the turn of this century, the imperial past was taken down to be rewritten, rebuilt and redesigned. This objective can be traced through a range of cultural disciplines, from rewriting the Soviet discourse in literature to re-imagining Soviet symbols, from privatizing public spaces and practices to rebuilding objects, as the chapters in this collection show.

Both the Soviet and the imperial past have been dismantled and reassessed in recent cultural output, but while the Soviet identity has played an active part in the creation of new definitions, the imperial past has been preserved and relegated to museums, turned into an object for contemplation. Contemporary culture hovers between past and present, unable to address the present alone. If the 1990s have been governed by an attempt to look for values and national identity in the imperial past, then the 2000s veer towards a return to Soviet values, without reinstating them as positive and desirable or idealizing the Soviet past, but perceiving the Soviet era both as a traumatic experience and at the same time inspiring nostalgia. Indeed, if we look at the political changes in the 'zeroes' and beyond, the rigidity introduced into political governance speaks of a centralized rule that is accused of vote-rigging and corruption, and challenged by the 'protest movement' (*protestnoe dvizhenie*) that grew out of the allegedly fraudulent parliamentary elections in December 2011.

If the fin de siècle at the turn of the nineteenth and twentieth centuries looked for answers towards the East, at the Orient, at the Other, then at the turn of the twentieth and twenty-first centuries the Other is no longer an attractive alternative to the Self, but an enemy. The Orient is perceived as dangerous: it is the land of the undesirable and poverty-stricken *gastarbeiter*, of violence and war, of religious fanaticism. In all this, the safe haven of the Soviet past offers stability in the chaos, especially of the Yeltsin years, but is also seen as a somewhat better society than the capitalist and globalization excesses of western societies where the masses tend to suffer at the expenses of the ruling elite.

The return to realism (or, as Mark Lipovetsky puts it in his chapter, the shift from complex to simple forms), underscoring the non-fictional mode, is signalled in the twenty-first century by the rise of documentary cinema and theatre. The works of teatr.doc, of the playwrights of New Drama and of the new wave of Russian film-makers are indicative of this minimalism in artistic devices that stands in sharp contrast to (and rejection of) the increasing glamorization of culture and society. Through this deliberate rejection of celebrity and glamour, to use the title of Helena Goscilo and Vlad Strukov's excellent collection of essays on the topic (2011), the decadence of that world becomes obvious: whether this is in the popular adulation of the figure of Vladimir Putin (see Goscilo 2013), the scandalous yet media-attractive behaviour of Kseniia Sobchak, the fake monumentality of Zurab Tsereteli or the grotesque father-image of Nikita Mikhalkov, as discussed in the above-mentioned collection; or whether this is through the official support lent to Vladimir Putin by many of the country's cultural elite (including actors Evgenii Mironov and Chulpan Khamatova, but also the provocative artist Sergei Bugaev 'Afrika') and the elevation of the empty lifestyle of the 'New Russians' featuring in the works of Sergei Minaev and Oksana Robskii – such acts and works expose what is repulsive, ethically wrong and morally condemnable in a manner that is aesthetically pleasant. This pattern of attraction and repulsion gives rise to a range of façades and masks that cover corruption and collapse: kitschy and iconic images of the president repeat the forced veneration of Soviet leaders while assimilating the commercial branding of public and celebrity figures in capitalist cultures. Julia Kristeva argues that the concept of the abject always hides (or uncovers) the horror before the self: the abject is the 'fear of the subject before its own identity' (1982: 5).

Yet many artists are engaged in social and political struggle, making their art works statements against the (political, social or cultural) establishment. In their style, these works are often repulsive, unflattering, vulgar: they live a deliberately decadent life – and in this way form a 'new' manifestation of a fin de siècle culture: not suggesting any future in this world, they turn to cosmism, mysticism and spirituality; rejecting any Utopia, they state depression, stagnation, resignation – in the sense disavowing any responsibility for the present. The actions of the anarchist art group Voina (awarded the innovation prize by the Ministry of Culture in April 2011) with their action of a phallus painted on the Liteinyi Drawbridge in St Petersburg in June 2010 or their overturning and arson attack of a police vehicle in December 2011; or of the rock group Pussy Riot with its 'punk prayer' on the soleas of the Cathedral of Christ the Saviour in Moscow on 21 February 2012 have highlighted not only the politically and socially provocative behaviour of protest groups, but also the complexities of their anarchic behaviour and refusal to be part of society, as is impressively and sensitively highlighted in Andrei Griazev's documentary *Zavtra/Tomorrow* (2012).

Many of the cinematic, artistic and literary works of the late twentieth and early twenty-first century share a concern with the void behind the mask or the façade: artists often understand perfectly well that reality is nothing but a display, a demonstration and a staged performance. Everyday life is the performance of a routine, where the reality seems to stand next to the invented set of roles and rituals that man performs. This situation is finely captured in Sergei Mokritskii's film *Den' uchitelia/ Protest Day* (2012), which captures the life of Afanasii Derkach, a teacher of Russian literature, who lives on his own, has separated from his wife, is estranged from his child and has to care for his elderly mother. He leads a life full of routines and void of any social function. On the way he runs onto the protests on Bolotnaia Square (which took place in December 2011, February and May 2012) and stands estranged from the action (for a fine review see Boele 2013). If the intelligentsia was the think-tank of social reform during the Soviet era, in present-day Russia it has lost its meaning, its role and its touch with the political reality entirely. It is a new generation of bloggers and social networkers that has taken the leading role and become the driving force of social change, reforms and protests. It is this shift in society, which has left a generation of educated people alienated and marginalized, that also contributes to a sense of an 'end of' a phase of social development.

The fin de siècle was doomed by pessimism, boredom and cynicism for the new era and artistic works governed by decadence, in the sense that the artifice ruled over description and realism, as we see perfectly in the works of Oscar Wilde and Audrey Beardsley, where ornamentation covers evil and violence, and an artistic portrait replaces a human being. If we apply these features – decadence, void, artifice – to Russian culture of the late 1990s and early 2000s, we may find a different, more universal explanation for the preoccupation with the (Soviet) past that governs Russian culture. Elements of the degeneration that announced a storm before the new age, that celebrated decay and that paved the way for a new modernity can also be found in contemporary Russian culture, which is engaged in the process of covering the void with glamour or, to the contrary, stripping the covers from the meaninglessness of the modern age through anarchic action. The contributions in this volume suggest a strategy of laying bare the meaninglessness and the non-real qualities of contemporary society, and of playfully engaging with the void.

This volume, then, explores Russian culture at the turn of the twentieth and twenty-first centuries, hovering between identities of Soviet and Russian, Europe and Asia, past and present/future, in an attempt to position itself in the here-and-now and in the context of global media. The contributions explore different aspects of culture – literature, visual arts, everyday culture and cinema – with regard to one overarching question: what is the impact of the 'Soviet' discourse on contemporary culture, at a time when Russia seems to integrate itself into European trends in arts and culture whilst enhancing its uniqueness, its orthodoxy and strong role of the church in the country's cultural and political life. Thus, the contributions investigate the phenomenon of 'post'-Soviet and try to define the relationship of contemporary art to the past, and ask questions about the reasons for this preoccupation with the Soviet era.

The book is divided into three parts, which investigate the return to old values as manifestations of decadence. The first part offers four approaches to contemporary Russian literature, exploring its trends in terms of the writers' engagement with the past and studying the reasons for a return to the Soviet tradition as trauma, as an act of remembrance and as a platform for an escape from reality; in all these ways, they are symptomatic of the loss of literature's (and the writers') role in contemporary society. Maria Litovskaya discusses the function of the Soviet experience in post-Soviet discourse. The values and stereotypes, texts and images of Soviet culture – in their historical development and in transformations – have become the subject for philosophical, ethical and sociological analysis in post-Soviet literature, recycling Socialist Realist patterns and deconstructing the authoritative Soviet system. Yet this partial nostalgia expresses no desire to return to the Soviet past, but simply to remember it. Mark Lipovetsky contests the traditional binary opposition on which readings of Russian culture hinge, suggesting instead continuities. Against this backdrop of the contemporary literary scene, the following chapters examine the ways in which Russian writers shy away from reality and invent worlds that resemble the contemporary world only. In her analysis of Victor Pelevin's novels Meghan Vicks finds a lack of meaning that is playfully covered, while Andrei Rogatchevski explores the role of mass media in contemporary Russian fiction, drawing on a range of author of different political views, from Victor Pelevin to Aleksandr Prokhanov, from Boris Akunin and Dmitrii Bykov to Sergei Minaev. These blurred borders between media reality and reality raises questions about the moral integrity of media professionals and about modern man's addiction to television.

The second part concerns visual culture and focuses on visual arts: artist engage on the one hand with the Soviet past in an attempt to reflect upon their relationship to a history they never experienced first-hand, on the other they echo the fragmentation and decomposition in order to give an impulse towards rebuilding, reconstruction. The end of the century highlights the instability of perception and insecurity of the artist, convinced only of his own techniques.

In the 1990s several underground art groups emerged in the two capitals; they significantly shaped the contemporary art scene. Amy Bryzgel explores the works of Afrika and Mamyshev-Monroe, who deal in different ways with the loss of Soviet identity: Sergei Bugaev 'Afrika' by replacing Soviet symbols with new, Russian ones; and Vladislav Mamyshev-Monroe, who turns himself into a symbol by taking on the guise of Marilyn Monroe and re-creating through montage the grand Stalinist musical films, impersonating the 1930s film star Liubov' Orlova. Maria Engström investigates the work of Aleksei Beliaev-Gintovt, the chief exponent of imper-art, a neo-conservative movement which draws on Eurasianism, mysticism, dandyism, while admiring the vital force of the masculine body as displayed in military and Soviet art. The combination in imper-art of spiritual values with a fascination for military and conservative imperialism highlights the overlapping of binaries which Lipovetsky finds in literary practice, while Bryzgel's analysis highlights the emptiness of the Soviet tradition that is being literally clothed by performances of identity. In popular culture, a similar process of window-dressing can be observed: Bettina Jungen looks at the change in chocolate packaging in post-Soviet Russia. During the 1990s designers turned back to the late nineteenth century rather than images of the Soviet era. The post-Soviet market displays Russian cultural myths and a mixture of old and new concepts of cultural hierarchies. Nataliya Danilova explores the practices of war commemoration in post-Soviet Russia, discussing new trends driven by political, economic and social transformations related to globalization. She demonstrates that the ceremonies and official acts of commemoration are a rehearsed display.

The third part explores cinematic culture. In cinema, we observe film-makers dwelling on the alienation of man from his surroundings and an increasing marginalisation, shown in locations that never change, but are depleted. Serguei Oushakine looks at *samosud*, or justice from below, in recent films such as *Voroshilovskii strelok/ Voroshilov Sniper* (1999) and *Elena* (2011), as well as the staged events of the art group Voina. Oushakine observes a shift from the normative vacuum of the 1990s to a set of fragmented communities and groups bound by local versions of justice and truth. Random distributions of violence are replaced by motivated acts of revenge and self-exercised trials. Stephen Norris explores the popular image of the Soviet hero on screen and demonstrates how it is used as a template for the media image of Vladimir Putin in the film *A Kiss for the Press*. In both instances, voids are being filled by cult images in a manner reminiscent of the political non-reality in Pelevin's *Generation 'P'*. The following three chapters in this part are devoted to the oeuvre of three individual film-makers with different fates and career paths that bridge Soviet and Russian culture. Peter Rollberg looks at the artistic evolution of Slava Tsukerman, a film-maker who opposed the Soviet system and left the country in the early 1970s to forge a new identity in the West, while developing an increasingly complex and contradictory attitude toward Soviet culture after 1991. Eugénie Zvonkine explores two films of Kira Muratova from the Soviet and post-Soviet era to highlight the film-maker's concern with the loss of identity that is embedded in her films even before the collapse of the Soviet Union and to show the disintegration of national and social structures in the context of a larger, more humanistic tradition. I conclude the volume with a chapter on Aleksei Balabanov, who is one of the few film-makers to repeatedly depict St Petersburg on screen: the city never changes its face, whether the films are set in the first or last years of the twentieth century. Balabanov challenges the centrality of the city and suggests an empty centre, focusing instead on outskirts and emptied streets in an attempt to suggest a move from centre to periphery, and with it the increasing marginalisation of social groups formerly belonging to the centre. Balabanov's oeuvre thus offers a diagnosis of social, political and artistic developments of Russian cinema at the end of the twentieth century.

In covering a range of disciplines, the volume hopes to make visible the parallel developments in visual, popular and literary works of the new Russia, which experiences a new fin de siècle only to emerge, it would seem, with a new face and a new identity: one that is no utopian or ideological construct, but a deliberately donned, refined and decorated stage mask – that can be changed and that can be lifted, that can true or false, that can lie in a courtyard among other façade fragments or be pulled down, only to be worn again.

Works cited

Boele, Otto (2013), 'Sergei Mokritskii: Protest Day', *KinoKultura* 39, http://www.kinokultura. com/2013/39r-protestday.html. Accessed 3 January 2013,

Condee, Nancy (2009), *The Imperial Trace. Recent Russian Cinema*, New York: Oxford University Press.

Goscilo, Helena (ed.) (2013), *Putin as Celebrity and Cultural Icon*, London and New York: Routledge.

Goscilo, Helena and Vlad Strukov (eds) (2011), *Celebrity and Glamour in contemporary Russia*, London and New York: Routledge.

Gudkov, Lev (2004), *Negativnaia identichnost'*, Moscow: NLO.

Kristeva, Julia (1982), *Powers of Horror. An Essay on Abjection*. New York: Columbia University Press.

Notes

1   A term applied to Russian culture and literature of the period from 1900–1920, which was particularly rich in poetry and set itself apart from the Golden Age in the first half of the nineteenth century. It is, in this sense, synonymous with the term fin de siècle applied to European culture of the same period.

2   The Triumphal Arch in Moscow was designed by Joseph Bové to commemorate the Russian victory over Napoleon in 1812 and built between 1827 and 1834. It was dismantled in 1936 in the context of Stalin's plans for the reconstruction of Moscow. In 1968 a new Triumphal Arch was built to Bove's plans on Victory Square (*Ploshchad' pobedy*). The original ornaments were stored in the Shchusev Museum of Architecture in Moscow.

3   The hotel Moskva opened in 1935 and was built to the plans of Aleksei Shchusev. It was demolished in 2004 and reconstructed to the original plans with its asymmetrical façade with two different avant-corps in 2012.

PART I

Written Discourse

Chapter 1

The Function of the Soviet Experience in Post-Soviet Discourse

Maria Litovskaya

The 'Soviet', whether we understand it as ideology or concrete social practice, is obviously a major cultural component of the contemporary social space in Russia. Twenty years have passed since the disintegration of the USSR. During this time, society at large and the individual who makes it up have gone through periods of euphoria, disappointment, hope, bewilderment and discontent. A new generation has grown up that has never seen Soviet rule. Many people who embodied the previous era have died. Many aspects of everyday life have drastically changed and the social structure has changed. However, despite these changes, Russia is still often referred to as a 'post-Soviet' society. This definition is symptomatic, because nobody in 1936 would have called Soviet society post-Tsarist or post-autocratic. The term 'Soviet' alone was quite sufficient, while the history of imperial Russia was the subject of academic interest, and used for propaganda purposes or personal memoirs.

If in the middle of 1990 Russian citizens (at least publicly) were divided distinctly into those who mourned and those who hated everything Soviet, while – gripped by the realities of a new life, actually little was said about the Soviet experience, then in modern Russia we witness the heyday of the recent past. It is sufficient to go into any Russian bookshop to see racks of books about the events of the Civil or Second World Wars, the collectivization or the space project or the Lenin-Stalin-Khrushchev-Brezhnev era. The radio and television programmes of the 'serious' channels are full of transmissions (both neutral and also admittedly controversial) about the Soviet past. Their number increases before significant historical dates for Soviet society, such as the 65th anniversary of the Victory over Fascism or the 50th anniversary of the first space flight. Finally, the popularity of historical (Soviet) themes in society and the ambiguity of their coverage are indirectly confirmed by the fact that the falsification of history has been declared a state problem,[1] obviously in the first instance concerning recent Soviet history.

Simultaneously with the quantitative growth of texts about the 'Soviet' experience, the range of evaluations of this past changed.[2] Today, even superficial surfing across sites of the Russian Internet shows the popularity of forums, blogs and bloggers,[3] who quite professionally, i.e., with an understanding of the opportunity of various interpretations of the facts, discuss aspects of Soviet history. An important factor of published academic works and sites is the description of Soviet practices and politics, whether this concerns the relationship between ideology and the everyday, the designing of rules and norms or the functioning of memory of the Soviet experience in a contemporary space.[4] As a result, on the one hand, these general efforts show the multifaceted nature of this phenomenon; on the other, there is a consecutive deconstruction of Soviet practices, which ultimately strips the Soviet experience of its demonic qualities as well as the conspiracy-charm inherent in its image, for example in 'dissident' literature.

Values, stereotypes, texts and images of Soviet culture are the subject for reflection of a broad layer of the population, and also for analysis not only of social scientists (researchers and academics), but also – in the Russian tradition – by social scientists-turned writers, artists or film-makers. The list of books which have received literary awards in 2009 makes apparent the increasing tendency of 'historicization'.[5] At first sight, such a tendency can be attributed to nostalgia. But even at first sight it is clear that it would be difficult to unequivocally assess this phenomenon in post-Soviet culture as an interpretation – even sympathetic – of the Soviet past just as 'nostalgic'. This phenomenon requires differentiation, because texts of different types are characterized by a varied zeal for diverse approaches to Soviet history and its modern interpretations.

The rehabilitating approach to the Soviet past is, above all, characteristic for the policies of state television channels. The state policy on the representation of the Soviet past is more or less clear. In the modern (not only Russian) world the demand for a return to the past has become the source of a rapid growth of the 'heritage industry', that well-developed sphere of media activity which aims at the effective visualization of history, allowing it to be turned into some kind of consumer good. In Russia such a theatricalization of 'our past' is generated regularly on the level of advertising, serials, television shows such as *Kakie nashi gody/These Were Our Years*, where a certain 'glamourization' of the Soviet past is achieved through one-sided reduction (see Shaburova 2009: 33–44).

The television channels offer the modern Russian spectator above all a well-censored idealized version of the past, where blemishes (or shortcomings, depending on the script) of the Soviet system are resisted by collectivism, mutual responsibility, patriotism, spirituality and heartfulness. Such texts reconstitute patriarchal relations, which society has considered lost but genuine and worthy, thus creating the basis for a regulated and predictable (with all its shortcomings) world of the past. Paradoxically this happens even with the scripts of serials built around the exposures of the official Soviet version of history (e.g., *V kruge pervom/ In the First Circle*; *Deti Arbata/Children of the Arbat*, *Moskovskaia saga/Moscow Saga*), not to mention texts obviously based on the idealization of the 'communal' past (e.g., *Sinie nochi/Blue Nights*, *Gromovy/The Gromovs*). Socially weak characters who have not lost their humanity despite the complexities of Soviet history form the basis for a nostalgic perception, and thus manipulate and stimulate the direction of nostalgia. This allows the spectators, who identify with the heroes, to experience afresh the feeling of belonging to the Soviet experience, perceiving their contemporaries as post-Soviet people without a feeling of shame.

At the same time the history of the Soviet period conceals many explosive themes, which give rise to a different sort of exposure and the formation of a 'repressive history' of Russia. This version, almost absent from television because of the 'falsification' component, is developed first of all in the space of Internet publications and non-fiction literature. It focuses on several themes connected with the problem of Stalinism. A similar – criminatory or revelatory – use of the Soviet experience is, on the one hand, characteristic of historical essays devoted to the disclosure of new secrets of Soviet history; on the other hand, it is typical of journalistic and publicistic essays, which see all the problems of modern Russia precisely in its Soviet heritage and instil in the country's population a sense of guilt for the past.

Although on the level of popular culture the attitudes to the Soviet past remain polarized, even this sphere of cultural activity sees ambivalent attitudes.[6] The further Russian society moves away from 1991, the less frequent become one-sided references that accuse or ridicule the Soviet experience. This also concerns research texts devoted to the deconstructive description of Soviet cultural policies and the rewriting of Soviet cultural history. The reference to the recent past more and more frequently includes both the representation of the negative experience and the attachment of a certain symbolical capital to the Soviet concept.[7] We mean here not the Soviet past and its research as such, but the use of facts or images concerning this experience in order to regulate certain moods in modern Russian society.[8] At the same time, the sense that the Soviet experience is prone to oblivion is omnipresent in society, including the demand to record its details, which is implemented in particular in numerous Internet-projects, such as sovietlife, sovietsongs and other sites on the Soviet everyday.

These tendencies are connected with the specific position of the Soviet past in post-Soviet space. One may argue that the Soviet past is a past like any other. The popular biographies of Boris Pasternak and Bulat Okudzhava written by Dmitrii Bykov, of Mikhail Prishvin, Aleksei Tolstoi and Mikhail Bulgakov written by Aleksei Varlamov, of Leonid Leonov written by Zakhar Prilepin at first sight differ little, say, from the biography of Anton Chekhov by Donald Rayfield, but the disputes around them are of a personal nature, where 'big history' corresponds to family and autobiography. Valerii Todorovskii's film *Stiliagi/Hipsters* (2008), made in the style of a musical, did not surmise a dispute about the credibility of Soviet reality of the second half of the 1950s which it represented, but precisely this aspect was most heatedly discussed among audiences and critics.

The turn to the past happens for different reasons, mostly because the original cult of the past is an organic consequence of the progress of modernity. The constant change of the conditions of life, which has become a normal condition of societies of the modern times, evoke in people the desire to return to more habitual and 'organic' past times, which can be described as 'good, old' and even ideal. But, as Etkind remarks, even in the 'ideal' case

modernization is a painful and traumatic process; some lose, others gain, almost everybody simultaneously loses and gains [...] People respond to traumas with fantasies, nostalgic and other, which should be understood and not condemned [...] This convenient and large, global narrative blurs distinctions between the feelings of the Russian intelligent, whose father was killed in the Gulag and whose children became alcoholics during the stagnation, whose savings disappeared during perestroika and, at last, whose culture – making sense of these events, was destroyed in the last decade, and the feelings of an Indian peasant, a French townsman, and an American house owner, who cannot hold at bay the global competition, lose their usual sources of income [...] Everybody is bad off (but when was it good?); but for everybody it's bad in different ways [...] The economy is irreversibly globalized, while culture answers with particularisation; whence arise problems that differ everywhere. The originality of the post-Soviet moment lies in its Soviet past.

(Lipovetskii and Etkind 2008)

The Soviet past can hardly be called ideal: few Russians would contest that. Endemic to texts of different sizes and genres about the Soviet experience created by former Soviet citizens with a greater or smaller degree of expressiveness are the authors' attempts first 'to get even' with the personal experience, i.e., to give an estimation of the country leaning on the experience where they lived and where their heroes lived; and second, to offer their version of the general concept of interaction between man and the Soviet state.

As Slavoj Žižek remarks, the interest in the past in modern post-socialist societies is usually explained by the 'immaturity' of the expectation of people who dreamt of 'another life', without imagining what, for example, capitalism meant: the inhabitants of the socialist camp wanted the capitalist democratic freedom while simultaneously preserving the guaranteed stability of socialism. When the people in the countries of Eastern Europe protested against communist regimes, the majority dreamt not of capitalism as a form of social organization, but about material prosperity and equity. They wanted to live outside rigid state control, beyond the primitive ideological brainwash and hypocrisy. When the lofty ideals of the Velvet Revolution were dispelled by a new reality, people reacted in different ways. The most natural expression of post-communist disappointment has been nostalgia for 'the good old times', which we should not take too seriously, since the desire to return to the grey and poor socialist reality is hardly genuine. Rather, 'it is a form of mourning, of gently getting rid of the past' (Žižek 2009). However, in the case of Russia, the mourning is complicated by an understanding that the Soviet experience – deprived of some of its important features – continues to exist.

On the one hand, a significant portion of modern post-Soviet society is composed of people who have spent part of their life in the USSR. In the state that exists no longer, they underwent their socialization process, and they became – many not of their own will – citizens of another country with essentially different rules and living conditions. For the majority, the massive changes implemented by the state were traumatic, and the condition of modern Russian society is in many respects the result of this trauma. Moreover, 'that country' (as Russia is called by its citizens) – did not enthuse many, and for quite different reasons.[9] On the other hand, according to Leonid Parfenov

before our eyes a certain third state has emerged: not the Soviet Union, of course, but also not Russia in the historical sense. We live in a country that should correctly be called post-Soviet Russia. In fact, the majority of people consider only the Soviet past its own. We have no mental link with imperial Russia. Well, just figure who of our compatriots would distinguish Alexander II from Alexander III?! The majority of Russians today serve in the army in Soviet style, they receive their education in institutes in the Soviet way, they are treated in hospitals in the Soviet way, they choose those in power, watch television and do lot of other things.

(Parfenov 2009: 4)

Addressing the same theme, Dmitrii Bykov emphasizes the paradox of the Russian perception of past and present:

The Fatherland has got used to failures and to the contrary, and we willingly weep for them. We are a very nostalgic people. We look, stooping our old shoulders, like the three-rouble sausage, like *The Pub '13 Chairs'* of the stagnation era[10] – and we weep, but back then we all spat! Where else can people despise and spit on something one day, and turn it into a gem the next? Either our life gets worse, or we do not like ourselves as we are: but life without a nostalgic flair always reminds us of the plague. We are sick of everything. But very soon, we might be weeping for everything.

(Bykov 2009)

The understanding that modern Russians live inside Soviet heritage and that this induces them to correlate an often contradictory knowledge of history with family and personal memory has gradually become a common phrase and enriches the notion of emotional links to previous epochs. Those who left Russia, in turn, construct their narrative about the ambiguous reasons that led them to make their choice. The first decade of the new millennium, when the first emotions about the disintegration of the Soviet state had subsided, saw a wide consideration of the Soviet experience not only through groundless denial or, to the contrary, absolute acceptance of the Soviet past, but also through the realization that condemnation/nostalgia are not the only emotions that arise during its representation and comprehension.

In the eyes of witnesses, the Soviet experience loses more and more of its palpability. The Soviet authorities have left no accessible corpus of objective data; even official information on the incomes of the population, on prices, living standards and medicine was either classified or falsified. The basic source of data lies in memoirs, in biased evaluations by Soviet citizens. In this story about the Soviet past, gaps cannot be avoided; these must be filled in a fragmentary manner, underlining the reliance on the imagination, on mythologizing on the basis of previous cultural experience and in the vein of new concepts.

The need for fantasies on the theme of the past is aggravated during periods of major social reorganization, when man loses sense of who he is and what rules he lives by. During the twentieth century, Russia has seen at least two major state reorganizations, each with not only global geopolitical consequences but also leading millions of people to a new self-definition. One of the consequences of the first 'revision' was the literature of the Russian Abroad with its powerful nostalgic pathos. But while we are inclined to justify the longing for an imperial Russia today, the grief for recent Soviet past, whose deficits and defects have been part of those living today, seems much less sound.

The analysis of lost/remaining, value/harm, necessity/uselessness of a more open conversation about those feelings that are experienced in relation to the Soviet past, of a recognition of the importance of these feelings which is still a topical and unresolved problem today, of course remains a subject for representation in literature: first, and most obviously, at the level of problems and themes; and second, at the level of formal, above all generic and stylistic, preferences.

Soviet figures may organically fit into new forms of mass culture. In Mikhail Shprits and Aleksei Klimov's film script *Pervyi otriad/First Commando* the story about sacred events of the Soviet past – the Leningrad siege or the deeds of pioneer-heroes – is fitted into the genre of modern mass culture, of a trash espionage novel or the Manga comics; then, Anna Starobinets takes the plot of *First Commando* as starting point for her adventure quest novel *Pervyi otriad: Istina/First Commando: The Truth*. Each new work in its own way links the Soviet past with the post-Soviet present, but a growing number of authors try to explain their vision of the Soviet experience. The fact of recognizing oneself as a former Soviet citizen is a theme for literature. Here again several strategies can be discerned.

At one end of the scale, there is the connection between private (personal, family) and state history, which demonstrates clearly the divergences between state policy and the private life of citizens. Aleksandr Arkhangelskii wrote the book *1962* about the events that occurred in the world, in the USSR and in his family during the year of his birth, showing their profound inner connection. Autobiographical books about the 'resistance of the weak', of private people with dramatic lives who, nevertheless, do not consider themselves victims of the century (*Podstrochnik/Line-by-line Translation* by Liliana Lungina, *Christened with Crosses* by Eduard Kochergin, or *Asistoliia/Asystole* by Oleg Pavlov) enjoy popularity among the broad readership.

At the other end of the scale there are phantasmagorical demonstrations, on the one hand of the absurdity, on the other of the unexpected efficiency of old Soviet practices. Mikhail Elizarov's *Bibliotekar'/The Librarian* about the war that flared up around a Soviet writer's books, which suddenly appeared vital to all those at a loss about post-Soviet life. His *Mul'tiki/Cartoons* represent the absurdity of Soviet education, transferred onto a new epoch where the best teacher is yesterday's re-educated murderer. In his novel *GenAtsid/GenAcide* Vsevolod Benigsen dwells on the inclusion of specific Soviet practices of the dissemination of culture, in particular the introduction of reading lists that are obligatory for the entire population. As a matter of fact, the author reviews not the qualities of society or literature, but that hypertrophied role which was invariably allocated to literature in Russian, and later Soviet, society. In *VITCh* Benigsen explores the image of Soviet dissidents, exiled by the Soviet authorities to a 'closed' city and – deprived of opportunities to express themselves publicly – without any interest in creative or political activity: they are simply not ready for an encounter with post-Soviet life.

Between openly autobiographical and phantasmagorical texts we find a number of 'ideological' novels, where problems connected with the Soviet experience drive the plot and are directly addressed by the characters in the body of the text.

In Anton Utkin's novel *Krepost' somneniia/Fortress of Doubt*, which structurally reminds of the late Iurii Bondarev's ideological novels, the heroes, who live on the threshold of the twentieth and twenty-first centuries indefatigably and verbosely argue about the specificity of Soviet/post-Soviet societies, offering a range of explanations of the USSR's disintegration. As many others who write about the USSR, they call it empire, placing the stress, however, not on the multinational state, but on its size and the multilayered social structure subordinated to a single will as a result of persistent efforts of Russian governors.

What in this past excites the contemporary, financially well-off character who has only benefitted from the new conditions of life? First, the secret of the USSR's disintegration, the 'state power that attracted both by a mysterious force and a sudden geriatric weakness' (Utkin 2010: 274). The instant and – as it seemed – painless collapse of the country incites one of the heroes to cautiously think of the future: 'He already had to learn how books become history, and with confusion he picked up an atlas. Those countries had already ceased to exist. There are other countries in their place [...] And here on the empire stands USSR, while it is the Russian Federation, but soon it will fold into a stack of newspapers and we don't yet know what will become true' (Utkin 2010: 82). The recognition of the greatness of the USSR at the cost of Soviet history, the unwillingness to reconcile with Russia's changed role in the modern world leads the heroes to attempt at least in their minds to change the history of the country's disintegration, but their reasoning leads them to the inevitability of such a disintegration, which repeats itself.

The destruction of Soviet ideology does not elicit pity in the heroes, unlike the pity for the loss of the huge country, of which they feel they are a part. On the one hand, the empire poses a threat to the individual compelled to subordinate his life, which continues in the established order – despite everything. 'In the central squares an unbridled minority challenges these, but in the side-streets and suburbs life continues in its usual flow: soups are made, children with satchels on their shoulders return from school, making their way along fences [...] and trains run according to schedule, and only the train drivers, digging their day through coal and cheap cigarettes, swear when they have to cross the front line' (Utkin 2010: 73).[11] At the same time, the imperial idea allows the character to feel himself as a part of some greater purpose, beyond the personal, which makes it easier to organize life within a certain framework. The specific 'convenience' of such an existence is particularly noticeable against the background of the amorphous Russian present. The destruction of the Soviet experience along with the imperial idea suggests the creation of a new purpose: 'There was a certain system of coordinates. Now – and he could see this very clearly – there was no such system at all. And when he thought about that, he would imagine that it might be a good thing, and useful: let them all forget, forget to the point of absurdity and then, maybe, something could be worked out' (Utkin 2010: 153).

In *Drawing Lessons* Maksim Kantor considers the development of the post-Soviet state as a special case altogether, satirically representing how, once again in world history, the revolutionary-minded Soviet intellectual-dissidents inevitably praise 'the civilized empire' after a shift of power (Kantor 2006: 2). At the same time the hero-narrator gives a geopolitical explanation for the events that have occurred and are occurring in the country.

Terekhov's *The Stone Bridge* (2009) reproduces in subject-matter and composition the modern Russian world view superimposing the traumatic and nostalgic. The novel's protagonist is our contemporary, a former agent of the Federal Security Bureau FSB (Federal'naia sluzhba bezopasnosti), a collector of Soviet toy soldiers, who – together with his colleagues – investigates a murder committed in Moscow on the Stone Bridge (Kamennyi most) in 1943. The investigation is quite meaningless, as the case has long been closed; there are hardly any witnesses left, and to understand the reasons which led a teenager from a stately Soviet family to shoot a girl of his circle is practically impossible. However, the book, written as an investigation novel from the perspective of the inspector, is not about solving a crime, but about interpreting the historical clues.

The real problem of the heroes is the immersion in the past. Having collected all the evidence, they – in a fantastic turn of the author's imagination, symbolically designating the limited readiness of the detectives to disclose the secret – are ready to participate in the court case which took place in 1943. Newspapers, magazines, letters of that time, confused statements of witnesses – all these help to reconstruct history and find here a hidden 'truth' which, however, as the hero admits, is not final. But the story that extends back into the past grips post-Soviet people: they really live only in it and for it, satisfying only their physiological needs in the present world, where they suffer from emptiness and loneliness.

By forming some integral story with a distinct plot from events of the past, the heroes give meaning to today's existence. They are deprived of the illusion that they might find some truth; on the contrary, in a postmodern manner they realize the essential impossibility of achieving this, because of the subjectivity of any narrated story, the multiple variants of connecting the same facts: 'we scraped together everything reflected in human hearts, counted up the numeral superiority in witness statements […] in fact any evidence, even given under torture, even false, originates somewhere! And we tied it together in a bouquet, according to *our* taste. Some pins are sticking out in different directions, and if you take it to the people, everyone will get hurt. […] None of them have the skill to handle the truth' (Terekhov 2009: 685; emphasis in the original). The detectives realize the inevitability of aberrations in human memory, the impossibility of an exact reconstruction of the details of the past: 'We are powerless even in establishing details for the police record: ten minutes of the emperor's agony at the summer residence in Kuntsevo with six (at least) adult, freezing witnesses produces no authentic reproduction of the event' (Terekhov 2009: 202). The heroes' sensation of history is often intuitive and based on personal experience:

[A]nd suddenly for a long instant I felt my past as you perceive separate instants as life: something from the outside, like a wind; iron tanks with boiled water, rolls of linen cords, molten lead that cooled down in the form of October stars with a curly-haired baby Christ, the black-and-white television, and most terrible – the death of the kinescope, as people moved out of the barracks, a crackling of newspapers torn apart in the toilet, the satin cap, the terrible language of the telegrams with condolences and congratulations that appeared on brownish, glued-together paper strips without vowels and prepositions, the stuffy booths of the hardly audible inter-city phone, the 'conscience of the passenger is the best ticket inspector', the last calls, tests, shooting, words and analyses, many rusty shells.

(Terekhov 2009: 612)

The memoirs of the Soviet experience are deliberately deprived of any idyll: the heroes experience no longing for the past, but nevertheless persistently gnaw at it, comparing their efforts with the defeated city: 'the truth of iron people was dried and varnished, their rest and silence already inaccessible. And year after year we besieged the city that no longer existed' (Terekhov 2009: 195).

What drives the heroes? What thirst do they quench and what, actually, are they looking for? On the one hand, by engaging with history they justify their own life, but even more so they are attracted by the opportunity to understand the destiny of the country where they live. Living on the splinters of a great power, they must try to understand the essence of the imperial project and the reason for the collapse of the enormous state. The investigation of the strange murder on the bridge gains meaning, because it helps understand the symptoms of the disintegration. Both the present and the past are shown as empty, monotonous and – at the level of an individual's everyday life – uninviting, but the past is capable of gaining closure in the context of a search for answers to the question about meaning; and this search for the invention of meaning is the most interesting feature of human life. The heroes' flight from contemporary problems into the past is not a form of escapism or a refusal to engage vigorously in the present, as they explain the reasons for the pitiable condition of state and society: 'The times came to an end, the dreams of the tsars were executed, our passages are secured, Russians are at the top; wherever you turn – only downwards, all that remains is to die' (Terekhov 2009: 410).

These and similar geopolitical explanations of what has happened and is happening in the country are, on the one hand, a justification, and, on the other hand, a self-justification. The USSR deserves respect if only because an experiment took place here to create one of the Utopias that captured the human imagination. The great secret, which the 'iron commissars' took with them to their graves, gave expediency to their actions, which are illogical and wild for their descendants, or cattle (*bydlo*) – as they are called in the novel.

Novels such as Terekhov's offer a form of support to post-Soviet man, a point of identification. The heroes think not in categories of nationality, generation or gender; they do not search for the Soviet in themselves; and they know neither self-humiliation nor mutual disparagement. The central question for them is who the Soviet people are: the others or they themselves. In such literature the answer is simple: Soviet is 'us' in the past; or, 'us' as heirs of the Soviet experience.

On the one hand, society – of course, its various parts to different degrees and for different reasons – fears the return of the Soviet; on the other hand, it recognizes the value of many practices of the socialist world. On the one hand, it constantly returns to the lost era, on the other, it is ashamed of this as an inadmissible weakness or – on the contrary – emphatically boasts of its predilection. Yet in none of the texts is there an exposure or praise of the Soviet, nor any form of longing.[12] Instead, we see an interested attempt to understand this part of the country's historical path, the mechanism of the bygone structure. Writers hold their own court, and this self-justice gives a social meaning to their role as writers. The decision of the judges is also more or less unequivocal. Sympathy for the people is required, both for those who lived in the empire and for those who have come through the hearths of reorganization. One can hold out in the modern world only by the stoicism of a soldier of the broken empire.

According to the modern Russian mass-media the Soviet past is not just sick, but also – to use another image – 'undigested'; neither society nor the individual has reached a unanimous position on this issue. In the eyes of its bearers the Soviet past loses its non-ambiguity, but it is placed into rigid external polarized ideological schemes which are protected so fiercely that there is a contradiction between them and personal histories and personal experiences. To deny the importance of the Soviet past for a person is to deny the importance of his life in that past. To recognize the Soviet past is to deny the meaning of the changes that have taken place.

Translated by Birgit Beumers

Works cited

Abramov, Roman (2009), 'Chto takoe nostalgiia? Puteshestvie po rossiiskoi blogosfere', *60-ia parallel* 35, pp. 36–41, http://www.journal.60parallel.org/uploaded_files/files/abramov.pdf. Accessed 20 September 2011.

Adon'eva, Svetlana (2009), *Dukh naroda i drugie dukhi*, Saint-Petersburg: Amfora.

Balina, Marina and Evgeni Dobrenko (eds) (2009), *Petrified Utopia: Happiness Soviet Style*, London: Anthem Press.

Baranov, N., with Konstantin Bogdanov and Iurii Murashov (2008), *SSSR: Territoriia liubvi*, Moscow: Novoe izdatel'stvo.

Bogdanov, Konstantin (2009), *Vox populi. Folklornye zhanry sovetskoi kul'tury*, Moscow: Novoe literaturnoe obozrenie.

Bykov, Dmitrii (2009), 'Kakoi byl god, kakie personazhi!', *Novaia gazeta* 25 December. http://www.novayagazeta.ru/society/42029.html. Accessed 20 September 2011.

——— (2011), 'Svoboda opredeliaetsia stepen'iu ee slozhnosti'. Interview with Lena Nikulicheva, *iUni* 15 September, http://iuni.ru/articles/article/?articleId=867. Accessed 20 September 2011.

Chizhova, Elena (2009), 'Vremia zhenshchin nel'zia nazvat' avtobiograficheskim v polnoi mere', *Vesti* 4 December, http://www.vesti.ru/doc.html?id=329403. Accessed 20 September 2011.

Epstein, Mikhail (2006), 'Epidov kompleks sovetskoi tsivilizatsii', *Novyi mir* 1. http://magazines.russ.ru/novyi_mi/2006/1/ep7.html. Accessed 20 September 2011.

Freidin, Gregory (2010), 'Mysteries at the heart of Stalin's empire', *Times Online*, 24 February, http://www.stanford.edu/~gfreidin/Publications/columns/Kamennyi%20most%20_TLS020242010.pdf. Accessed 20 July 2012.

Kantor, Maksim (2006), *Uchebnik risovaniia*, Moscow: O.G.I.

Kukulin, Il'ia, Mark Lipovetskii, Mariia Maiofis (eds) (2008), *Veselye chelovechki. Kul'turnye geroi sovetskogo detstva*, Moscow: Novoe literaturnoe obozrenie.

Leonteva, S. and K. Maslinskii (2008), *Uchebnyi tekst v sovetskoi shkole*, St. Petersburg and Moscow: Institut logiki, kognitologii i razvitiia lichnosti.

Lipovetskii, Mark and Aleksandr Etkind (2008), 'Vozvrashchenie Tritona: Sovetskaia katastrofa i postsovetskii roman', *Novoe literarurnoe obozrenie* 94, http://magazines.russ.ru:81/nlo/2008/94/li17.html. Accessed 20 September 2011.

Parfenov, Leonid (2009), 'Naslednik neporotogo pokoleniia', Interview with Sergei Grachev, *Argumenty i fakty* 50 (9 December), http://www.aif.ru/society/article/31392. Accessed 20 September 2011.

Rezanova, Zoia (ed.) (2011), *Nostal'giia po sovetskomu v sotsiokul'turnom prostranstve sovremennoi Rossii*, Tomsk: Tomsk University.

Shaburova, Ol'ga (2009), 'Nostalgiia: strategii kommertsializatsii ili Sovetskoe v glamure', in N. Kupina and O. Mikhailova (eds), *Sovetskoe proshloe i kul'tura nastoiashchego*, 2 vols., Ekaterinburg, vol. 1, pp. 33–44.

Terekhov, Aleksandr (2009), *Kamennyi most*, Moscow: Astrel'.

Utkin, Anton (2010), *Krepost' somneniia*, Moscow: Astrel'.

Žižek, Slavoj (2009), 'Post-Wall: Neo-Anti-Communism', *London Review of Books* 31.22 (19 November). http://www.lrb.co.uk/v31/n22/slavoj-zizek/post-wall. Accessed 20 September 2011.

Notes

1 Decree (Ukaz) of 19 May 2009 'About a Commission under the President of the RF on counteraction to attempts at the falsification of history to the detriment of Russia's interests' (O kommissii pri prezidente RF po protivodeistviiu popytkam fal'sifikatsii istorii v ushcherb interesam Rossii).

2 It is sufficient to look at the expansion of contexts for the analysis of the ideological complex of Sovietness. Thus, Mikhail Epstein (2006) considered Soviet as a display of the Oedipus complex; Konstantin Bogdanov (2009) wrote a book titled *Vox populi. Folklornye zhanry sovetskoi kul'tury* [*Vox Populi. Folklore Genres of Soviet Culture*]; Svetlana Adon'eva republished a corrected version of her monograph *Kategoriia nenastoiashchego vremeni* [*The Category of Artificial Time*; 2001] under the title *Dukh naroda i drugie dukhi* [*The Spirit of the People and Other Spirits*; 2009], where she considered the Soviet in the context of rituals of Russian folklore. Numerous other books and articles by researchers with a wide range of approaches and interests have appeared which cross over the Soviet experience.

3 See, for example, the web communities: sovietlife.ru; sovietschool.ru, sovietchildhood. ru; sovietsongs.ru, sovarch.ru and others. About the Soviet theme in the blogosphere see Abramov (2009).

4 Some collections show the variety of aspects of the Soviet that are investigated: *Uchebnyi tekst v sovetskoi shkole* [*The Textbook in Soviet Schools*] (Leonteva and Masklinskii, 2008); *SSSR: Territotiia liubvi* [*USSR: Territory of Love*] (Baranov, Bogdanov, and Murashov, 2008]; and *Veselye chelovechki: kul'turnye geroi sovetskogo detstva* [*Cheerful Little Men: Cultural Heroes of Soviet Childhood*] (Kukulin, Lipovetskii, Maiofis 2008); *Petrified Utopia: Happiness Soviet Style* (Balina and Dobrenko 2009). The Shevchenko Institute of Literature in Kiev has published (since 2009) a series of collections 'Studia Sovetica'; an international journal on the study of Stalinist and post-Stalinist culture (*BLOK*) appears in Bydgoszcz (Poland).

5 The award 'Book of the Year' for 2009 went to Leonid Parfenov for 'the nostalgic encyclopaedia' *Namedni/Lately*. the 'National Best-seller' was awarded to the novel *Stepnye bog/Steppe Gods* by Andrei Gelasimov in 2009, and in 2010 to *Kreshchennye krestami/Christened with Crosses* by Eduard Kochergin. In 2009 the novel *Zhuravli i karliki/Cranes and Dwarfs* by Leonid Iuzefovich received the 'Great Book' (Bol'shaia kniga) award, alongside Aleksandr Terekhov's *Kamennyi most/The Stone Bridge*, whose protagonists are engaged in historical research, including recent Soviet history. The winner of the Russian Booker 2009 Elena Chizhova admits herself that one of her purposes in writing the novel *Vremia zhenshchin/The Time of Women* was the aspiration 'to understand the phenomenon of historical memory' (Chizhova 2009). Texts about heroes of the Soviet era appear in the popular series of fictionalized biographies *Zhizn' zamechatel'nykh liudei/Life of Remarkable People* on a regular basis.

6 See, for example, the practice of the publishing house Yauza, which simultaneously publishes popular science books on military history with diametrically opposed interpretations. Thus the series 'Viktor Suvorov's Truth': Suvorov was a former agent of the State Intelligence Service, emigrant, popular historian who proved that Stalin initiated World War II. This is opposed by another collection of the same publishing house 'Viktor Suvorov's Untruths', which deny all these claims.

7 This is indicated by television programmes such as *Sud istorii/Court of History* where two sides (in this case S. Kurginyan and N. Svanidze and six experts for either side) clash over the events of June 1941 or the financing of industrialization. The stalemate result of such disputes appears to be stipulated by the script.

8 Nostalgia for the Soviet past is activated through socially significant events stimulating the revival of the object (objects) of nostalgia in collective/group/individual memory. Events of global (for example, the economic crisis), regional (for example, the dismissal of construction workers), all-Russian (for example, Victory Day) significance stimulate social reflection, the appearance of nostalgic texts that revive strong collective emotions directly connected with the gone/going cultural objects, causing emotional experience in groups of subjects. For more detail see Rezanova 2011.

9 Thus, for example, Dmitrii Bykov calls the contemporariness of the times which dethroned the Soviet system, but did not offer any alternative ways of development: 'everything that was most loathsome in the Soviet Union has become hardy and long-playing. And we turned out to be the heirs to it all. The most abominable of what existed in the Soviet Union

has been kept. Except for the closed borders. Everything that was more or less decent – the educational tradition, the humanitarian tradition, the anti-clerical or non-clerical tradition, the internationalism, many good things, including the strange Russian cosmism, – all this waned in the first instance, as happens in such cases' (Bykov 2011)

10 *Kabachok 13 stul'ev/The Pub 13 Chairs* (dir. Georgii Zelinskii): television comedy aired between 1966–80.

11 Such a juxtaposition of life with political reorganization can be found frequently in the description of the disintegration of the Russian empire after the Revolution.

12 In a review of *The Stone Bridge* Gregory Freidin, using the metaphor from the title of Terekhov's novel, reaches the following conclusion: 'A conventional allegory – life floating on the river of time – has replaced the stone bridge, a rigid metaphor for constructing identities and meaning. Welcome to post-imperial Russia in the post-nostalgia age' (Freidin 2010).

Chapter 2

Cycles, Continuity and Change in Contemporary Russian Culture

Mark Lipovetsky

As Boris Gasparov suggested in his article on Pushkin 'History without Teleology', reading the cultural process through the dichotomies of prose/poetry, archaists/innovators, culture/explosion etc., despite the shared anxiety of binary oppositions, can still be productive if one would 'release these categories from the concept of the progressive historical development, within which they are typically invoked' (Gasparov 2003: 274). Furthermore, according to Gasparov, typically parallel developments of opposite trends can be detected in any given period. The fact that one of these tendencies gains the spotlight, manifesting the tenor of the time, while the others are marginalized and less visible, permits the use of these dichotomies as a sensitive research tool.

Following this prompt, I focus here on cycles and continuities connecting post-Soviet culture with the cultural phenomena of the Soviet period. I have no ambition of constructing an overarching and universalizing model. I fully realize that contemporary culture – Russian or any other – cannot be reduced to a generalized construct. Rather, I would like to suggest that the following be taken as an intellectual provocation simultaneously demonstrating the need for historical typologies for the study of the contemporary cultural process and the multiplicity of models that can be applied to it. I am not worried therefore about the contradictions between descriptions of the post-Soviet cultural process suggested below. Each approach taken separately would inevitably turn reductive; however, multiple overlapping approaches have a better chance of capturing a three-dimensional image of the cultural dynamics.

'Simplicity' vs. 'complexity'

In the early 2000s the talk about the tiredness of overly 'complex' forms, i.e., postmodernist, avant-gardist and modernist experiments, became endemic in Russian literary criticism. Out of this discourse emerged the notion of the 'end of postmodernism', followed by a wave of manifestoes declaring the 'new realism' in prose, drama and even poetry (see, for example Basinskii 2000; Beliakov 2009; Bol'shakova 2009; Ermolin 2006). The shift from 'complex' (sophisticated, self-reflective and fragmentary) forms to more 'simple' (transparent, coherent and democratic) is not a new phenomenon in twentieth-century culture.

Probably Heinrich Wölfflin (1966) was the first to suggest a dichotomy of styles dominated by either an 'open' or a 'closed' form. Dmitry Cizevsky (1952) had argued that literary styles alternate between two extremes: the quest for unity and the quest for complexity; while the former produces completed forms, the latter generates the free-form and even 'formless' phenomena. A similar dichotomy is reflected in the typology of 'primary' and 'secondary' styles developed by Dmitrii Likhachev (1973) and applied to nineteenth- and twentieth-century literature by Igor' Smirnov (2000). Recently, Georgii Knabe (1993: 26–72) maintained that the development of art is defined by fluctuations within the dichotomy of 'culture vs. life'. In his last book on the theory of genre, Naum Leiderman (2010) divided grand styles as gravitating towards the opposed poles of cosmological and chaological strategies in the aesthetic world-modelling.

All these dichotomies implicitly presuppose life or reality as something independent of cultural production. Unlike these great scholars, I suggest that 'life' cannot be anything but a product of 'culture'. In other words, a new 'simplified' cultural process is always the result of another, preceding 'complex' period. During 'complex' periods new constructs of the real are introduced and tested; during the ensuing 'simple' periods these new concepts seem congruent with 'life', which testifies to the fact that they are already adopted in the culture. Therefore, a shift between 'complex' and 'simple' forms may be described as a fluctuation between the creation of new, yet incessantly changing, concepts of the real, and the appropriation of already-existing models that are mistaken for actual reality by authors and audiences alike. Thus, it would be more accurate to speak about an ongoing competition of two modalities: one reader-oriented ('simple') and the other author-oriented ('complex') – in the same way as an utterance can be speaker- or listener-oriented.

Also, unlike the scholars cited above, I doubt that such dichotomies – should they be detectable in the cultural process – necessarily produce new styles or aesthetic systems. These modalities can develop within (or above) any aesthetic language – modernist, postmodernist or even avant-gardist – without changing its inner structure. For instance, the case of the 'simplification' of avant-garde can be illustrated through the use of avant-garde tropes in posters of the late 1920s and early 1930s, or even in Sergei Eisenstein's films of the 1930s and 1940s (see, for example, Bonnell 1999; Neuberger 2003: 25–135).

The discussion in the 2000s about 'the end of postmodernism' appears to be quite symptomatic for this case. In my book *Paralogies* (*Paralogii*, 2008) I have argued that the attempts to conceptualize contemporary Russian literature in terms of the end of postmodernism, post-postmodernism, new realism, etc. are indeed misleading. Such trends as New Drama, contemporary poetry and even the recycling of Socialist Realist tropes in popular culture of the 2000s still employ postmodernist strategies: the 'reality effect' appears here as a mutable product of language games, and even when binary oppositions seem to be restored, the authors leave a loophole for their ironic interpretation. The latter device was successfully tested for the first time in Aleksei Balabanov's *Brat 2/Brother-2* (2000) – a film that can well be interpreted as a straightforward manifestation of xenophobic ideology, yet leaves open the opportunity to perceive it as a mockery of post-Soviet nationalism. This opportunity was gladly taken up by many liberal-minded critics, who lauded this film despite its protagonist's explicit nationalistic views.

Speaking of postmodernism, it is worth recalling that bridging the gap between high-brow modernist and popular culture was declared to be one of the central goals of western and especially American postmodernism in the late1960s–70s (Fiedler 1972). For Russian postmodernism, developing in the underground simultaneously with its western counterparts, this task was quite irrelevant. However, since Victor Pelevin's *Generation 'P'* (1999) and Vladimir Sorokin's *Goluboe salo/Blue Lard* (1999), Russian postmodernism launched a quest for a broader readership which, in turn, brought into play easy-to-follow plots rather than self-reflective meditation; references to current politics and popular culture rather than broad and sophisticated cultural allusions; (quasi-) relatable and recognizable characters rather than metamorphosing narrative masks and multi-layered voices; monological narratives rather than polyphonic discourses; coherence rather than fragmentation; an interest in social and political subjects rather than philosophic questioning. Another quite significant indicator of such a shift in the 2000s can be detected in the transition from the deconstruction of various cultural myths to myth-making; even if these are individual myths, they are still presented by the authors as universal and usually enforcing binary oppositions. This tendency is exemplified by such works as Sorokin's *Ice Trilogy* (*Led/Ice* (2002); *Put' Bro/ Bro* (2004); *23,000* (2005), in English 2011), Dmitrii Bykov's novels – especially *ZhD/ Live Souls* (2006), the evolution of Evgenii Grishkovets's plays, Nikita Mikhalkov's films of the 2000s or Andrei Khrzhanovskii's much-acclaimed cinematic recreation of the romantic myth of the Nobel-laureate Joseph Brodsky in *Poltory komnaty/A Room and a Half* (2009). The exponential growth and popularity of non-fictional forms or forms imitating non-fictionality is also reflective of this turn, manifested in such documentary genres as memoirs or blogs, the emergence of numerous quasi-documentary phenomena such as teatr.doc, mockumentaries (*Pervye na Lune/First on the Moon* (2005) by Aleksei Fedorchenko) and various essayistic genres.

The turn in the new millennium to reader- or viewer-oriented discourses may be seen as part of the waves that run through the entire twentieth century. The Silver Age of Russian modernism (1890s–1910s) clearly demonstrated the radical innovation and complication of poetic discourses. In the 1920s this process extended to prose, and coincided with a trend towards an oversimplification of artistic language. In the 1930s the latter tendency took the upper hand – not only because of the pressure of Socialist Realism: Boris Pasternak's striving for 'unheard of simplicity', Anna Akhmatova's inclination towards 'epic' forms detectable in *Requiem* (1940) do not necessarily fit the Socialist Realist doctrine, while resonating with the reader-oriented vector of the period. The 1950s witnessed the transformation of Socialist Realism into highly codified art, ornate and sometimes almost baroque in its fantasticality, while the 1960s were invigorated by a drive towards 'sincerity' (to use Vladimir Pomerantsev's catchphrase from the title of his famous article 'Ob iskrennosti v literature'/'On Sincerity in Literature', 1953), as well as the emergence of a specific kind of Social Realism, the so-called lieutenant and youth prose. This 'sincerity', understood as a direct, if naive, reaction to the catastrophic twists of history and attention to the details of everyday life is also responsible for the success of the poets Evgenii Evtushenko, Bulat Okudzhava and Andrei Voznesenskii, as well as Aleksandr Volodin's plays, and Leonid Gaidai's film comedies. By contrast, the long 1970s (1968–86) clearly demonstrated the surge of 'complex' literature and film, not only through the development of underground phenomena belonging to modernist, avant-gardist and even postmodernist aesthetics, but also due to the highly complex system of hints, ellipses and allusions employed by published Soviet authors and film-makers.

Perestroika and the 1990s are somewhat similar to the 1920s: during this period the simplistic social (not socialist!) realism derivative from the Thaw existed alongside postmodernism as it rose from the underground and started to affect the cultural mainstream. This period witnessed not only the parallel dynamic of 'simplistic' and 'complex' tendencies; it was also characterized by the revival of the so-called returned literature. Texts that had been banned during the Soviet period for political reasons created an unprecedented situation when the high modernism of the 1920s–30s with all its complexity suddenly acquired a new cultural and political urgency.

Finally, since the late 1990s and throughout the 2000s one can observe another turn to 'simplicity' as manifested by the adoption of the languages of mass culture, a turn to 'human documents', verbatim, naturalism as exemplified by New Drama and new poetry. The rise of Internet-based forms of literature is especially telling for the reader-oriented modality: in blogs, fan fiction and other forms of net-literature the reader functions as the writer and the borderline between the categories of reader/writer is demonstratively and deliberately problematized.

Having said that, it is important to remark that the opposite tendency did not vanish in the 2000s either: sophisticated and multi-layered 'high modernist' novels,[1] or films by Kira Muratova and Aleksandr Sokurov – all designate the presence of a 'complex' counter-current underneath the 'new simplicity' of the 2000s. It would be a stretch to consider this literature as missing an audience: Mikhail Shishkin's reading of chapters from his newest novel *Letter-Book* was certainly among the most attended events of the Moscow Book Festival in June 2010.

The 'complex' counter-current can be found in other periods of 'simplicity' as well, and vice versa. Silver Age poetry enjoyed less popularity in the 1900–10s than the neo-realist prose. Indeed, Andrei Platonov's most complex works, such as *Kotlovan/The Foundation Pit* (1930), *Schastlivaia Moskva/Happy Moscow* (1933–36) were created in the 'simplistic' 1930s. Or the aforementioned 'returned' modernist masterpieces of Zamiatin and Nabokov were misread during the perestroika period as predominantly political and anti-totalitarian statements, i.e., their meaning was reduced to a narrow spectrum of simple political ideas.

The meaning of 'post'

What conclusions can we draw from all this? Apparently, such transitional periods as the 1920s or the 1990s are marked by a balance between reader- and author-oriented tendencies. Periods dominated by author-oriented, 'complex' poetics, such as the Silver Age or the 'long seventies', typically precede catastrophic or revolutionary historical shifts. But what is the common feature between the Stalinist 30s, the Thaw, and the 2000s? Consumerism? A relative stabilization after historical turmoil? Perhaps it would be more productive to seek common characteristics not in the inherent features of any given period, but in their self-descriptions, which appear to be surprisingly similar. All these periods are perceived from within as those following times of troubles or periods of havoc and chaos, radical shifts and the accompanying muddle: in short, traumatic events concerning society at large – be it the Revolution and Civil War, the Stalinist terror or the anarchic nineties. Thus, it would be possible to suggest that those periods marked by the domination of a reader-oriented tendency imagine themselves as post-traumatic.

From this premise I would like to propose another hypothesis, one of many relevant for contemporary cultural situation: that 'simplistic' and 'complex' tendencies in cultural history correlate to two opposing scenarios of dealing with traumatic experiences: of acting-out and of working-through. Certainly, any artistic work in some ways already 'works through' traumas – personal and historical alike. But the resonance between various texts created in the same period suggests that certain tendencies of dealing with trauma acquire more urgency and gain more limelight in 'complex' periods, while others dominate, relatively speaking, 'simplistic' periods.

Perhaps the reader-oriented modality arises as an attempt to address and reflect recent traumatic experiences in a most direct way. Socialist Realism is not an exception in this context: it only mandates a compulsory positive outlook on the traumas of the Revolution and the Civil War, but most importantly, of Stalinist modernization. For post-Soviet culture of the 2000s, the concept of trauma is multifold, but mainly consists of two contradictory and overlapping components: the trauma of Soviet history seen in its wholeness, from the Revolution to 'developed socialism' and the trauma caused by the collapse of Soviet civilization in the 1990s (see Oushakine 2010).

Following Dominique LaCapra's interpretation of Freud, one may define such cultural attempts to generate immediate and direct responses to traumatic experiences as the acting-out of trauma (which is frequently mistaken for realism): 'Acting-out is related to repetition, and even the repetition compulsion – the tendency to repeat something compulsively [… a tendency] to repeat traumatic scenes in a way that is somehow destructive and self-destructive […] Acting-out is a process, but a repetitive one. It's a process whereby the past, or the experience of the other, is repeated as if it were fully enacted, fully literalized' (LaCapra 1998: 2, 5). This definition corresponds to many phenomena of recent Russian culture, such as the fascination with non-fiction and (quasi-) documentary forms, a new wave of hypernaturalism as manifest in New Drama (see Beumers and Lipovetsky, 2009) and photographic representation (from a minimal distance) of everyday traumatic experiences in poetic texts similar to blogs and blogs similar to a lyrical diary. The repetition compulsion can be also detected in the frantic recycling of Socialist Realist tropes endemic in popular culture of the 2000s (see Lipovetsky 2004, Martynova 2009) and the newly-found fascination with Soviet songs (*Starye pesni o glavnom/Old Songs about the Main Thing* (1995–8)) to the literal and metaphorical recolouring of Soviet 'cult' series such as *Semnadtsat' mgnovenii vesny/Seventeen Moments of Spring* (1973), as well as Sergei Ursuliak's miniseries *Isaev* (2009), a prequel to the above spy saga about Stirlitz) and remakes of popular Soviet films.

However, the acting-out of trauma has internal limitations, which are most evident in the evolution of New Drama. Its hypernaturalist poetics constructed by various performances of violence aim at acting out the trauma of the nineties generation, of those who did not experience the euphoria of the perestroika period, but got the full load of disappointments, frustrations and, most importantly, violence associated with the collapse of the Soviet economy and system in the 1990s. This is the generation traumatized by everyday violence, who knows violence as a basic, common language: the isomorphism between trauma and the language of its performance creates a powerful emotional impact carried in the rough plays of New Drama. However, its effect did not last for more than a few years.

In the plays of New Drama, communication through violence and the transformation of violence into a language of a transcendental quest not only eliminates all alternative strategies of self-identification and self-realization, but also leads New Drama's characters to ultimate self-destruction, or at least reduces them to empty shells. The semiotic mechanism of New Drama is presented self-reflexively in Kirill Serebrennikov's film *Izobrazhaia zhertvu/Playing the Victim* (2006), based on the Presnyakov brothers' play of the same title: the protagonist Valia has no identity beyond performance. The performance (of violence, of crime victims) constructs his – as well as others' – reality as the process of interaction through violence only. Valia cannot find any way out of this 'reality' except through the realm of death: the murder of his entire family by poison that Valia administers in the finale is both a penalty for Valia's relatives' desire to live in a false world and his own logical conclusion to the actual nature of the real. This is where the acting-out of trauma reaches its limit, obviating that the reproduction of languages of violence as the main source of trauma does not generate any other languages or forms of communication. The traumatic is first presented as an identity-forming device; then aestheticized (and sometimes ritualized); and finally – inevitably – automatized and commercialized. Yet all these operations remain within the repetition-compulsion (i.e., they also belong to the realm of the traumatic) and, most importantly, they fail to produce – in La Capra's words – a 'necessary critical distance' that allows one 'to engage in life in the present, to assume responsibility – [which] does not mean that you utterly transcend the past' (LaCapra 1998: 5).

Notably the crisis of New Drama has led to the migration of many of its authors and theatre directors into cinema and the translation of the aesthetics of New Drama into cinematic language. This process is responsible for some key Russian films of recent years.[2] These films obviously depart from the orientation towards viewers' expectations, as testified by the public scandals associated with the film almanac *Korotkoe zamykanie/Crush* (2009) with five shorts by Petr Buslov, Ivan Vyrypaev, Boris Khlebnikov, Aleksei German Jr. and Kirill Serebrennikov, and the series *School* on the Russia's First Channel. In their own way, the creators of these new films return to auteur cinema with its meditative tempo, long shots and reduced plot intensity, in other words – they seek a new complexity. These films manifest the destructive effects of communication through violence in a suggestive rather than descriptive way, leaving gaps in the film's texture and forcing the viewers to seek their own, emotional rather than rational, justifications of the filmic logic.

Thus, it is not explained explicitly why Valia in *Playing the Victim* decides to kill his entire family; why Pasha in Popogrebskii's *How I Ended this Summer* does not immediately tell his boss about the tragedy that had befallen the latter's wife and son; why Proskurina's road movie is titled *Truce*; and why Loznitsa's hopeless and violence-saturated version of another road movie with a similar plot to that of Proskurina bears the title *My Joy*.

I would like to argue that these inner gaps create a critical distance that constitutes the process of working-through the same traumatic experience that was acted out in New Drama. According to LaCapra, 'in the working-through, the person tries to gain critical distance on a problem, to be able to distinguish between past, present, and future' (LaCapra 1998: 2). Most importantly, this distinction is based on the demonstration of the instability of binary oppositions. The working-through, unlike the acting-out of trauma, tries to avoid by all means the scapegoat mechanism that is, in turn, based on pure binaries between past and present, self and other, etc. Furthermore, this turn towards a new complexity revitalizes some significant strategies elaborated in the literary underground of the 1970s–80s. Here the subject of continuity and change arises.

The Underground Inheritance

From 2009 to 2012, I served as a judge on the jury of the literary prize NOS (*Novaia slovesnost'* – *novaia sotsial'nost'*), the first Russian literature award where both the shortlistees and the finalists are defined in the process of an open debate. The first award went to Lena Eltang for her experimental novel *Kamennye kleny/Stone Maples*; in 2010 the prize was awarded to Vladimir Sorokin's *Metel'/Blizzard*. In order to make the logic of our choices more visible and even performative, a public debate was staged about an imaginary, faux-prize NOS that would be awarded in 1973. Obviously, in the historical 1973 nobody would ever have consider combining works of Russian literature belonging to such disparate areas as non-conformist Soviet publications, political and aesthetic underground, as well as émigré literature into one shortlist.[3] This exercise was not just a play of wits, but tried to establish a certain parallel between cultural periods. In our joint opinion, 1973, or more broadly speaking the early 70s, deeply resonate with the current period. The early seventies may serve as a model for the beginning of a new 'author-oriented' period, when new models of reality, and most importantly, new strategies of working through the historical trauma were elaborated. The literature of that period dealt with the trauma of Stalinism and applied it to the entire Soviet experience, coupled with the trauma of the failed attempts at de-Stalinization – which sounds not so different from the current sociocultural disposition. In the shortlist of 1973, one can detect an entire spectrum of strategies each of which, in its own way, inserts critical distance into a traumatic discourse. Further, I will try to characterize these strategies by looking at how they were continued and radicalized in contemporary culture.

First, the strategy of social idiocy represents the Soviet world as though there was no Soviet regime, i.e., removing the ideological content from the Soviet social and historical context and focusing on its phantasmal effects only. As an alternative to social phantasms arises the power of language or, more broadly, art as the sole force capable of turning horrifying phantasms into a new individual myth. This strategy is best represented by Sasha Sokolov's *School for Fools*, as well as his subsequent novels. Outside of this imaginary shortlist, and in a different way, this strategy was also epitomized by Joseph Brodsky in poetry and Tarkovsky in cinema, although both of these artists can hardly be reduced to one strategy only. This tendency continues to develop in the post-Soviet period. Its best representatives in the 1990s and 2000s are, perhaps, Aleksandr Sokurov in film, and Elena Shvarts and Aleksei Parshchikov in poetry. Through the years this discourse became marked by signs of a hermetic fixation on the power of language that blocked its engagement with new traumatic experience.

The trickster strategy is well tested throughout the course of Soviet cultural history as an effective method of inner distancing from the social condition which, meanwhile, exposes its hidden mechanisms and exploits its hidden contradictions. The trickster in Soviet culture became the epitome and poetic justification of the cynical 'shadow world' comprising everything unofficial – the Soviet shadow economy (*blat*), politics, psychology and sociality. In the gallery of Soviet tricksters shine Erenburg's Julio Jurenito, I'lf and Petrov's Ostap Bender, Aleksei Tolstoi's Buratino and Aleksandr Tvardovskii's Vasilii Terkin. Iskander's Sandro of Chegem appears as a late addition to this venerable team (see Lipovetsky 2011). However, it is Abram Tertz/Andrei Sinyavsky who, in his book *Strolls with Pushkin*, written when its author was serving a term in the Gulag, transformed trickery into a method of cultural critique – a powerful tool for the estrangement of the cultural tradition. A lot has been written about the scandals generated by this book within the émigré community as well as in the perestroika period. In my view, the major reason for these scandals lies in the fact that Tertz inserted the trickster into the very heart of the cultural tradition – not only does he depict Pushkin as a cultural trickster, but he thus creates a utopian model of culture that will not, or rather cannot become repressive, and – unlike the actual Russian cultural tradition – would never sponsor terror of any kind. This line of trickery has in its own way been developed by Dmitrii Prigov who directly works through the traumatic effects of various cultural discourses by creating a mock *Gesamtkunstwerk* of the entire contemporary culture. Notably, in the post-Soviet period the infatuation with the trickster as a personage faded away, because in social life the trickster, and the entire shadow, *blat*-based realm associated with him, moved from alternative culture to Soviet establishment, into the post-Soviet cultural, political and economic establishment exemplified by such trickster-like figures as Vladimir Zhirinovskii, Boris Berezovskii, Kseniia Sobchak or Vladimir Putin himself. At the same time, the effect of cultural trickery as exemplified by Tertz's Pushkin started to play a central role in visual art as represented by such professional tricksters as Oleg Kulik,

Vladislav Mamyshev-Monroe, the Blue Noses group or the groups Voina (members of this group were arrested for their performances in 2010) and Pussy Riot (arrested in 2012).

Cultural trickery as a method of working through historical traumas (as opposed to the representation of the trickster as a character) is exemplified in contemporary literature by Vladimir Sorokin in his masterful artistic personification with and ensuing deconstruction of any authoritative discourses taken from a broad range of sources from Socialist Realism to classical literature. Sorokin also passed through a phase of 'acting-out' trauma. In this respect his *Ice Trilogy* is especially symptomatic, since there he imitates, yet does not deconstruct, a universal totalitarian mytho-ideology with all its effects. However, in his most recent works, such as *Den' oprichnika/Day of the Oprichnik* (2006), *Sakharnyi Kreml'/The Sugar Kremlin* (2008) and *Metel'/Blizzard* (2010), his method is quite different both from the *Ice Trilogy* and his early conceptualist works. In each of these texts he displays contemporary discourses of power – neo-traditionalist in *Day of the Oprichnik* and *The Sugar Kremlin*, and modernizing in *Blizzard* (for an analysis of these texts see Etkind and Lipovetsky 2008, 2010; Lipovetskii 2010). Yet, at the same time, Sorokin's representation includes critical distance formed by the tropes and stylized idiom of *oprichnina* (mediated through imagery borrowed from Eisenstein's second part of *Ivan Groznyi/Ivan the Terrible* (1946); released in 1956) in *Day of the Oprichnik* and *The Sugar Kremlin*, the discourse of the late nineteenth-century heroic intelligentsia's narrative in *Blizzard*. The effect in both cases is similar: the sources of contemporary political practices are located within authoritative cultural traditions, and instead of making a binarist accusation at the 'wrong-doers' Sorokin insinuates the reader's empathy towards a fusion with the central character, be it the *oprichnik* Komiaga in *Day of the Oprichnik* or doctor Platon Garin in *Blizzard*. In turn, the reader's reverberation with the protagonist also suggests a shared responsibility for the traumatic effects of the authoritative discourses of the traditionalist Order and the intelligentsia's driven 'modernization'. Notably, this semiotic mechanism was not at play in Sorokin's earlier conceptualist works, where he estranged authoritative discourses through the sudden alienation of the reader from a conventional central character due to disgust bordering on physiological loathing.

Although Venichka in Venedikt Erofeev's *Moscow to the End of the Line* can be also interpreted as an ultimate cultural trickster, the significance of this book is far greater. *Moscow to the End of the Line* pioneers a novel strategy in working through the historical trauma that can be called *Menippean* in agreement with Mikhail Bakhtin's concept of Menippea as the genre of 'ultimate questions' discussed in a serious, yet comic, way, where metaphysical concepts are tested by lowlife conditions, liminal situations, existential and social thresholds (see Bakhtin 1983: 101–37). Not only does Erofeev translate the question of moral repercussions of power into the quest for God, but also his quest results in the eventual demise of binary oppositions between the supreme spiritual authority and brutal murderers, metaphysical hierarchy and the persecution of individual logos in the finale (Lipovetsky 2011: 151–91).

In the post-Soviet period this line of cultural enquiry found its most talented heir in Victor Pelevin. In his novels he consistently fuses the mythical sacred with contemporary political and media discourses, thus performing a Menippean 'testing of the idea', applied to the idea of the sacred and to post-Soviet concepts of power and authority. Although his works are uneven, and frequently after brilliant ground-breaking texts like *Chapaev i Pustota/Buddha's Little Finger* (1996), *Generation 'P'* (1999; translated also as *Homo Zapiens*), *Sviashchennaia kniga oborotnia/The Sacred Books of Werewolf* (2004), he slips into recycling his own insights. His novel *t* and the collection of short(er) prose *Ananasnaia voda dlia prekrasnoi damy/Pineapple Water for a Beautiful Lady* (2011) prove the productivity of this method for the interpretation of the present-day global condition and not only of the Russian version of capitalism.[4]

If the Menippean strategy inscribes the historical trauma into the multifaceted context of mythical and philosophical discourses, Shalamov's *Kolymskie rasskazy/Kolyma Tales* remains in the contemporary cultural context an unsurpassed example of the strategy that can be defined as non-literary, if not anti-literary. For a good reason Shalamov insisted that his work be treated neither as conventional literature nor as conventional non-fiction; he stated that

> the author destroys the division between form and content, or rather defies the difference between them. The author believes that the significance of the subject dictates certain principles. The subject of *Kolyma Tales* cannot be expressed through conventional stories, which would trivialize the subject. Instead of a memoir, *Kolyma Tales* offers new prose, the prose of living life, which at the same time appears as a transfigured reality, as a transfigured document.
>
> (Shalamov 1965)

The reason for this rejection of any literary conventions can be found in Shalamov's perception of the Gulag, or more broadly the Soviet experience, as an anthropological catastrophe that had drawn its participant beyond the human condition, let alone modern cultural conventions. This method, however, despite its declared minimalism of artistic means, is most radical in its innovation of the aesthetic arsenal. Shalamov defined his style specifically as non-literature: it was a daring attack on all literary conventions similar to the most radical forms of the zero degree of writing. Shalamov sought such forms that would go beyond literary discourses. Mainly, these are either mythological structures (frequently not marked by an appropriate allusion and sometimes not even registered by the narrator), which grow through a thick layer of everyday horror; or performative, frequently hyper-naturalist, elements situated beyond the realm of a verbal utterance.

Either way, Shalamov's methods of 'working-through' trauma resonate with the artistic strategy of Liudmila Petrushevskaia as a playwright and prose-writer and, to a certain extent, with Evgenii Kharitonov, the author of highly unconventional texts dealing with queer existential and social traumas. In film, this very method can be detected in the works of Kira Muratova (especially in *Nastroishchik/The Tuner* and *Dva v odnom/Two in One*) and Aleksei German Senior (*Khrustalev, mashinu!/Khrustalev, My Car!*). All these authors follow Shalamov's footsteps. First, they shift the focus of representation from the Gulag or similar sites of terror to everyday life, which surprisingly reveals a prison- and war-like nature; second, they perceive Soviet and post-Soviet everyday existence not only as a trace to the anthropological catastrophe that happened in the past but also as a manifestation of its routine and unnoticeable continuation in the present; third, they demonstrate the comical inapplicability of traditional cultural discourses to this experience; and finally, they present their individual style as non-literature or non-film, as an imprint of raw life, as a document – although, of course, each of them creates a carefully designed illusion of such an escape from the realm of cultural convention.

Petrushevskaia directly influenced New Drama, but the latter, as mentioned above, slipped into the mode of acting-out instead of working through trauma. Paradoxically, New Drama lost the estranging, distancing power that was inscribed in the non-literariness of the method. The hypernaturalism displayed by New Drama authors came from their incapability to analyse their own experience, while Shalamov, Petrushevskaia or German created the illusion of hypernaturalism which was derivative from their intentional severance of aesthetic conventions as a key to achieving an analytical distance from the horrifying material.

This strategy acquires new strength in contemporary cinema, especially in the aforementioned directors and their films, many of which focus on characters who are either deliberately isolated from their current social context and are trying to function despite the unwritten rules of the social game (typically based on the communication by and valorization of violence); or, on the contrary, are trying to master the languages of violence and thus succeed in life. Thus, in Boris Khlebnikov's *Help Gone Mad* and Aleksei Popogrebskii's *How I Ended this Summer* the protagonist who does not understand the world around him intuitively reinstates its brutal principles in their most grotesque forms. Aleksei Mizgirev's *The Hard-Hearted* is constructed like a *Bildungsroman*, which transforms the traumatized subject into a brutal cop, a powerful reproducer of today's systemic violence. In *Truce*, the protagonist's inability to say no to the opportunities offered by the fantastic, illogical world around him is presented as a paradoxical, yet accidental, way of his moral survival in his travelogue through the territory ruined by an anthropological catastrophe. The world depicted in the film methodically and routinely turns cultural conditions and myths upside down. Quite indicative is a scene when a new Eva (after having sex with the hero in a cucumber hothouse as pitiful imitation of paradise) is sincerely offended by his equally sincere proposal to marry him. A provincial philosopher brilliantly played by Sergei Shnurov uses the example of Pugachev from Pushkin's *Kapitanskaia dochka/The Captain's Daughter* as a justification or even an imperative to kill anyone.

This new wave of Russian cinema works through historical traumas in a paradoxical way – by presenting the post-catastrophic condition as a unifying cultural and social norm, albeit horrifying and tragicomic. This had already been done by Petrushevskaia and Sergei Dovlatov, but recent films focus not on the existential and social conditions as manifestations of an anthropological catastrophe, but on various individual scenarios of social adaptation and resistance to this fantastic normalcy. In this respect, the new cinematic wave offers something similar to the studies of Soviet subjectivity, addressing not the Stalinist period but the ongoing present. This similarity is based not only on a common attention to 'human documents' but also on the understanding of the realm that in the preceding generation was perceived apocalyptically, as a space of human existence, self-realization and resistance. Thus, in Fedorchenko's *Silent Souls* an entire mythological world is invented in the course of the filmic depiction of the Meryas' funeral rites. Yet this constructed myth does not emerge as antithesis to a brutal reality, as one may expect: the new myth, centred here around the inseparability of Eros and Thanatos, is inscribed into the prosaic and dilapidated (post-catastrophic) texture of the contemporary Russian province, and is also presented in a (quasi)-documentary manner.

Conclusion

The approaches to post-Soviet culture proposed are above all an intellectual provocation designed to demonstrate the vital need of going beyond a binary opposition between Soviet and post-Soviet culture. The interpretations of post-Soviet cultural phenomena as contrasting with Soviet discourses or, alternatively, reviving the lost grandeur of the Soviet epoch, have lost their heuristic power and no longer reflect the actual intricacy of contemporary cultural processes.

By focusing on a cyclical gravitation of culture towards the poles of 'complexity' and 'simplicity', on interconnected, yet dissimilar, methods of 'working-through' historical traumas, and on lines of continuity linking post-Soviet literature and film with the late Soviet underground, I tried to draw attention to mechanisms of culture that sit deeper than ideological and political change. Contemporary research into Soviet culture in cultural anthropology (Yurchak) or history (Halfin, Hellbeck and others) challenges the worn-off binarist paradigm, according to which Soviet cultural phenomena were split between two universes: official culture controlled by the state and non-conformist culture rebelling against state ideologies and practices. In line with this vision, either all 'official' Soviet culture has been rejected as a totalitarian aberration, or anything aesthetically valuable has been directly linked to pre-Soviet paragons, over the head of the Soviet milieu.

The focus on tendencies over the entire twentieth century of Russian culture, including the Soviet period, links seemingly unrelated phenomena – especially, from the standpoint of their ideological content and sociocultural positioning. This seems to be necessary for an adequate (self)-conceptualization of Russian culture in the twenty-first century not as a culture in a 'transitory' condition (which has been lasting for over two decades now!), but as a furtherance of a newly discovered non-binarist complexity of the Soviet period. The development of such an approach (or rather a whole new spectrum of approaches) is necessary for the historization of contemporary phenomena, a task which is crucial both for scholars of Russian culture and cultural figures alike.

Works cited

Bakhtin, Mikhail (1983), *Problems of Dostoevsky's Poetics*, ed. and transl. by Caryl Emerson, Minneapolis: University of Minnesota Press.

Basinskii, Pavel (2000), 'Kak serdtsu vyskazat' sebia', *Novyi mir* 4, http://magazines.russ.ru/novyi_mi/2000/4/basin.html. Accessed 6 September 2011.

Beliakov, Sergei [2009], 'Istoki i smysl "novogo realizma"', *Rossiiskii pisatel'* http://rospisatel.ru/konferenzija/beljakov.htm. Accessed 6 September 2011.

Beumers, Birgit and Mark Lipovetsky (2009), *Performing Violence: Literary and Theatrical Experiments of New Russian Drama*, Bristol, Chicago: Intellect.

Bol'shakova, Alla [2009], 'Sovremennyi literaturnyi protsess: Tendentsii i perspektivy', *Rossiiskii pisatel'* http://www.rospisatel.ru/konferenzija/bolshakova-doklad.htm. Accessed 6 September 2011.

Bonnell, Victoria (1999), *Iconography of Power: Soviet Political Posters under Lenin and Stalin*, Berkeley: University of California Press.

Cizevsky, Dmitry (1952), *Outline of Comparative Slavic Literatures*, Boston: American Academy (*Survey of Slavic Civilization*, vol.1).

Ermolin, Evgenii (2006), 'Sluchai novogo realizma', *Kontinent* 128, http://magazines.russ.ru/continent/2006/128/ee27.html. Accessed 6 September 2011.

Etkind, Alexander and Mark Lipovetsky (2008), 'The Return of a Triton: The Soviet Catastrophe and the Post-Soviet Novel, *Novoe Literaturnoe Obozrenie* 94: 174–206. Published in English in *Russian Studies in Literature* 6.4 (2010): 6–48.

Fiedler, Leslie (1972), *Cross the Border – Close the Gap*, New York: Stein and Day.

Gasparov, Boris (2003), 'Istoriia bez teleologii (Zametki o Pushkine i ego epokhe)', *Novoe literaturnoe obozrenie* 59, http://magazines.russ.ru/nlo/2003/59/gas3.html. Accessed 6 September 2011.

Halfin, Igal (2003), *Terror in My Soul: Communist Autobiographies on Trial*, Cambridge: Harvard University Press.

Hellbeck, Jochen (2006), *Revolution on My Mind: Writing a Diary under Stalin*, Cambridge, London: Harvard University Press.

Knabe, Georgii S. (1993), *Materialy k lektsiiam po obshchei istorii kul'tury i kul'ture antichnogo Rima*, Moscow: RGGU.

Kobrin, Kirill, Aleksei Levinson, Mark Lipovetskii, Irina Prokhorova, Vladislav Tolstov and Elena Fanailova (2011), 'NOS -1973', *Novoe Literaturnoe Obozrenie* 109, http://magazines.russ.ru/nlo/2011/109/kk23.html. Accessed 6 September 2011.

Konrad, Nikolai (1966), 'O nekotorykh voprosakh istorii mirovoi literatury' (1965), in Konrad, N. *Zapad i Vostok: Stat'i*, Moscow: Nauka, pp. 456–69.

LaCapra, Dominique (1998), 'An Interview with Professor LaCapra by Amos Goldberg', Shoah Research Center, 9 June http://www1.yadvashem.org/odot_pdf/Microsoft%20Word%20-%203648.pdf. Accessed 6 September 2011.

Leiderman, Naum (2010), *Teoriia zhanra: Issledovaniia i razbory*, Ekaterinburg.

Likhachev, Dmitrii (1973), *Razvitie russkoi literatury XI–XVII vekov: epokhi i stili*, Leningrad: Nauka.

Lipovetskii, Mark (2008), *Paralogii: Transformatsii (post)modernistskogo diskursa v russkoi kul'ture 1920–2000-kh godov*, Moscow: Novoe Literaturnoe Obozrenie.

——— (2010), 'Metel' v retrobudushchem: Sorokin o modernizatsii,' http://www.openspace.ru/literature/projects/13073/details/17810/. Accessed 6 September 2011.

Lipovetsky, Mark (2004), 'Post-Soc: Transformations of Socialist Realism in the Popular Culture of the Recent Period,' *Slavic and East European Journal* 48.3, pp. 356–77.

——— (2011), *Charms of the Cynical Reason: The Transformations of the Trickster Trope in Soviet and Post-Soviet Culture*, Boston: Academic Studies Press, 2011.

Martynova, Ol'ga (2009), 'Zagrobnaia pobeda sotsrealizma,' *Neue Zürcher Zeitung* 28 August, http://news.a42.ru/news/item/153067/; also at http://www.openspace.ru/literature/events/details/12295. Accessed 6 September 2011.

Neuberger, Joan (2003), *Ivan the Terrible*, London: I.B.Tauris.

Oushakine, Sergei (2010), *The Patriotism of Despair: Nation, War, and Loss in Russia.* Ithaca, London: Cornell University Press.

Pelevin, Viktor (1999), *Generation 'P'*, Moscow: Vagrius.

Pomerantsev, Vladimir (1953), 'Ob iskrennosti v literature,' *Novyi mir* 12. English translation (abridged) at http://www.thedrawers.net/pomerantsev.htm. Accessed 20 July 2012.

'Proekt NOS-1973,' http://www.prokhorovfund.ru/projects/own/108/444/. Accessed 6 September 2011.

Shalamov, Varlam (1965), 'O prose,' http://shalamov.ru/library/21/45.html. Accessed 6 September 2011.

Smirnov, Igor' (2000), 'Ocherki po istoricheskoi tipologii kul'tury,' in his *Megaistoriia: K istoricheskoi tipologii kul'tury*, Moscow: Agraf, 2000: 11–195.

Sorokin, Vladimir (1999), *Goluboe salo*, Moscow: Ad Marginem.

Wölfflin, Heinrich (1966), *Renaissance and Baroque*, Ithaca: Cornell University Press.

Yurchak, Alexei (2006), *Everything Was Forever, Until It Was No More: The Last Soviet Generation*, Princeton and Oxford: Princeton University Press, 2006.

Notes

1   For example, Mikhail Shishkin's *Vziatie Izmaila/The Taking of Izmail* (2000); *Venerin volos/Maidenhair* (2005); *Pis'movnik/Letter-Book* (2010); the meditative prose by Aleksandr Gol'dshtein (*Pomni o Famaguste/Remember* Famagusta, 2004, *Spokoinye polia/Quiet Fields* (2006)); and Andrei Levkin (*Golem, russkaia versiia/Golem, Russian version* (2000); *Mozgva*, 2005; *Marpl*, 2010).

2   For example, Kirill Serebrennikov's *Playing the Victim* and *Iuriev den'/Yuriev Day* (2008), Ivan Vyrypaev's *Eiforiia/Euphoria* (2006) and *Kislorod/Oxygen* (2009), Vasilii Sigarev's *Volchok/Wolfy* (2009), Aleksei Popogrebskii's *Kak ia provel etim letom/How I Ended this Summer* (2010), Boris Khlebnikov's *Svobodnie plavanie/Free Floating* (2006) and *Sumasshedshaia pomoshch'/Help Gone Mad* (2009), Valeriia Gai-Germanika's *Vse umrut, a ia ostanus'/Everybody Dies But Me* (2008) and her television series *Shkola/School* (2010), Aleksei Mizgirev's *Kremen'/The Hard-Hearted* (2007), Bakur Bakuradze's *Shultes* (2008), Aleksei Fedorchenko's *Ovsianki/Silent Souls* (2010), Svetlana Proskurina's *Peremirie/Truce* (2010) and Sergei Loznitsa's *Schast'e moe/My Joy* (2010).

3   Among the 'finalists' were Solzhenitsyn with the first volume of *Arkhipelag Gulag/Gulag Archipelago*, the first book publications (outside the USSR) of Venedikt Erofeev's *Moskva-Petushki/Moscow to the End of the Line*, Andrei Siniavskii's *Progulki s Pushkinym/Strolls with Pushkin*, Varlam Shalamov's *Kolymskie rasskazy/Kolyma Tales*; Sasha Sokolov's *Shkola dlia durakov/School for Fools* (completed in 1973 but published in 1975). The list comprised some seminal texts published in Soviet journals and publishing houses in 1973, such as Vasilii Shukshin's *Kharaktery/Characters*, Iurii Trifonov's *Neterpenie/Impatience*, the Strugatskii Brothers' *Piknik na obochine/A Roadside Picnic*), later transformed by Andrei Tarkovsky into his famous film *Stalker*, 1979), and select chapters from Fazil' Iskander's mock epic *Sandro iz Chegema/Sandro of Chegem* (1973). The shortlist also included some works not published until the late 1980s–90s, but written around 1973, such as Evgenii Kharitonov's and Igor' Kholin's prose, as well as Liudmila Petrushevskaia's first full-length play *Uroki muzyki/Music Lessons*.

4   Aside from Pelevin, one may list as practitioners of the Menippean method Vladimir Sharov (*Do i vo vremia/Before and During Time* (1995); *Repetitsii/The Rehearsal* (1997); *Voskresenie Lazaria/The Resurrection of Lazarus* (2003); *Staraia devocka/The Old Little Girl* (2000); *Budem kak deti/Be like Children* (2008)) or Pavel Peppershtein (*Mifogennaia liubov' kast/The Mythological Love of Castes* (1999–2002); *Vesna/Spring* (2010)). Among the younger generation, Vyrypaev's dramatic Menippeas *Oxygen* (2002; also a film of 2009), *Bytie No. 2/Genesis 2* (2004), and especially *Iiul'/July* (2006) are living proof of the rich potential of this strategy of working-through traumas in contemporary culture (see Beumers and Lipovetsky 2009: 241–69).

Chapter 3

Victor Pelevin and the Void

Meghan Vicks

The void is a paradoxical and complicated concept in Victor Pelevin's writings, just as the eponymous 'P' of his novel *Generation 'P'* (1999)[1] is an ambiguous referent, suggesting a number of possible meanings. Most obviously, 'P' stands for Pepsi, signifying those 'children of the Soviet seventies [who] chose Pepsi in precisely the same way as their parents chose Brezhnev' (Pelevin 2003: 1). This indicates a generation whose identity and ideology are defined by consumer culture. However, Pelevin has suggested in an interview that the 'P' may also stand for the obscene term *pizdets*, whose linguistic root is *pizda*, meaning 'cunt'. *Pizdets* generally means 'the end of everything', or, to be more literarily crass, a 'cuntastrophe'. As such, 'Generation *Pizdets*' is a generation that has come to a vulgar end – 'a generation that faces catastrophe', proposes Pelevin (2000). In that same interview, Pelevin puts forward yet another interpretation of the 'P', that is to say Putin, but then concedes, 'it's whatever you like'. In other words, the 'P' can signify whatever one wants or needs it to signify; it has no stable meaning of its own. This points to yet another understanding of the 'P': as Sally Dalton-Brown notes (2006: 246 n12), it may stand for *pustota*, which means 'emptiness' or 'void'. Indeed, *pustota* is a central theme in Pelevin's writings, not only foregrounded in one of his earliest novels, *Chapaev i pustota/Chapaev and Voyd* (1996, transl. 1999), but also recurring throughout his literary oeuvre up till the present day. Of course, the concept of 'emptiness' also figures predominantly in Pelevin's well-known study and practice of Buddhism.[2]

Thus, the novel's title may signify a brand-crazed generation defined by consumerism (Pepsi); a dead, already-ended, catastrophic generation without meaning or direction (*pizdets*); or an empty generation (*pustota*). While these various understandings of the meaning of 'P' may seem to contradict one another, I would like to suggest that they are unified in the concept of nothingness that permeates Pelevin's writings. While Pepsi and *pizdets* represent a nihilistic form of nothingness that results from (the loss of) grand narratives such as Soviet communism and post-Soviet capitalism, *pustota* signifies a spiritual form of nothingness that may provide meaning, beauty, agency and respite to those mired in the nihilistic nothingness of Pelevin's world. In fact, Pelevin's fiction repeatedly demonstrates how nothingness is both the crisis of and the salvation from modern day existence.

In what follows, I analyse three of Pelevin's most famous novels – *Chapaev and Voyd*, *Generation 'P'* and *Sviashchennaia kniga oborotnia/The Sacred Book of the Werewolf* (2004, transl. 2008) – demonstrating how nothingness is both a predicament of today's world and the means to transcendence. *Chapaev and Voyd* and *The Sacred Book of the Werewolf* focus more upon the empowering and freeing condition of nothingness, whereas *Generation 'P'* highlights the abject terror and meaninglessness inherent in the nihilistic nothingness produced by an ideology-ridden society (in this specific case, capitalism). When we look at the trajectory of these three novels, we find that Pelevin begins by exploring the positive aspects of the void with *Chapaev and Voyd* in 1996, then shifts to the nihilistic and pessimistic void in 1999's *Generation 'P'*, before returning to a more optimist treatment of the void in 2004 with *The Sacred Book of the Werewolf*; I will return to the meaning of this trajectory in the conclusion.

Nihilistic nothingness in *Generation 'P'*

Generation 'P' presents a newly post-Soviet Moscow that is simultaneously grappling with the loss of Soviet society, and the ushering in of capitalism where Soviet ideology once reigned. Pelevin presents this situation in both comic and horrific lights: on the one hand, the replacement of Soviet ideology with capitalism provides ample material for the carnivalesque mocking of any ideological system that dictates reality; on the other hand, the situation reveals the lack of stable meaning and dearth of truth in the world, which Pelevin's hero, Babylen Tatarsky, experiences as horror and abjection. This shift from one ideology to another, and the accompanying influx of media and consumerism, blur so greatly the distinctions between high and low culture (high art is used to market cheap goods), between self and object (you are what you buy) and between politics and propaganda (the media control the political) that nothing harbours secure meaning. It is in this way that nothingness takes centre stage in Pelevin's post-Soviet Russia: through the perpetual deconstruction of various binary oppositions – a deconstruction that is fuelled by capitalism – society loses its stable foundation of meaning-making structures. *Generation 'P'* demonstrates how capitalism produces a nihilistic nothingness, and renders its subjects empty vessels through which to channel money.

One method Pelevin employs to demonstrate the consequent meaninglessness caused by the replacement of one ideology for another, and capitalism's production of nothingness, is to utilize sacred cultural emblems to market goods. The use of art for such consumer ends undermines the ideals and disinterestedness of art itself: art is no longer under the control of an aesthetic judgement, which operates by virtue of the fact that there is no yardstick by which to measure the worth of art; nor is art the vessel of the ideal anymore. Instead, art becomes something used to make money, which in turn renders art the sum of its monetary worth. For example, Tatarsky reads Pugin's advertisement for the Gap chain of clothing stores Anton Chekhov is shown with his bare legs splayed, creating the outline of a gap. The advertisement reads, 'RUSSIA WAS ALWAYS NOTORIOUS FOR THE GAP BETWEEN CULTURE AND CIVILISATION. NOW THERE IS NO MORE CULTURE, NO MORE CIVILISATION. THE ONLY THING THAT REMAINS IS THE GAP. THE WAY THEY SEE YOU' (Pelevin 2003: 63). The use of a pant-less Chekhov to advertise a brand known for its jeans implies the degradation (literally, the bringing down to the lower-bodily stratum) of a symbol of Russian literature, and also suggests the urgent need for this degraded, pant-less symbol to improve its grade and fill its lack by purchasing a pair of jeans at the Gap. High art is in need of a new image and ideology, one that can be bought, embodied in a brand name and resold to others. Furthermore, the advertisement's turn on the pun – the Gap (the store) and the gap (a figuration of nothingness) – allows for a significant double reading: the first, that nothing remains but the Gap, which is consumerism; the second, that nothing remains but the gap, which is nothing itself. The products of capitalism – consumerism and nothingness – become synonymous, even indistinguishable.

Additionally, even when art is not used as fodder for advertisements, but instead is presented as a valuable object in its own right, the artwork itself is not actually presented at all; a description of the piece and a price tag are displayed in its place. Art's worth has been reduced to its monetary value: as Tatarsky's boss, Azadovsky, explains, Russia has invented a new wave of art called 'monetaristic minimalism' (Pelevin 2003: 232). As a result, art, which used to transcend any measurement of worth, has been reduced or 'minimalized' to a single measurement – how much one pays for it. Furthermore, the pieces of art represented by the price tags may not actually exist. Alla, Azadovsky's secretary, reads descriptions of paintings and sculptures that are similar to real artworks by artists such as Goya, Picasso and Velasquez. However, the descriptions do not perfectly match up to existing pieces. It appears that what is described are artworks that seem like they very well could exist (they have characteristics of well-known works by Goya, Picasso and Velasquez), but in fact do not. With this possibility in mind, I would like to suggest that in Pelevin's novel, there is no artwork actually for sale behind the price tag. In Tatarsky's world, art has literally been minimized, reduced to its price tag; nothing exists besides its monetary value, and this is what is truly meant by 'monetaristic minimalism'. This serves as a metaphor for what Pelevin perceives as the newfound status of art in post-Soviet Russian culture: it is only as valuable as its monetary worth (as we will see, he applies this status to his own novel, *Generation 'P'*, as well).

The wave of 'monetaristic minimalism' that has swept through the realm of art parallels man's (d)evolution from Homo sapiens to Homo zapiens (from a television 'zapper'). Pelevin presents man as existing in a condition where binary oppositions are chimeras: 'the dualism that imposes the division into subject and object […] has never existed and never will' (Pelevin 2003: 77). It follows that man is no longer able to perceive himself as separate from the objects around him, many of which attempt to market themselves as expressions of his 'self'. Illustrative of this new state is 'The Path to Your Self', the fittingly named store Tatarsky stumbles upon that sells, among other items, T-shirts that advertise one's personal rebellions and beliefs; that is, the store sells one's image – who one will become. *You are what you buy* becomes quite literal in Tatarsky's world, just as art is reduced to how much one will pay for it.

As such, man is no longer able to distinguish himself from the spectacle surrounding him, which includes advertisements, branding, media and television: man no longer perceives a difference between the reality that is the material world, and the reality that is the material world as seen on television. This new condition of man is dubbed 'collective non-existence' and the 'unreal':

> There are no words to describe the degree of its unreality. It is a heaping of one unreality upon another, a castle constructed of air, the foundations of which stand upon a profound abyss. […] The position of modern man is not merely lamentable; one might even say there is no condition, because man hardly exists. Nothing exists to which one could point and say: 'There, that is *Homo Zapiens*.' *HZ* is simply the residual luminescence of a soul fallen asleep; it is a film about the shooting of another film, shown on a television in an empty house.
>
> (Pelevin 2003: 80, 82; emphasis in the original)

Man's new non-condition is reminiscent of art's material minimalism. As paintings and statues – art's material and visual nature – have been exchanged for price tags, so *Homo sapiens* has evolved into *Homo zapiens*: that is, men that can hardly be called men, can be said not to exist, as they are nothing but a conglomeration of images and brands that are themselves built upon a 'heaping of one unreality upon another'. To paraphrase Pelevin, the condition of modern man would be lamentable if modern man could still be said to exist at all. By the end of the novel, Tatarsky fulfils this fate of modern man by being himself reduced to the servile adjunct of his own televised image.

The novel blames capitalism for man's newfound non-existence, and capitalism itself is figured as the all-consuming and all-being oranus – another emblem of the void, as we will see. As humans have evolved to the post-reality state of *Homo zapiens*, they now exist only insofar as they are characterized (given an identity) by images; that is, they only exist to the extent that they are branded. The consumerist impulses that compel *Homo zapiens* to purchase their identities and experiences (and thereby come into being), along with the sum total of *Homines zapientes* themselves (which continue to want to be, and establish their beings, through further purchases), together comprise a giant, all-encompassing oranus. Each *Homo zapien* equals a single cell of the oranus, whose existence depends entirely upon a continuous flow of money streaming through it. To ensure that money is constantly exchanged between each of its cells, the oranus has developed a central nervous system known as the media, whose never-ceasing advertisements fuel the *Homo zapiens'* desires to buy and sell. Besides its raison d'être – to perpetuate a stream of money – the oranus has no other characteristic or function; it is itself an emblem of zero, a signifier and conveyor of nothing: 'Oranus has neither ears, nor nose, nor eyes, nor mind. […] In itself it wishes for nothing, since it is simply incapable of wishing in the abstract. It is an inane polyp, devoid of emotion or intention, which ingests and eliminates emptiness' (Pelevin 2003: 84). Again, *pustota*/emptiness is reiterated as the definitive nature of all things in the new cultural non-condition. The void is the culminating product of capitalism, the essence of man, the status of art and culture and the only truth and reality in the novel's post-Soviet world.

In *Generation 'P'*, then, Pelevin diagnoses post-Soviet culture much in the same way as western postmodernists characterize twentieth-century western culture. The vanishing of the subject in postmodern existence may be witnessed in the transition of man from *Homo sapiens* to *Homo zapiens*. Jean Baudrillard writes extensively on the simulative nature of reality, and this crisis of meaning occasioned by the rule of consumerism and commercial images is a common theme in western postmodernism, especially in the work of Fredric Jameson. However, Pelevin figures these postmodern notions quite literally, not just as a metaphor: art is no longer displayed in galleries, and humans can no longer be said to exist. In her excellent study 'From Homo Sovieticus to Homo Zapiens: Viktor Pelevin's Consumer Dystopia' Sofya Khagi argues that 'if Baudrillard still leaves room for a metaphorical reading of his provocative thesis about the Gulf War, with some provisional "reality" beyond the virtual warfare presented for the benefit of the populace, then Pelevin's politicians are literally disembodied' (Khagi 2008: 563). More importantly, Pelevin develops his postmodern theories with a Russian twist, one which inserts a meta-awareness into the system that displays how all existence is, and always has been, empty, and how all cultural conditions have really been non-conditions; only the realization that such is the case is new. This focus on the emptiness inherent in culture is a staple of Russian postmodernism, an early manifestation of which appears in the sots-art movement, as well as in the work of other Russian conceptualists during the second half of the twentieth century.[3] An intentional play-off of Andy Warhol's 'pop art', sots-art likewise utilizes images from popular culture and brings them into a sacred space (e.g. the museum, Soviet ideology). However, the main distinction between sots-art and Russian conceptualism and their western counterparts, (besides the former's play with the familiar images of Socialist Realism), is their insistence on 'emptiness as the ultimate signified of all signifieds' (Epstein 1995: 200). As Ilya Kabakov, one of the foremost Russian conceptualists, writes:

In contrast with the West, the principle of 'one thing instead of another' does not exist and is not in force, most of all because in this binomial the definitive, clear second element, this 'another', does not exist. It is as if in our country it has been taken out of the equation, it is simply not there. [...] What we get is a striking paradox, nonsense: things, ideas, facts inevitable with great exertion enter into direct contact with the unclear, the undefined, in essence with emptiness. This contiguity, closeness, touchingness, contact with nothing, emptiness makes up, we feel, the basic peculiarity of 'Russian conceptualism'.

(Kabakov 1992: 247)

Russian conceptualism explores the nothingness that makes up existence. In 'Like a Corpse in the Desert', Epstein reiterates Kabakov's view when he describes conceptualist poetry as 'the poetry of crossed-out words, words that cancel themselves out at the moment of utterance, as if devoid of meaning. [...] They present the riddle of self-manifest emptiness' (Epstein [1987] 1999: 136). And Alexander Genis famously describes the cultural condition of Russia through the metaphor of a 'cored onion' – a culture with many layers surrounding an absent centre:

Here, in the 1990s [...] we may draw on a new metaphor, signaling the emergence of a new cultural paradigm, born of the emptiness or *nothingness* that was perceived as fatal to the earlier paradigm. [...] In the paradigm of the onion, the emptiness at the center is not a cemetery but a source of meaning. This is the cosmic zero point, around which being germinates. This emptiness, which is both everything and nothing, is the focus of the world. The world is made possible only because of the emptiness at its center. It structures being, bestows form on things, and allows things to function.

(Genis 1999: 411; emphasis in the original)

As we will see, Genis's optimistic view of nothingness as the ultimate potentiality, or creative force, is present in *Chapaev and Voyd* and *The Sacred Book of the Werewolf*.

However, this optimism is largely absent in *Generation 'P'*; instead, the atmosphere and narrative style of the novel pivot back and forth between carnivalesque carousing and abject horror, ultimately offering neither meaning nor salvation from meaninglessness. The aesthetics and mood of this post-Soviet non-condition are at once distinguished by both Mikhail Bahktin's notions of the carnival, and by Julia Kristeva's theories of abjection. Pelevin's novel reveals how carnival and abjection are two sides of the same coin, and share at their core a liminal state of zero – neither absence nor presence of being, but an utterly ambiguous, *pustoi/empty* being (e.g. moth-eaten images, soulless Homo zapiens). These liminal and out-of-bounds states of carnival and abjection have become permanent features of Pelevin's post-Soviet empty world: the perpetual deconstruction of binary oppositions highlights the fleeting nature of meaning and the non-existence of transcendental truth, which, on the one hand, is accompanied by revelry in the freedom produced by the release from officialdom, and, on the other hand, incites terror in the face of borderless existence. As such, a full appreciation of Pelevin's conception of this Generation Pustota, or, this non-condition of culture, must take into account how his notions of emptiness are intimately related to theories of carnival and abjection. Emptiness, carnival and the abject together comprise an aesthetic trinity in *Generation 'P'*.

Much of the imagery, plotting and characters of Pelevin's post-Soviet empty world seem plucked from the aesthetic arsenal of Bakhtin's carnival. First of all, in Pelevin's novel, the sacred (high culture, art, literature, religion, God, truth, etc.) is ubiquitously combined with the profane (low culture, everydayness, advertisements, ribald jokes, cigarettes, drugs, sex, etc.); the degradation of the sacred is, of course, one of the chief elements of the carnivalesque tradition.[4] Second, the novel presents a world in which the spectacle (images) has taken the place of reality. This is another important motif in the carnival: a spectacle without spectators, wherein everyone is a participant in a sweeping performance that has become the world.[5] The power and authority of the spectacle is emphasized repeatedly throughout the novel, and not just at the end when Tatarsky is subjected to his televised image. For instance, when Morkovin takes Tatarsky to Daft Podium, he shows him an expensive Silicon Graphics computer installed with a Soft Image program that is twice as expensive as the computer itself; the images are literally more valued than the material machine that displays them. Another carnivalesque element consists of parodic pantomimes of official figures that have taken the place of all official figures – reminiscent of the jester's replacement of the king during carnival.[6] For instance, Tatarsky discovers that Boris Yeltsin has long been dead, and that the Boris Yeltsin that continues to serve as president is actually a digital dummy of the man whose jester-like antics – perpetual drunkenness, stumbling over important foreign and state officials, continual mess-making – are the combined efforts of advertisers and television executives who strive to secure high ratings. Last, while the novel's oranus is analogous to the collective and unfinished grotesque body of the carnival tradition, there are two significant differences: first, whereas Bakhtin's notion of the 'grotesque body' is the literal embodiment of the corporeal condition of the world during carnival time, Pelevin's oranus is a figurative representation of the non-condition of post-Soviet culture; and second, the grotesque body is temporary and only exists for the period of carnival, while the oranus is a seemingly permanent fixture of Pelevin's world. In all, these signifiers and motifs of carnival found throughout the novel are expressions of the culture's emptiness and non-condition. The freedom produced by the collapse of universal truths, and by the deconstruction of binary oppositions, renders the world topsy-turvy, equalizes high and low cultures and unleashes a celebratory, blithe mood.

However, in this permanent carnival state that never returns to an official order, the lack of meaning and emptiness at its core soon becomes horrific. Carnival quickly turns into its dark twin, the abject, which famously resides in the realm where meaning and distinctions have completely collapsed – or never existed. In *Powers of Horror*, Kristeva defines the abject as something akin to absolute otherness, or 'the jettisoned object' (Kristeva 1982: 2). The abject is neither subject nor object, but that impossible and unthinkable ambiguity that resides outside of any and all systems of meaning, in 'the place where meaning collapses' (Kristeva 1982: 2). She writes, the abject is 'a "something" that I do not recognize as a thing. A weight of meaninglessness, about which there is nothing insignificant, and which crushes me. On the edge of nonexistence and hallucination, or a reality that, if I acknowledge it, annihilates me' (Kristeva 1982: 2). In Pelevin's novel, the emptiness that resides at the core of culture jettisons the post-Soviet world into the realm of the abject. The opening scenes present a world saturated by a sinister ambiguity and a dark mood provoked by the fact that everything once life-affirming and positive has been rendered meaningless waste: 'It wasn't possible to say that the essential nature of the world had changed, either, because now it no longer had any essential nature. A frighteningly vague uncertainty dominated everything' (Kristeva 1982: 6). Here, the notion of emptiness is symbiotically connected to an abject aura: a 'frighteningly vague uncertainty' dominates everything, the essential nature of which is non-existent. This symbiotic relationship between emptiness and the abject is reiterated in a later passage that describes how the Soviet realm, which no longer exists, has been replaced by a putrid uncertainty: 'Lenin's statues were gradually carted out of town on military trucks […], but his presence was merely replaced by a frightening murky grayness in which the Soviet soul simply continued rotting until it collapsed inwards on itself' (Kristeva 1982: 19). The abject that accompanies the post-Soviet non-condition of culture continually threatens to annihilate those characters, including Tatarsky, who recognize it. As Kristeva explains that the abject is 'what [is] permanently thrust aside in order to live'

(Kristeva 1982: 3), so Pelevin's novel illustrates how awareness of the meaninglessness and emptiness of the world must be repeatedly kept at bay, oftentimes through drugs and self-inflicted pain. Suffering and hallucinations become methods for constructing at least the appearance of borders (and therefore, the appearance of a self) in a borderless, abject and empty world in which the death of the self has transpired.

A certain paradox emerges when we consider the role that both carnival and the abject play in the creation of meaning (often in the form of art and literature) out of chaos, together with the death of literature and meaning that Pelevin's novel suggests. Many critics have interpreted the novel as a parable for the death of the intelligentsia, and the end of the sacred literary word, in post-Soviet culture. These readings point to still another form of emptiness suggested by the novel: the reduction of literature to zero as depicted in and embodied by the novel itself. Such interpretations focus on the trajectory taken by Tatarsky in the novel – he begins as an idealistic student who aspires to be a great poet, and ends as a cynic who writes and stars in advertisements. This suggests that the intelligentsia – traditionally the main producer and consumer of literature – has also been reduced to a meaningless zero. Lyudmila Parts, for instance, reads the novel as an allegory for the transformation of the concept of the intelligentsia in the post-Soviet period, and demonstrates how this transformation is embodied in Tatarsky: '[Pelevin] presents the story of the conversion of an *intelligent* into a copywriter [...]. In this story, the degradation of the word accompanies and precipitates the degradation of its carrier, the intelligentsia' (Parts 2004: 441). In Parts's view, the novel tells the story of the death of Russia's literary class and the accompanying de-mythologizing of the intelligentsia, which is brought about by the destruction of language's sacredness. When we recall that Tatarsky's background shares many similarities with Pelevin's own personal history, we can add an additional dimension to Parts's claim: Tatarsky's story also represents Pelevin's own implied status as a member of the degraded intelligentsia who no longer writes literature.[7] Pelevin therefore reduces himself to zero – a signifier of nothing – as well.

Furthermore, the form of *Generation 'P'* evokes the process of watching television, and thereby suggests that Pelevin's novel itself is not literature. Stephen Hutchings points out that the main narrative thread is repeatedly interposed by proposals for advertisements that Tatarsky is writing, and therefore 'resembles a televisual anti-novel', functioning much in the same way as a television show that is constantly interrupted by commercial breaks; as such, the novel 'enacts the end of literature' (Hutchings 2004: 177). The cover for the novel's first edition (published by Vagrius) also reiterates the notion that Pelevin is not writing literature, but instead selling a brand. Foregrounding Che Guevara wearing a beret that bears the Nike logo, with a background composed of tiled Coke logos to his right versus tiled Pepsi logos to his left (together comprising a commercialized yin-yang), the cover image suggests that the novel is 'a visually packaged commercial product, rather than a product of the spirit' (Hutchings 2004: 177). Especially the yin-yang comprised of Coke and Pepsi indicates that the opposing forces that give rise to the natural and spiritual worlds are the ebb and flow of consumerism. Coke and Pepsi, of course, figure in the novel as metonyms for western capitalism and Soviet communism respectively, with the former taking the place of the latter in the course of the novel. Such a shift from Pepsi to Coke, however, essentially amounts to no shift at all – merely the replacement of one brown liquid for another; likewise, the shift from Sovietism to capitalism is figured in the novel as an exchange of one meaningless ideological system for another.

The aforementioned edition of *Generation 'P'* was not the only edition of the novel that was published by Vagrius during the year the novel was released. Khagi argues that, 'to appeal to the widest target group, both "high cultural" and "pulp" editions of the novel were issued' (Khagi 2008: 571). In effect, Pelevin adopts Tatarsky's theory of 'positioning' in order to market his novel: goods must be 'positioned' in such a way as to appeal to their target group. The above edition represents the 'mass market' positioning, while the 'high cultural' edition is much more modest, with Vagrius' typical black and white cover, and an image of Bruegel's *Tower of Babel*. Likewise, when the first English edition of the novel was released in 1999, it was published as *Babylon* in the United Kingdom, and as *Homo Zapiens* in the United States; these different titles reflect how the novel has been positioned according to the perceived tastes of its given consumer. Ultimately, the commercial packaging of the novel, coupled with the Russian-logos-to-western-advertising narrative, put forward the notion that literature itself has witnessed its end point, and has, like post-Soviet culture, become empty.

This idea that *Generation 'P'* is not a novel at all, but rather an anti-novel that embodies, in form and content, emptied literature – the logos brought to zero, logos without meaning – is complicated and even brought into a paradox when we consider the carnival and abject aesthetics that the novel employs. For both carnival and abjection are semiotic systems of liminality that produce the transcendental signified. One of the most important ideas in Bakhtin's *Rabelais and His World* concerns the corporeal word itself, and specifically, how it is born out of carnivalization and the grotesque body. The carnival uncrowns what was once a highly sacred act of naming and creating language, and brings the word down to the lower, material, bodily level in order to refresh it anew and manifest a richness of novel meanings. During carnival, the word becomes the offspring of the high and the low; it is at once of the body and of the mind, the oxymoronic fleshy idea and, significantly, re-links the proverbial golden chain between the signified and the signifier. As such, carnival rejuvenates the word, and, by proxy, the world with meaning. Likewise, the abject, as Kristeva argues, is closely (and even, perhaps, *necessarily*) tied to the production of art and religion. Kristeva makes the case that the best modern literature investigates the abject, the place where boundaries begin to break down, where we are brought face to face with an archaic and tenuous space that resides before linguistic, social or psychological binaries such as self/other or subject/object. The transcendental project, for Kristeva, is really our effort to smooth over the fractures of meaning associated with the abject: 'On close inspection, all literature is probably a version of the apocalypse that seems to me rooted, no matter what its socio-historical conditions might be, on the fragile border where identities do not exist or only barely so – double, fuzzy, heterogeneous, animal, metamorphosed, altered, abject' (Kristeva 1982: 207). The abject conditions, even necessitates, the aesthetic or religious project that creates the transcendental signified. For both Bakhtin and Kristeva, then, the apocalyptic moment generates a creative impulse that produces meaning, which makes Pelevin's employment of these systems to depict the post-Soviet non-condition of culture, and the accompanying death of literature, all the more troubling: *Generation 'P'* implies that carnival and abjection, which once produced meaning out of the apocalyptic moment, have lost their power to do so in the postmodern condition. Or, that the meaning that *is* produced – consumerism – is empty, no longer related to anything beyond the image.

This is a further way in which Pelevin dismantles his novel as novel, and denies his novel's literary art: he removes the meaning-making power and ability to produce ideals from aesthetic and theoretical systems (such as carnival and abjection) that have been studied and celebrated for their ability to generate meaning in an otherwise chaotic world. In all, *Generation 'P'* performs in its narrative and published forms as 'voided writing': it does so by marketing itself like a consumer product (which the text establishes as inherently empty), by reading as a television show interrupted by commercials (which functions to deny the novel's status as literary art), by dismantling aesthetic systems that traditionally produced meaning and by featuring a protagonist whose history reflects Pelevin's, thus implying that Tatarsky's journey from a meaningful to a meaningless logo is also the author's. The content of the novel figures as 'writing about the void': the story of Tatarsky in post-Soviet Russia demonstrates how art has reached its zero-point (literature has been replaced by advertisements; 'monetaristic minimalism'), how the human subject no longer exists (*Homo sapiens* have become *Homo zapiens*) and how the current cultural condition is a 'non-condition' (the oranus is the figuration of an all-consuming cultural void). While we might be tempted to read the novel as a dystopian critique of consumer culture, the novel's own consumerist form empties it both of its ability to satirize and of literature's traditional capacity to champion ideals that society strives to realize. *Generation 'P'* ultimately paints a pessimistic portrait of the post-Soviet world and the void, and echoes many well-known anxieties concerning the postmodern condition – in a world where everything is empty, how can one avoid nihilism? *Generation 'P'* diagnoses the state, but offers no remedy for this anxiety.

Bifurcated realities and the sacred, productive void: *Chapaev and Voyd* and *The Sacred Book of the Werewolf*

The deconstruction of binary oppositions that is ubiquitous in *Generation 'P'*, and that is at once the symptom and the cause of an empty culture, is found throughout many of Pelevin's other works – often taking the form of opposing realities that coexist. By setting up these coexistences that are inherently at odds with one another, reminiscent of Borgesian 'gardens of forking paths',[8] Pelevin's writings explore the nature of reality itself, always asking the question *what is 'is'?* His answer, as it is in *Generation 'P'*, is always nothingness; however this ontological void is not always accompanied by such pessimism as is found in *Generation 'P'*.

Intimately related to these multiple realities is the paradoxical notion that the void is at the centre of them all, and that nothingness is the essence of each reality or being – that is, the void is the creative force, the necessary element for anything to exist. It is in this way that Pelevin's preoccupation with the void as a cultural condition takes on a positive aspect and creative power, and even becomes a means to transcend the nihilistic nothingness that is portrayed in *Generation 'P'*. Emptiness becomes the only true state of being, the force that allows for existence, and is therefore a vessel of the sacred; it becomes the transcendental signified.

Bifurcated realities that are generated by a void is a theme that is central to Pelevin's *Chapaev and Voyd*, which is a literal translation of the novel's original Russian title, *Chapaev i Pustota*. Like *Generation 'P'*, the novel has been translated into English under two different titles: *The Clay Machine Gun* (United Kingdom, 1998) and *Buddha's Little Finger* (United States, 1999). The main character of the novel is also variously known as Peter Null in the UK edition, and Pyotr Voyd in the US edition. These divergent translations embody one of the main philosophies of the novel: alternative realities that simultaneously coexist in the same single entity. As Voyd/Null is the central character upon which these narratives are built, this indicates that these divergent narratives are also generated by the void. Moreover, when we place the US and UK translations side-by-side, they together form a visual and material representation of the novel's most significant symbol: the clay machine gun, which is also Buddha's little finger; likewise, Pyotr Voyd is Peter Null. At the core of both Voyd/Null, and the clay machine gun/Buddha's little finger, is the void of existence. As we discover in the course of the novel, when one shoots/points the gun/finger at something, its true nature is revealed as nothingness; that is, it disappears.

Thus, the image of the gun/finger represents the bifurcated realities that inhabit Pelevin's novelistic world, and moreover symbolizes the emptiness that is this world's essence: when one holds a mirror up to the gun/finger, the mirror reveals the true nature of the gun/finger by causing it to disappear. These realities only seemingly exist, they are only the appearance of realities, and beneath them there is literally nothing. As the novel's hero, Petka, puts it, existence is 'a golden label on an empty bottle … A shop where everything is displayed in a magnificently arranged window-setting, but that tiny, tender, narrow little room behind it […] Yes, that room is empty [void]' (Pelevin 1999: 287). His familial name, Voyd/Null (*Pustota*), draws Petka's statements to a full circle – there is a void (*pusto*) behind all existence, and there is Voyd (*Pustota*). Petka's statement at once affirms and erases his own being, and establishes him simultaneously *as both the creator and the created of his world, as both the signified and the signifier*, thereby exhibiting Pelevin's notions of a transcendental void generating the world, and the world, in turn, regenerating the very void that generates it. The void, in other words, is the sacred, productive space in *Chapaev and Voyd*.

In *The Sacred Book of the Werewolf*, Pelevin revisits the theme of bifurcated realities and the void as truth, but he more acutely explores how realization of these notions can become a source of creativity and power over one's existence. Whereas in *Chapaev and Voyd*, Pelevin's oxymoronic enlightened/insane hero is largely unaware of *why* he is simultaneously living in two separate realities, and for the most part must be taught the nature and power of the void, in *The Sacred Book of the Werewolf* Pelevin's heroine is fully aware of the power of emptiness, and uses this knowledge to control the world around her. A Hu-Li, the were-fox heroine of *The Sacred Book of the Werewolf*, understands the empty nature of the world, and her status as a shape-shifting were-creature symbolizes her corporeal and physiological embodiment of this enlightenment. As Pelevin's novels suggest, if the nature of existence is emptiness, and if the void is the only true and stable reality, it follows that any number of realities, even mutually contradicting realities, can exist simultaneously. The figure of a were-creature personifies Pelevin's philosophy: she can adopt different shapes or 'realities', because she truly, *viscerally* understands that she has no true stable nature – or that her stable nature is nothing itself.

This shift from *Chapaev and Voyd* to *The Sacred Book of the Werewolf* exhibits the evolution of Pelevin's exploration of the productive void and its enabling of bifurcated realities. Following the trajectory of Pelevin's fiction, we find that most of his stories and novels take place in different varieties of bifurcated existences, and that his more recent fiction increasingly portrays this forked nature in hybrid creatures: that is, the heroes of his later novels include more were-creatures and vampires (beings who corporeally embody a bifurcated nature), whereas the heroes of his earlier novels simultaneously exist in two or more realms, but are not themselves hybrid beings. In other words, the trajectory of Pelevin's fiction begins with bifurcated realms and increasingly narrows to bifurcated, hybrid beings. The emergence of these hybrid beings that embody Pelevin's notions of bifurcated realities is accompanied by his heroes' increasing agency and control over their worlds. Thus, the heroes of Pelevin's earliest novels – Omon of *Omon Ra* (1991), the cast of insects/humans in *The Life of Insects* (1993), Petka of *Chapaev and Voyd* – each exist simultaneously in opposing realities: Omon believes he has performed a mission on the moon, only to discover that it took place in an abandoned subway tunnel; the characters in *The Life of Insects* simultaneously live both as humans and as insects; and Petka, of course, exists both in 1919 Soviet Russia and 1991 post-Soviet Russia. None of these early characters, however, have any consistent control over which existence they occupy. In contrast, Pelevin's more recent hybrid characters *do* have control over their worlds: this is especially apparent in *The Sacred Book of the Werewolf, Empire V* (2006) and *t* (2009).

The void is therefore figured as a productive and creative force in *The Sacred Book of the Werewolf*, even though A Hu-Li is fully aware of the consumerist and nihilistic emptiness that is ubiquitously present in her world, and that is so pessimistically depicted in *Generation 'P'*. In fact, this destructive and meaningless emptiness is embodied in the other main were-creature of the novel, the werewolf Alexander. A Hu-Li therefore lives in a culture that is still entirely empty and fuelled by meaningless price tags; however, she directly confronts the empty nature of the world, and manipulates it to her own ends. In doing so, she demonstrates how the void can be the ultimate generative source, can transcend the nihilistic emptiness left in the wake of delegitimated grand narratives and can refashion the truth (that is, the void) to be anything she wishes.

Conclusion

Since the late 1990s, a prominent trend in various branches of Russian postmodernism has been to 'restore the reality which had been destroyed by the aggression of simulacra' (Lipovetsky 2001: 12). This desire to restore reality and re-mythologize cultural myths coincides, paradoxically, with the deconstruction of binary oppositions, delegitimization of ideological paradigms and with the demythologization of myths. We view this paradox at work in Pelevin's literary corpus, which illustrates, on the one hand, the lack of reality occasioned by the precession of simulacra and deconstruction of ideology (thereby evoking feelings of nostalgia at its best and nihilism at its worst), and on the other hand, attempts to restore reality by granting this 'lack of reality' the utmost meaning. That is, Pelevin mythologizes the void itself; he makes meaninglessness meaningful. The absence of reality – the void – that is revealed through deconstruction, and that generates simulacra, becomes mythology, ideology and meaning in Pelevin's writings: the void becomes the transcendental signified. This is how Pelevin 'restores the reality which had been destroyed by the aggression of simulacra': he makes meaningful this very lack of reality.

As a concept in Pelevin's work, the void cannot be reduced to a single meaning. In *Generation 'P'*, the void is horrifying, reduces all to meaninglessness, creates inertia and empties culture. But Pelevin also relates the void to writing literature (creating meaning and beauty), and with the production of reality itself. He first explores the positive and productive potentials of the void in 1996 with *Chapaev*, and then takes a pessimistic turn in 1999 with the nihilistic void of *Generation*. After a long pause, he produces the sacred book in 2004, and in doing so returns to the productive void – indeed, a sacred void that has taken the place of the transcendental signified. In all three cases, the void is immanent reality, but its own characteristics are just as varied and infinite as the 'realities' it enables: it is both the predicament and salvation of postmodern culture, just as it produces the depressing world of Babylen Tatarsky, the freedom for Pyotr Voyd to chose to live in early Soviet Russia and the power for A Hu-Li to create and control the world around her. In the trajectory of these three novels, then, we witness Pelevin debating the various meanings and possibilities of the void, ultimately arriving at a paradoxical solution: the void generates perceptions of the world that precede the material reality of the world, perceptions that actually generate their own reality; in so doing, these perceptions regenerate the very void that enables them to be.

Works cited

Bakhtin, Mikhail (1984), *Rabelais and His World*, Bloomington: Indiana University Press.

Dalton-Brown, Sally (2006), 'The Dialectics of Emptiness: Douglas Coupland's and Viktor Pelevin's Tales of Generation X and P', *Forum for Modern Language Studies* 42.3, pp. 239–48.

Epstein, Mikhail (1995), *After the Future: The Paradoxes of Postmodernism and Contemporary Russian Culture*, Amherst: The University of Massachusetts Press.

——— (1999), 'Like a Corpse in the Desert: Dehumanization in the New Moscow Poetry' (1987) in Slobodanka Vladiv-Glover (ed.), *Russian Postmodernism: New Perspectives on Post-Soviet Culture*, New York: Berghahn Books, pp. 134–44.

Genis, Alexander (1999), 'Onions and Cabbages: Paradigms of Contemporary Culture', in Slobodanka Vladiv-Glover (ed.), *Russian Postmodernism: New Perspectives on Post-Soviet Culture*, New York: Berghahn Books, pp. 394–422.

Hutchings, Stephen (2004), *Russian Literary Culture in the Camera Age: The Word As Image*, London: RoutledgeCurzon.

Kabakov, Ilya (1992), *Zhizn' mukh/Das Leben der Fliegen/Life of Flies*, Ostfildern: Cantz.

Khagi, Sofya (2008), 'From Homo Sovieticus to Homo Zapiens: Viktor Pelevin's Consumer Dystopia', *The Russian Review* 67, pp. 559–79.

Kristeva, Julia (1982), *Powers of Horror: An Essay on Abjection*, New York: Columbia University Press.

Lipovetsky, Mark (2001), 'Russian Literary Postmodernism in the 1990s', *Slavonic and East European Review* 79.1, pp. 31–50.

Mozur, Joseph (2002), 'Viktor Pelevin: Post-Sovism, Buddhism, & Pulp Fiction', *World Literature Today* 76.2, 1 May.

Parts, Lyudmila (2004), 'Degradation of the Word or the Adventures of an *Intellect* in Viktor Pelevin's *Generation П*', *Canadian Slavonic Papers* 46.3–4, pp. 435–49.

Pelevin, Victor (1999), *Buddha's Little Finger*, translated by Andrew Bromfield, New York: Penguin Books.

Pelevin, Viktor (2000), 'I Never Was a Hero', interview with *The Observer* 30 April, http://www.guardian.co.uk/books/2000/apr/30/fiction. Accessed 9 January 2012.

——— (2003), *Homo Zapiens*, translated by Andrew Bromfield, New York: Penguin Books.

——— (2008), *The Sacred Book of the Werewolf*, translated by Andrew Bromfield, New York: Penguin Books.

Notes

1   The novel has been translated into English (by Andrew Bromfield) both under the title *Babylon* (London, 2001) and *Homo Zapiens* (New York, 2003). I refer to the novel as *Generation 'P'* throughout this chapter and references are to the American editions, with my own amendments when needed. Spellings of proper names follow the translations.

2   For a discussion of the Buddhist elements of Pelevin's writings and philosophy, see Mozur 2002.

3   'Sots-art' is a term coined in 1972 by the Russian artists Vitalii Komar and Aleksandr Melamid to refer to their work that combines pop art with imagery from Socialist Realism.

4   Bakhtin writes that the essential principle of grotesque realism and the carnivalesque is 'the lowering of all that is high, spiritual, abstract; it is a transfer to the material level, to the sphere of earth and body their indissoluble unity' (Bakhtin 1984: 19–20).

5   'Carnival is not a spectacle seen by the people; they live in it, and everyone participates because its very idea embraces all people. While carnival lasts, there is no other life outside it' (Bahktin 1984: 7).

6   Bakhtin writes that during carnival, 'the jester was proclaimed king, a clownish abbot, bishop, or archbishop was elected at the "fest of fools", and in the churches directly under the pope's jurisdiction a mock pontiff was even chosen' (Bakhtin 1984: 81).

7   Like his hero, Pelevin was born in the sixties, studied briefly at the Gorky Literary Institute in Moscow and worked as an advertising copywriter. They also share an affinity for the writings of Boris Pasternak. See also Khagi (2008: 570–71), who points out many biographical and stylistic similarities between Tatarsky and Pelevin, and makes a case for the novel as an intensely self-referential text.

8   Pelevin alludes to Borges' famous garden in the preface to *Chapaev and Voyd*, which is written by the fictional Urgan Jambon Tulku VII. Here, the fictional editor suggests an alternative title of the text, 'The Garden of the Divergent Petkas', which is in reference to the main character who exists in at least two separate realities. A complete comparative analysis of Pelevin and Borges lies outside the scope of the present project.

Chapter 4

From Homo Zapiens to Media Sapiens: Post-Soviet Television in Russian Fiction

Andrei Rogatchevski

Different art forms reflect and influence reality differently, and therefore not only complement each other but also often find themselves in competition against each other. It would be interesting to find out how television – a medium that evidently plays an ever-increasing role in people's lives – is reflected in fiction, which arguably plays an ever-diminishing role in their lives.[1]

Russia is not an exception to this trend.[2] Although Russian television was a relatively late developer,[3] when it finally burst onto the cultural scene with all its might in the late 1980s, it acquired a 'monstrous power' (Limonov 2005: 252) – and did so at the expense of belles-lettres, which had hitherto striven to play a leading role in society.[4] Andrei Voznesenskii's prescient 1980 poem, called 'Farewell to the Book' ('Proshchanie s knigoi', Voznesenskii 2005), symptomatically expresses grave concern over the lack of future for literature in a world dominated by television:

> What is a book? It is difficult
> for you even to imagine it now.
> Is it a TV screen with subtitles, linked
> to people's souls for a power supply? [...]
> If the foolish freedom
> results in a total
> annihilation of literature,
> can it still be called freedom?

As television in Russia has always been heavily politicized (which may well be the only constant feature of this otherwise rather vibrant and flexible medium), it would make sense to limit a selection of its recent fictional representations of Yeltsin's and Putin's era to representatives of different political views, to see if their attitude to television in any way depends on which side of the political spectrum they are. With this goal in mind, *Generation 'P'/Babylon* (1999) by the leftist Victor Pelevin, *Gospodin Geksogen/Mr Hexogen* (2002) by the nationalist Aleksandr Prokhanov, three satirical 'tales' from the turn of the century by the liberals Boris Akunin and Dmitrii Bykov, as well as *Media Sapiens* (2007) by the nihilist Sergei Minaev, are going to be examined. To try and separate fact from fiction, where possible, excerpts from memoirs and journalistic responses to TV programmes will be quoted.

The first theme, common to almost all of the above-named authors, is their concern with mediality, i.e., the inability to distinguish between television broadcasts and reality, stemming from and/or leading to a concern that the audience is being constantly manipulated. Pelevin's *Generation 'P'* (a story about a copywriter, based on the narrative principles of a computer game) is a seminal text in this respect because it creates, possibly for the first time in Russian fiction, a philosophical framework dealing with the premises that 'reality is the material world as it is shown on television' (Pelevin 2000: 81). Since 'every few seconds there is either a change of camera angle or a fade into close-up on some object, or a switch to a different camera', it is possible to say that

> [these] changes in the image [...] can be correlated with a virtual psychological process in which the observer is forced to switch his attention from one event to another and select the most interesting content from what is taking place – that is, to manage his own attention as the makers of the programme manage it. This psychological process creates its own virtual subject, which for the duration of the television programme exists in place of the individual, fitting into his or her consciousness like a hand into a rubber glove. [...] The virtual subject that replaces the viewer's actual consciousness is absolutely non-existent – it is merely an effect created by the collective efforts of editors, cameramen and producers. [...] The viewer becomes a remotely controlled television programme, [...] the residual luminescence of a soul fallen asleep; it is a film about the shooting of another film, shown on a television in an empty house.
>
> (Pelevin 2000: 79, 81–82)

Pelevin calls this phenomenon homo zapiens (derived from 'zapping', or channel surfing), a new human breed emerging among the audiences as a result of their manipulation by means of television programmes.

In such a context, it is hardly surprising that in *Generation P* politicians and media personalities, frequently shown on TV, such as President Yeltsin, financier Boris Berezovskii and Chechen resistance leader Salman Raduev, turn out to be virtual. One character in the book, a TV company employee, explains to another:

> By his very nature every politician is just a television broadcast. Even if we do sit a live human being in front of the camera, his speeches are going to be written by a team of speechwriters, his jackets are going to be chosen by a group of stylists, and his decisions are going to be taken by the Interbank Committee. And what if he suddenly has a stroke – are we supposed to set up the whole shebang all over again?
>
> (Pelevin 2000: 166)

These lines may well have been inspired by carefully edited TV appearances of the gravely ill President Yeltsin and, some 20 years before him, the General Secretary of the CPSU Leonid Brezhnev.[5] Admittedly, in the late 1990s–early 2000s, there also was a distinct general feeling that even Russian 'members of Parliament, government ministers, TV presenters, [...] leaders of political parties and factions, as well as Prosecutors General [...] were mere ghosts, a mirage, someone's fabrication' (Bogomolov 2004: 63). However, the picture Pelevin paints is global: virtual politicians include President Reagan, and the expensive and complex technology necessary for manufacturing 3-D images has been supplied to the Russian TV executives by their American colleagues.

By contrast, in his own version of what went wrong with Russian television in the 1990s, Prokhanov is very specific about who to blame (although the reasons for his unease – the use of television for falsifications and brain-washing, the latter being the *second* common topic in the fiction about post-Soviet Russian TV broadcasting – are not dissimilar to Pelevin's). His *Mr Hexogen* (the story of Putin's rise to power, based on rather persuasive conspiracy theories) features, among others, two rival media tycoons, Astros and Zaretsky, who can easily be identified as Vladimir Gusinskii of the NTV channel and Boris Berezovskii of the ORT channel, respectively. Astros speaks of his TV channel:

> We neither inform nor entertain. We form the reality. With the help from new technologies, we have learned how to influence history. We focus on a selected individual and turn him into a historic figure, or starve another individual, who might already be a significant politician, of sustenance (*pitanie*), and he becomes useless.
>
> (Prokhanov 2002: 169)[6]

To further his goals, Astros does not shy away from combining the latest computer technologies with the ancient art of voodoo. In a workshop at his TV station, he keeps a hunchback magician, who makes the dolls of future political stars and tortures the dolls of those politicians who have fallen out of favour with Astros (the famous NTV show *Kukly/ Puppets*, reminiscent of the British *Spitting Image* and the French *Les Guignols de l'info*, has been satirised in this scene).[7] Astros explains:

> Our puppet show is not a farce, not a political caricature and not a funny act performed by marionettes, as simple-minded men in the street might believe. It is a magic ritual, a mystery play, based on a mystical correlation between an Image and a Prototype. Their simultaneous extrasensory impact merges with the television's electromagnetic wave – and a route to follow is imposed upon the world.
>
> (Prokhanov 2002: 171)

Ordinary people also have a place in Astros's designs. For them, a number of game shows have been produced, from aiming darts at a target formed by Alexander Pushkin's portrait to an electronic imitation of syphoning capitals from a Moscow bank to a bank in New York. Astros points out:

> These game shows, with all their seeming simplicity and naivety, suppress or stimulate different parts of people's subconscious, and model their individual and group behaviour. At the time of social tension, civil unrest and mass display of chauvinism and

residual emotions of imperial grandeur, these game shows function like psychotropic medication.

(Prokhanov 2002: 165–66)

Needless to say, Pelevin's and Prokhanov's anxieties, ranging from existential to paranoid, received an additional boost when Yeltsin's heir, President Putin, and his team started interfering with the TV programme content on a regular basis. This trend was promptly parodied in the satirical 'tale' 'Blesk i nishcheta telepuzikov'/'The Splendors and Miseries of Teletubbies', by Dmitrii Bykov. In it, for the first time in his life, Putin chances upon a Teletubbies episode on Russian television and, not knowing that the programme is aimed at a preschool audience, gets quickly bored. He complains to the Minister of Culture that such programmes cannot assist the state in training the Russian youth for their future existence in a bipolar world where things tend to explode unexpectedly and youngsters often have to live on the streets and sniff glue. Producer General of Channel One (a caricature of Konstantin Ernst) is given the task of doing something about it. To get rid of the foreign odour, he renames Tinky Winky as Mitya, Dipsy as Vitya, Laa-Laa as Lyalya and Po as Pyotr (altering Po's sex as a result in order to turn her into a role model for future defenders of Mother Russia). The dubbing team receives the following instructions on re-recording: Mitya is supposed to say when jumping: 'This is how high our economy peaks!'; Vitya (when marching): 'This is what we'll do in the army!'; Lyalya (while crawling on her belly): 'This is what we do out of love for our president'; and Pyotr (when landing on his bottom after a jump), 'Those who won't crawl will be confined to the Naughty Step' (*budut sidet*') (Bykov 2005: 415).[8] The baby face of the sun that appears at the beginning and the end of each episode is replaced with Putin's face. The Minister of Culture is suitably impressed with the alterations and goes off to report to the President.

To the best of my knowledge, no author has yet described Putin the fictional character feeling unease because of the responsibility he carries for reducing television to a Kremlin mouthpiece again.[9] Probing the moral integrity of media professionals, however, is *yet* another topic common to a number of works of fiction under consideration. Thus, Boris Akunin's satirical tale 'Nevol'nik chesti'/'A Slave to Honour', from his 2000 collection *Skazki dlia idiotov/Tales for the Idiots*, mocks a slur campaign waged by the ORT against the then Moscow mayor Iurii Luzhkov, when he participated in the 1999 Duma election as a leader of the Fatherland/All Russia (*Otechestvo/Vsia Rossiia*) movement. The anti-Luzhkov campaign was spearheaded by the presenter Sergei Dorenko, known as 'Telekiller'.[10] Luzhkov filed a defamation suit against him – and won. In Akunin's story, Dorenko serves as a prototype of Ippolit Viazemsky, host of the 'objective and impartial' analytical programme 'To Be Honest' (*Chestno govoria*). Viazemsky is asked by his Boss (who is given no name – the reader knows only that he is working in the Kremlin) to destroy the reputation of Moscow's 'Governor General', called Gubok (Luzhkov is known among Muscovites as Luzhok). Overwhelmed by disgust, Viazemsky divulges to the electorate that Gubok, whose official political slogan is 'Buy Russian Goods' (*Pokupaem otechestvennoe*), has installed about a dozen foreign toilets for private use in all of his numerous residencies (a proof of that has been provided by hidden cameras). After such an exposé, the Governor General's chances of winning the election become very slim. The sensitive Viazemsky is full of remorse, but he cannot deny his Boss any request, because years ago the Boss paid half a million dollars for a successful operation separating Viazemsky's daughters, born as Siamese twins, from each other, and Viazemsky feels eternally indebted to him for that (Akunin 2000: 14–22).[11]

If such pangs of conscience were apparently still imaginable before the start of Putin's first presidential term, the end of his second presidential term is associated with the emergence of a different type of media professionals (*mediishchiki*), namely those, whose loyalty is first and foremost to the ruthless logic of the deified mass media, which decrees that a media objective (especially when it comes to generating events rather then covering them) should be achieved by any means necessary. Sergei Minaev's *Media Sapiens* and *Media Sapiens-2* (two parts of the same novel, published separately in 2007, within a one-month interval) is an example. It tells the story of the journalist and 'political technologist' Anton Drozdikov who is sacked from the Foundation for Effective Politics (a real-life organization established by the PR guru Gleb Pavlovskii), when it transpires that the speeches he wrote for various Russian politicians have been modelled on talks by Dr Goebbels. Subsequently, he is employed by the anti-Putin opposition (funded from London, in a hint at the London-based exile Boris Berezovskii) to scupper Putin's attempts at being re-elected as president for the third consecutive term. To demonstrate to the electorate the incompetence of powers-that-be, Drozdikov, a master of conjuring up an event out of the thin air, commissions a false documentary about homeless children (played by actors in a heavy make-up) and spreads rumours that a soldier arrested for selling weapons to the criminals has had his leg amputated as a result of cruel treatment (the 2006 real-life story of the private Andrei Sychev, who had been severely beaten by his fellow soldiers to make him impersonate a working TV set, has been creatively utilized here), and launches misinformation that there have been explosions on the Moscow underground and an exchange of fire on the Russian-Georgian border (thereby predicting the 2008 South Ossetia War approximately 18 months in advance). Drozdikov openly admits that he and his colleagues are 'callous and amoral creatures, motivated by vanity and greed', and claims that 'it is not important if something has happened for real. The main thing is whether or not the event has been reported in the media and, therefore, has entered people's minds' (Minaev 2007a: 208, 285). Furthermore, Drozdikov states that 'there are only two reasons as to why one particular event overshadows other events in the eyes of the audience: either it has been orchestrated according to our own script, or we have taken an insignificant piece of real news, worked on it and turned it into a headline' (Minaev 2007: 151). Making sure that you have been paid for your work forms the first postulate of the mass media according to Drozdikov: 'The royalties for your tomorrow's news segment should be paid to you today, and it does not matter if that news segment is ever aired'. The second postulate of the mass media says: 'A slow death by hunger is better than being rude to your investor' (Minaev 2007: 161), which, in other words, means 'he who pays the piper calls the tune'. As an example, Drozdikov mentions young designers who make visually striking political advertising for both the Putin camp and the anti-Putin camp (Minaev 2007: 255–56). Insofar as one's conscience is concerned, Drozdikov believes that it is safer to 'shove it up the arse' (Minaev 2007: 195).

Remarkably, the responsibility for such a cynical work ethic is laid at the feet of the consumer: 'Media structures are much cleverer than their audience. How else would you explain the fact that the audience keeps allowing others to manipulate it, and accepts blindly all the daftness and deception it receives from television screens [...] on a daily basis?' (Minaev 2007: 6)[12] For Drozdikov, the audience's low intelligence level deserves nothing but contempt: 'If the three national channels broadcast [the stand-up comedian] Petrosian non-stop, except for commercial breaks and farming news, nobody will ever turn the thing off. [...] A [typical] audience consists of naïve retards (lokhi i debily), who perceive the world through television and react to it the way they are dictated to by anchormen' (Minaev 2007: 19, 149). In Drozdikov's opinion, the media's main attraction lies in offering audiences 'not so much a SPECTACLE but a DIFFERENT LIFE', which turns viewers into addicts (see Minaev 2007: 71, 265; and Minaev 2007a: 312).[13] Drozdikov likens media audiences to grazing cows, who 'raise their heads from the ground occasionally, to heed the sound of a shepherd's horn' (Minaev 2007: 306). According to Drozdikov, 'politics of the future will be about ruling an idle flock via television by remote control', while exploiting the feelings of fear and hatred (Minaev 2007a: 44, 68). Drozdikov predicts that one fine day the borderline between the mass media (exemplified by television) and reality, 'already quite blurred, will disappear altogether. This will be the first day of a new era, when the mass media amalgamate everything around them and become God', whose first commandment is 'Thou shalt turn thy TV on and love it more than thyself' (Minaev 2007a: 290, 293). The name of this deity is Media Sapiens.

Although the biggest punishment for media professionals in Drozdikov's vision of hell consists of turning them into members of the audience (see Minaev 2007a: 173), he does have at least one thing in common with the viewers: he is also addicted to television, if only at the opposite end, i.e., as a manufacturer and merchandiser, not as a consumer.[14] When Drozdikov is mistakenly believed to be dead and is publicly elevated to the status of a martyr by the anti-Putin forces (which makes a return to his life as a media executive no longer possible), he responds by wrapping a suicide belt around his body, sneaking into the Ostankino TV tower and threatening to blow himself (and the tower) up by detonating the explosives in the belt with electric current from the main transmission cable. This is a symbolic gesture of someone who has been a faithful servant of the media God and now aspires to become God himself, by turning his body into a hybrid of human flesh and television transmitter and dying in the process[15] – only to experience resurrection as a news headline.

Is it at all possible to overcome the omnipresent dependency on television[16] and stop watching it? In Drozdikov's view, life without a TV would not be worth living (see Minaev 2007a: 311). Bykov, however, considers just such a possibility, inspired by the August 2000 fire at the Ostankino TV tower, which led to a temporary disruption of television broadcasts.

In his satirical tale 'O tom, kak buria snesla bashniu'/'How a Hurricane Destroyed a TV Tower', he describes one typical Russian family, which, after the TV signal vanished, would not know any more what to clean their teeth and kitchen sink with and what to use against dandruff, because they had lost their long-term memory and could only remember the names of the advertised products for as long as their trip to the supermarket lasted (there was no reason to memorize the products' names because they were constantly repeated on TV anyway). A teenager, for whom Beavis and Butthead felt 'closer than Mum, Dad and Motherland' (Bykov 2005: 381), got so frustrated over his favourite characters' disappearance that he went outside and started looking for someone to kill. Even President Putin felt helpless, because he would normally get his instructions on where to travel from television:

> Television helped him to play up to people's expectations. If the RTR channel announced that, according to rumours, Putin was on his way to Samara, Putin did go to Samara. If, however, the NTV channel announced that well-informed sources reported that Putin was going to the Middle East, he would go to the Russian Far East instead, to spite his political opponents yet again. Putin enjoyed this game and never knew in the morning where he would end up at night. Now the television remained silent, though.
>
> (Bykov 2005: 383–84)

By the time the broadcasts resumed a week later, people had discovered that they could actually live without a television. Alas, things like that can only happen in fiction.[17]

To sum up, regardless of the authors' political affiliations, their vision of Russian television in all of its main aspects (strategy, content and impact) is decidedly negative and offers no redeeming features, which is unusual for the mainstream criticism levelled at the television medium (and journalism at large) in the West. The traditional dichotomy between the Journalist Hero and the Journalist Villain,[18] stemming from the western fiction and reinforced by various forms of popular culture, such as films, comic books and TV series, seems to lose its relevance for post-Soviet Russian television as depicted in fiction, because in such depictions Hero Journalists are rather thin on the ground. Instead, Russia's own dichotomy appears to consist of the abusive deity of Media Sapiens, on the one hand,[19] and the mistreated species of Homo Zapiens, on the other.[20]

Furthermore, the charges levelled against Russian television in the analysed texts offer hardly anything new,[21] but the scale and bleakness of these charges, although evidently exaggerated in virtually every work of fiction under consideration,[22] are highly remarkable. This can probably be partly explained by the fact that in the 1990s, the main Russian TV channels, far from being impartial and often acting as a proxy for either the government or the opposition:

> together and separately, lobbied for, appointed, compromised and removed Prime Ministers [...], patently provoked miners' strikes and blockades of the railway tracks. If this manipulative cynicism (*igrovoi tsinizm*) was obvious to the viewer, those who

functioned as journalists must have been corroded from the inside in an even more spectacular way.

(Bogomolov 2004: 283)

Is the current situation with Russian television, which is allegedly breeding docility with impudence, really that bad? Possibly.[23] It is worth noting that, with the exception of Pelevin, who shuns the mass media as a matter of principle, all the other authors act as regular contributors to television programmes, either as guests or as hosts; hence they are supposed to know exactly what they are talking about. Yet the impartiality of these authors may be called into question at any time, because they stand vulnerable to the accusations of jealousy, owing to the fact that their readership is considerably smaller than the viewing figures of the TV programmes they participate in, and it is anybody's guess whether some of their books would be read or published if it was not for their TV appearances. After all, to quote from Sergei Minaev again, 'In the beginning there was the Word. Television appeared afterwards' (Minaev 2007: 12).

Works cited

Akunin, Boris (2000), *Skazki dlia idiotov*, Moscow: GIF.

Bogomolov, Iurii (2004), *Khronika pikiruiushchego televideniia, 2000–2002/Taking the Plunge: A Chronicle of Television Broadcasts, 2000–02*, Moscow: MIK.

Bykov, Dmitrii (2005), *Kak Putin stal prezidentom SShA: Novye russkie skazki*, St Petersburg: RedFish.

Dunn, John (2004), 'Humour and Satire on Post-Soviet Russian Television', in L. Milne (ed.), *Reflective Laughter: Aspects of Humour in Russian Culture*, London: Anthem, pp. 181–92.

Ehrlich, Matthew C. (2009), 'Studying the Journalist in Popular Culture', *The IJPC Journal*, 1, pp. 1–11, http://ijpc.uscannenberg.org/journal/index.php/ijpcjournal/issue/view/18. Accessed 5 July 2011.

Isani, Shaeda (2009), 'Journalism FASP and Fictional Representations of Journalists in Popular Contemporary Literature', *ILCEA: Revue de l'Insitut des langues et cultures d'Europe et d'Amérique*, 11, pp. 1–15, http://ilcea.revues.org/index251.html. Accessed 5 July 2011.

Jenkins, Henry (2010) 'The Image of the Journalist in Popular Culture: An Interview with Joe Saltzman (Part Three)', http://henryjenkins.org/2010/07/the_image_of_the_journalist_in_1.html. Accessed 5 July 2011.

Kononova, Svetlana (2011), 'A Disappearing Habit', *Russia Profile*, 4 July, http://russiaprofile.org/culture_living/40137.html. Accessed 5 July 2011.

Kravchenko, Leonid (2005), *Kak ia byl televizionnym kamikadze*, Moscow: AiF Print.

Kuznetsov, Aleksandr (2005), *Kamera dlia prezidenta*, Moscow: AiF Print.

Limonov, Eduard (2002), *V plenu u mertvetsov*, Moscow: Ul'traKul'tura.

—— (2004), *Kak my stroili budushchee Rossii*, Moscow: Presskom.

—— (2005), *Takoi president nam ne nuzhen! Limonov protiv Putina*, Moscow: [s.n.]

Mehegan, David (2007), 'Young People Reading a Lot Less', *The Boston Globe*, 19 November.

Minaev, Sergei (2007), *Media Sapiens: Povest' o tret'em sroke*, Moscow: Astrel'-Ast.

—— (2007a), *Media Sapiens-2: Dnevnik informatsionnogo terrorista*, Moscow: Astrel'-Ast.

Pelevin, Viktor (2000), *Babylon*, trans. by Andrew Bromfield, London: Faber and Faber.

Prokhanov, Aleksandr (2002), *Gospodin Geksogen*, Moscow: Ad Marginem.

Shenderovich, Viktor (2002), *Zdes' bylo NTV i drugie istorii*, Moscow: Zakharov.

Voznesenskii, Andrei (2005), 'Proshchanie s knigoi', *Novaia gazeta*, 24 February.

Notes

1 Thus, in the United States, 'the average person between ages 15 and 24 spends 2 to 2 ½ hours a day watching TV and 7 minutes reading', while 'almost half of Americans between ages 18 and 24 never read books for pleasure' (Mehegan 2007). These figures are indicative of a trend common to many other countries.

2 'On average, Russians spend about nine minutes reading books per day, while they watch television for about four hours [...] every day' (Kononova 2011).

3 Owing to a particularly strict censorship, it did not make the most of its potential until the Perestroika years. According to head of Soviet Television from 1985 to 1988, only 0.5 per cent of its programmes were broadcast live in the mid-1980s (Kravchenko 2005: 48). Live TV programming, often perceived as an evidence of free speech, has decreased again since Putin's ascent to power (see Limonov 2002: 60).

4 The collapse of the centralized all-Russia book distribution system in the 1990s hit the Russian provinces especially hard, leaving those outside Moscow and St Petersburg with few viable alternatives to television and the Internet as the chief sources of information and entertainment.

5 Cf. the reminiscences of Yeltsin's personal cameraman on how the footage of Yeltsin was scrutinized and repeatedly re-edited before going on air, by Yeltsin's daughter, his press-secretary and one of his senior office administrators (Kuznetsov 2005: 256–58). As for Brezhnev, in his final years he could not pronounce certain words clearly any more, and these words had to be found in his previously televised speeches and edited in, which required skills of the highest quality (Kravchenko 2005: 175).

6 This and subsequent translations are mine, unless indicated otherwise.

7 The process of making puppets for *Kukly/Puppets* was described in some detail by an erstwhile scriptwriter on the programme (see Shenderovich 2002: 93). For more on the programme's style and content, see Dunn 2004: 187–89.

8 In the same piece, Bykov satirizes the proliferation of drama series on Russian television (up to 27 weekly, on five main Russian terrestrial channels in 2001–02, see Bogomolov 2004: 248). According to Bykov, who parodies the titles of several well-known shows, the typical daily TV listings in the early 2000s were: '9am – the TV series *Polichinelle's Fatal Secrets;* 10am – the *Wild Angel* TV series; 11am – the *Tame Devil* TV series; then came *The Lifeguards of the Sunset Beach, A Slave without an Aura* [a play on words to make fun of the popular 1976 Brazilian 'telenovela' *A Escrava Isaura*. – AR] and *Bloody Divorces'*

(Bykov 2005: 410). The *Field of Wonders/Pole chudes* game show, modelled on *The Wheel of Fortune* and 'combining values of consumerist society with purely Soviet naivety': the show's presenter Leonid Iakubovich distributes electronic goods among the participants and gets home-grown foodstuffs in return, not by way of a 'barter exchange, but out of the goodness of people's hearts' (Bogomolov 2004: 277), also got mocked: 'At 7pm came *The Field of Wonders* in a modified version: instead of asking questions, Iakubovich received gifts […] thanking donors after every other one, and shouting like a cockerel, 'Commercial break!', after every third. The programme's ratings were unbelievable' (Bykov 2005: 410). Furthermore, in Bykov's view, Russian news programmes are hardly distinguishable from comedy shows: 'At 8pm [the husband and wife team of stand-up comedians], Evgeny Petrosyan and Elena Stepanenko split their sides with laughter merely because of looking at each other. The channel's comedy night ended with a news programme, which made the entire country laugh' (Bykov 2005: 410).

9 Contrary to the situation shortly before (and during the early stages of) Putin's presidency, when 'the ORT and RTR channels lionised [Yeltsin and Putin], while the TVTs laughed at them. […] The NTV and TVTs channels specialised in counting the wounds of the anti-terrorist campaign [in Chechnya], while the ORT and RTR channels presented the public opinion with its victories and feats of valour. The audiences therefore had no reason to complain about getting an incomplete picture of events' (Bogomolov 2004: 6).

10 Dorenko was reportedly among those Russian television presenters who 'elevated a vulgar character bashing (*mochilovka*) to a form of art, enjoyed both by its makers and the audiences' (Bogomolov 2004: 10).

11 Dorenko does have two daughters, Ekaterina and Kseniia, but they are not twins. Such a ridiculous explanation of Viazemsky's behaviour is evidently given to demonstrate that it cannot really be justified at all.

12 In fact, many members of the audience do protest, by rather limited means at their disposal, against what they see as substandard television. Iurii Bogomolov, a long-standing television observer of the *Izvestiia* and *Rossiiskaia gazeta* newspapers, thus summarizes the reaction of his readers on the basis of their letters and telephone calls: 'They disapprove of the conformist position of our well-known TV journalists. […] They criticise […] reality TV ('*telebytovukha*') for its soft porn genre. They slam American thrillers and their Russian imitations. They complain about too many game shows, morals in decline, the neglect of purely Russian values, as well as the destruction of Russian mentality, culture and other sacred things' (Bogomolov 2004: 330).

13 This may well be true of soap operas, but, according to some impressions, typical Russian TV talk shows apparently represent a cross between a flea market and a sewer: private stories, shared with the viewers, are frequently reminiscent of 'rusty screws, punctured bicycle tires, purulent wounds, second-hand wigs, monstrous deformities and ugly complexes – if not for sale than at least to stare at. […] [The producer and the presenter of the talk show *Bol'shaia stirka/The Big Laundry* claim that] they graciously perform a useful operation of opening a valve to let out the shit […] which has been gathering inside people for decades. The shit gets removed and the society becomes purer and more dignified' (Bogomolov 2004: 181, 362).

14 Cf. an observation of an audience member: 'Broadcasting, especially its live variety, captivates you in the same way as the backstage smell does. Once inhaled, it knows no substitutes. From then onwards, our newsmakers thinks only of further pretexts to appear in front of TV cameras. It's an illness, of course' (Bogomolov 2004: 103–04). This has been confirmed by an industry insider: 'Those who have worked for television, even for a short term, know how this crazy job with no regular hours sucks you in, envelopes you, captivates you, penetrates your entire body like a virus and never lets go. The employee falls ill once and for all. No doctor can cure such a person from an obsessive desire to stay in the atmosphere of TV-related creative activity' (Kravchenko 2005: 113).

15 In view of an audience member, 'having a multi-channel TV implanted into your sub-cortex' is the worst torture imaginable (Bogomolov 2004: 315).

16 Cf., for instance, Prokhanov's comparison of the Ostankino TV tower to a syringe, which 'at night would get filled with a bluish solution and injected into the sick, swollen veins of Moscow' (Prokhanov 2002: 298).

17 Bogomolov's reports about the real Muscovites' reaction to the Ostankino fire and its consequences give little ground for optimism: 'some people's pain was almost physical. A citizen by the name of Elizaveta Petrovna said on the NTV: 'It was as if something precious had been taken out of my house. […] Houses felt empty – and so did people's heads. […] The street sweeper Mar'ia Ivanovna heard during the day that television had started working again, [on a decimal channel]. She did not believe it at first, but at night, when she came home, tuned her indoor aerial in and saw the picture, she started calling her friends and relatives. From different corners of Moscow, they gathered at Mar'ia Ivanovna's place to commune with [the presenter] Tat'iana Mitkova' (Bogomolov 2004: 53, 55).

18 Professor Joe Saltzman, Director of the Image of the Journalist in Popular Culture (IJPC) project (see www.ijpc.org), characterizes these basic stereotypes as 'either a hero righting a wrong or the last one standing up for freedom of speech and press, or a villain in cahoots with the government in power' (Jenkins 2010).

19 Cf. an accusation addressed to the Russian television executives: 'You are turning Russian people into imbeciles. You are forcibly lobotomising the nation' (Limonov 2004: 115).

20 Cf. a claim that one part of the Russian viewers' collective conscience retains the tradition represented by 'Pushkin, Pasternak and Akhmatova, while its other part has a new content, i.e. vulgar Western hits, adverts and fashion shows. Ordinary citizens' brains are fragile: several years of "public television" have turned them into quiet lunatics without a nation, a will power and a history. Soon they'll be fed through their noses, like catatonic patients' (Limonov 2004: 115–16). Apparently, even professional television critics are not immune from the debilitating influence of television. Thus, Bogomolov admits that his vigil at the small screen is responsible for his constant bad mood, as it does not take much effort to find serious faults with the TV repertoire (see Bogomolov 2004: 247–48).

21 Cf. Bogomolov's reaction to the American film *Switching Channels* (1988), whose previous incarnations are known as the famous Broadway comedy *The Front Page* (1928) and its another film adaptation, *His Girl Friday* (1940): 'the same concern about ratings […], the same production problems […], the same moral collisions […] and the same basic principle:

if there is no news, it should be invented [...]. Feature films are pure fiction, of course, but they contain so many hints of reality ...' (Bogomolov 2004: 163).

22 Cf.: none of the fictional 'depictions, whether positive or negative, ever should be taken as wholly faithful and literal representations of what the press has done or how it operates' (Ehrlich 2009: 2).

23 In the West, we are witnessing a general decline of the public trust in journalism too, which is also reflected in American and West European fiction (see, for example, Isani 2009: 12–13). Unfortunately, it is hard to determine whether it is people's perception that feeds the negative fictional representation of journalism, or vice versa. This text has appeared within the framework of the research project 'Models of Representation in Literary Discourses' (OPVKCZ.1.07/2.3.00/20.0125), co-financed by the European Social Fund and the state budget of the Czech Republic.

PART II

Visual and Popular Culture

Chapter 5

Afrika and Monroe – Post-Soviet Appropriation, East and West

Amy Bryzgel

Sergei Solov'ev's film *ASSA* (1987) presented Russian artist Sergei Bugaev (Afrika)[1] to the greater Soviet population as Bananan: a bohemian hipster who dreamt in Technicolor and listened to only the coolest western music. On the night that he brings his love interest, Alika, back to his apartment, he impresses her with a Sony drum machine and sings a quirky love song with her, a pin-up of David Bowie watching over them in the background. Bananan's orientation, as a Russian, from the East, could not have been more western. In the 1990s, however, with the Soviet Union crumbling in the wake of the wave of freedom and democracy that was washing over Russia, Afrika changed direction, by travelling back in time, both literally and figuratively, to archive the Soviet past before it would be ultimately lost to posterity. In 1993 he travelled to Simferopol (Crimea), Ukraine, to spend two weeks as a patient in a mental institution. He used this time, which he considers an artistic performance, to explore signs, symbols and language within the context of mental illness and schizophrenia. In 1995 he exhibited the results of his investigations in the institution, along with much of his extensive collection of Soviet memorabilia, at his largest solo exhibition to date at the Museum of Applied Arts (MAK) in Vienna.

Like Afrika, when Vladislav Mamyshev debuted to the art world of Leningrad at the opening of the 1989 exhibition 'Women in Art', his orientation had changed as well – he appeared as Mamyshev-Monroe, a cross-dresser/performance artist. From there, his personality split into a myriad of other personae, from Catherine the Great and Vladimir Lenin to Charlie Chaplin and Dracula, perpetually straddling the border between East and West. Perhaps his most successful balancing act was his performance as Liubov' Orlova, Stalin's favourite actress, in his 2006 remake of her 1938 classic film, *Volga-Volga*. The artist did not entirely *become* her, but rather embodied her, hijacking her body with his head superimposed over her torso. He also imposed his own voice over hers in this re-appropriation of the film, leaving the speech of the other actors intact.

While Afrika delved into both his own subconscious and that of the nation with an aim towards recovering the lost Soviet past, Mamyshev-Monroe's creations utilized disguise and costume in order to negotiate the expansion of the world around him to include the West. This chapter will examine the diverse manners in which two St Petersburg-based artists, Sergei Bugaev (Afrika) and Vladislav Mamyshev-Monroe, attempt to navigate the changing face of the Russian landscape during a period of great social and political change, by appropriating various elements from the past, both East and West. I argue that their appropriation differs very much from that postmodern practice as we know it in the West, because it represents a deliberate strategy on the part of the artists to experience a past that was denied to them because of the socio-political circumstances in which they found themselves.

Afrika

Timur Novikov's 1984 portrait of Afrika sends a clear message. Painted in a primitivist style reminiscent of Mikhail Larionov, the artist is depicted wearing jeans, Nike sneakers, and sporting a Walkman – not exactly the picture of the new Soviet Man, as originally envisaged by Soviet ideologues. In the 1980s the artists in Novikov's circle, Afrika among them, craved the West. They made contact with artists and philosophers from beyond the Iron Curtain, for example Jacques Derrida and Felix Guattari. In 1985 Afrika wrote to Andy Warhol, who sent him six (real) Campbell's Soup cans that he had autographed. When John Cage appeared in Leningrad for a concert in 1989, the artists waited backstage, eager for an audience with their so-called guru. The composer accepted their invitation to be a guest in Afrika's studio the next day. When he arrived, they created a performance together, titled *Water Music*, which they photographed; afterward, Cage remained for conversation with the participants. (See Photos 5.1 and 5.2)

Solov'ev's film *ASSA* came at a pivotal moment in these nonconformist artists' lives. They had just begun to become famous through their exploits with rock music groups

Figure 5.1: Sergei Bugaev (Afrika), John Cage, and some of Afrika's artist-friends *Water Music*. Performance in Afrika's studio, Leningrad, 1989. John Cage is seen pouring water. Courtesy of the artist.

Figure 5.2: Sergei Bugaev (Afrika) and John Cage in Afrika's studio, Leningrad, 1989. Courtesy of the artist.

Pop Mekhanika (headed by Sergei Kurekhin) and Viktor Tsoi's Kino, receiving invitations to travel and perform abroad. The film presented a love triangle, with Alika, the heroine, caught between her mobster boyfriend Krymov and Bananan, her artist lover. In the end, the mob wins one battle, when Krymov has Afrika killed; Alika trumps him by then killing Krymov herself. As Anna Lawton has written, 'Krymov's death, and Bananan's murder, mark the end of an era and open the door to a new beginning' (Lawton 2004: 189). Indeed, this is not only true of the film, but also with regard to Soviet reality, as it was just shortly after the film's premier across the Soviet Union that the foundations of that 'empire' began swiftly to crumble and ultimately disintegrate.

Afrika's avant-garde forebears

If Afrika's filmic orientation was pointed westward, his two-dimensional work from the late 1980s and early 1990s was angled not only back on the East, but also back in time. Afrika's initial engagement with the past focused on the Soviet avant-garde, a history that had been largely suppressed until the Thaw. His re-workings of artists such as Alexander Rodchenko and El Lissitzky share similarities with appropriation art that one could find in the West around the same time, by the likes of Sherrie Levine, for example. However, his is an 'appropriation' of a past that had only just been rediscovered. Fellow Russian artists Vitalii Komar and Aleksandr Melamid declared themselves the 'children of Socialist Realism and the grandchildren of the avant-garde' (in Erofeev 1995: 37), because it was the former, and not the radical experimentation of artists from the 1920s, that pervaded the immediate consciousness and imagination of Russian artists everywhere. Afrika attempts to digest and engage with this foundation of Russian art that had been neglected, forgotten and forbidden for the majority of the twentieth century. For the artist, it was the avant-garde's investigations into sign systems that made their work significant. According to Afrika, Vladimir Maiakovskii was 'in some sense, the creator of the sign system on whose grandiose ruins we are currently standing' (Afrika and Mazin 1994b: 14), and like an archaeologist on a dig, he attempts to resurrect those ruins by engaging in dialogue with them. Afrika begins his artistic career with a study of the sign systems of the avant-garde, by attempting to work through them and even subvert them.

Afrika's 1989 'Anti-Lissitzky' series effectively turns the work of that artist on its head. *Klinom belym bei krasnykh/Beat the Reds with the White Wedge* reverses the colour scheme of the original 1919 *Klinom krasnym bei belykh/Beat the Whites with the Red Wedge* by El Lissitzky, which also reverses its meaning. In Afrika's version, the Mensheviks should win the Civil War. In *Klinom golubym bei rozovykh/Blue Wedge Beats Pink*, the colours turn from Soviet red and black to pastel; from serious to light-hearted. Although both of these images look identical to the original, save the colour and lettering changes, each include a coda that was not present in the original: a margin containing text. For example, on the side of *Blue Wedge Beats Pink* Afrika adds the statement 'grandfather – I am with you' thus declaring Lissitzky his artistic grandfather in the same manner that Komar and Melamid did.

In 1990 the artist-pacifist created *Don't Beat Anybody with Anything*, which consists of three panels; from left to right, they are: a board containing a copy of the graphic elements of Lissitzky's *Beat the Whites with the Red Wedge* done in a green-and-black colour scheme, without text; a central panel consisting of simply a solid green, with the following message scrawled across it in Russian: *don't beat anybody with anything* (written in red in italics). PENETRATE INTO THE VOID (written in black block letters); and a final panel that is identical to the first one, with the colours inverted. Here the artist references not only Lissitzky, but also Malevich, who quite notably transformed himself 'in the zero of form' (in Bowlt 1988: 118) in 1915, with his Suprematist manifesto, his painting of the *Black Square*, and his exhibition of Suprematist work at the 0.10 exhibition in St Petersburg. With Malevich's project, the artist aimed to find a form of painting that was truly non-objective, and one that would clearly and seamlessly express the ideals of the burgeoning communist state. Conversely, Afrika's alteration renders the original message created by Lissitzky meaningless, if the 'wedge' closing in on the circle is not, in fact, 'beating' any one or any thing. His reworking creates a disjuncture between image and word, insofar as the shapes are still in their fighting positions, with the text contradicting that stance.

Afrika's statements in the Anti-Lissitzky series represent the artist's engagement with and exploration of signs systems that he continues throughout his career. His appropriation participates in the nostalgic yearning that is typical of post-Soviet Russia. While nostalgia is a longing for an irrevocable past, Svetlana Boym adds that nostalgia can be a longing for a home 'that no longer exists or has never existed' (Boym 2001: xiii). The cultural heritage of Malevich and Lissitzky was denied to all artists in the pre-perestroika era, along with the trajectory of the western modernism in art history.[2] In his quest for the West, Afrika circumvents the Socialist Realist past and engages in dialogue with his artistic grandparents. By subverting the signs in the original images, he demonstrates how signifiers used in language are arbitrary, and how meaning can shift and change when commonly understood sign systems are disrupted. His later studies of signs in the post-Soviet era then rest on this foundation of the exploration of the work of the originators of these new, modern methods of communication – the work of the historical Russian avant-garde.

Crimania

When the Soviet Union began to dissolve, the system which Afrika had not only fought against, but defined himself in opposition to, fell apart along with it. Subsequently, the artist experienced a feeling of loss, which manifested itself in a depression. Boym has noted that in the sixteenth and seventeenth centuries, nostalgia was considered a medical affliction, and one that was curable at that (Boym 2001: 3–4). After the fall of the Soviet Union, Afrika complained of 'a feeling of uncertainty, confusion about "which country I live in"' (Afrika, in Noever 1995: 55), and expressed a desire for his friend, the French psychoanalyst Felix Guattari, to examine him. While that never came to pass, the artist

Figure 5.3: Republican Psychiatric Hospital No. 1, Simferopol, Ukraine. The lower floor is the men's ward, where Afrika stayed during his performance *Crimania*. Photograph taken by the author in 2008.

sought healing in a different direction – in a return to his roots on the Black Sea.[3] As Boym has written about this time, 'Soviet popular culture of the 1970s and 1980s was permeated by dreams of escape; Russian popular culture of the 1990s featured many stories of return' (Boym 2001: 65). Thus Afrika's road to healing began with a return to the East, in the form of a journey into the Soviet past, with his two-week stay in the mental institution. He aimed to use his time there as a patient to explore 'the dissociation of a remarkably powerful social structure [that created] circumstances of geopolitical changes comparable in size to the end of the Roman Empire' (Afrika, in Noever 1995: 64).

Titled *Crimania*, this two-week-long performance,[4] which took place in the Republican Psychiatric Hospital No. 1 of Simferopol (see Figure 5.3), was Afrika's attempt come to terms with the period of uncertainty of the early 1990s, which he labelled the time of Great Aphasia, or 'pseudo-aphasia' (Afrika, in Noever 1995: 64), in recognition of the dissolution of shared tropes and values in Soviet official as well as public discourse. While clinical aphasia is usually the result of an injury to the brain, aphasia can also appear in a symbolic sense, when a structure that keeps a sign system intact is disrupted. The catalyst for what Afrika referred to as the time of Great Aphasia was the dissolution of the Soviet Union. A patient afflicted with aphasia will be unable to string words together to make coherent sentences; it is a disruption to the order of the sign system that is common language between all human beings. For Afrika, this relates to the post-Soviet condition with regard to the changing of country names, street names, currencies, acronyms, among other terms.

Afrika's Soviet signs and symbols

Two years after the performance in Crimea, the artist exhibited the 'results' of his experience in the mental institution at MAK, which consisted primarily of banners from the Soviet era that the artist reworked to adapt to the new circumstances of the Russian Federation. The exhibition, titled *Crimania: Icons, Monuments, Mazàfaka*, also consisted of installations and displays of Afrika's collections of other Soviet memorabilia, such as busts of Lenin and Stalin, Soviet flags, banners and medals. Throughout his career, the artist had been collecting these symbols of the former Soviet Union, and this aspect of his personality (collecting) was examined by Viktor Mazin, Afrika's friend who acted as a relative visiting him during the performance. Mazin sought to determine the connection between the artist's emotional state and the objects that he collected, and to seek the cause for his desire to collect. Mazin referred to these objects as 'representation[s] of things which act as objects of power, i.e., which actually represent representation' (Mazin 1995: 41). In the end he hoped 'to determine those mechanisms which force the artist to a.) collect and b.) exhibit "totems", i.e., sacred objects from the zenith of the Soviet Empire' (Mazin 1995: 41).

When Jacques Derrida visited Afrika's studio in 1991, he noticed, among other pieces of Soviet memorabilia, a large portrait of Stalin in the hall, the possession of which he interpreted as the artist's desire 'to give these objects the status of objects existing outside history, taken out of the context of their time' (Derrida, quoted in Ryklin 1995: 16). Indeed, in decontextualizing the objects, Afrika reduces them to mere signifiers, whose meaning can shift, depending on the context. Just as he destabilizes Lissitzky's red wedge, he undermines the original meaning of this Soviet totem by removing Stalin's portrait from its original ceremonial context and placing it in the studio of a non-conformist artist. Furthermore, Derrida commented that in preserving Stalin's portrait, he isolates the grief over the utopian dream, which died along with this man among others. In Derrida's words, Afrika turns 'that grief about this concrete body [...] into an abstract grief about the universal fact that the world has de-realized, that reality has no way of supporting itself anymore' (Derrida, quoted in Ryklin 1995: 16). With the fall of the Soviet Union, the structure that supported the world of the Soviet utopian dream had disintegrated, along with its rhetoric, leaving only the signs intact. Afrika isolates those signs, collects them and preserves them for posterity.

After having amassed a collection of Soviet banners, the artist attempted to recycle the images contained therein and adapt them to the new circumstances of the country, to create a new cultural heritage, much in the same manner that his earlier paintings resurrected the historical avant-garde. Following conversations with patients in the hospital as to what new flags could look like, he added other signs to the original banners, layering the symbols. He left the original elements intact, for example the images of Lenin and Stalin, the coat of arms of the Soviet Union, slogans such as 'Glory to the CPSU' and 'Onward Toward the Victory of Communism'. On top of those elements and integrated within them, he had familiar imagery from different times and places embroidered, for example Donald and Daisy Duck, the CNN Logo, figures of Roman soldiers and stylized Byzantine angels, to name a few. In many instances, these additions contribute a layer of humour to what was

Figure 5.4: Sergei Bugaev (Afrika). *Flag*, no date. Photograph taken by the author in the artist's studio, 2008.

originally grave and ceremonious.[5] By re-contextualising the images, Afrika levelled the Soviet symbols, placing them side by side with other signs representing various periods and aspects of human culture. The effect was one of cataloguing, whereby the Soviet images on the banners were relegated to the annals of history, from which the added symbols had come themselves. Afrika deprived the flags of their old meaning by corrupting them, but the new meaning is not exactly clear. With the re-worked banners the artist has created a visual equivalent to the nonsense language of aphasia. By uniting images from East and West, Afrika disengages the Soviet meaning of the banner, shifting the tone from official to playful. This new amalgamation of symbols, East and West, represents Afrika's attempt to unite both aspects of his artistic heritage (see Figure 5.4).

The stochastic pendulum

By merging the Soviet symbols with western ones, Afrika invokes a new artistic language that is still under development. The central piece in the MAK exhibition demonstrates how Afrika achieves balance between East and West. It is an installation titled *Morphology of an Image (MZF 1* [Mazàfaka 1; A.B.]*) with the Stochastic Pendulum (Prigogine 1)*,[6] and consists of a monumental statue of Lenin whose body forms part of a rocket. The stochastic pendulum referred to in the title is based on regular chaotic movement, which means that while the motion of the drum that propels the pendulum is regular, the resultant behaviour of the bob is irregular, but within certain parameters that can be relied upon.[7] Applying these characteristics to the situation in the former Soviet Union, we can conclude that after the initial disturbance that sent shock waves through the language of Soviet socialism (the collapse of the USSR), the system then adjusted itself by incorporating the disturbance into its movement. In this sense, there was no possibility for escape from the chaos of everyday life.

The pendulum first appeared in Afrika's 1990 installation *Donaldestruction* in an exhibition at the Lenin Museum in Leningrad. It consisted of a background collage of black-and-white images taken in the Soviet period, including pictures of collective farm workers, labourers and even images from the Great Patriotic War. In the centre of the collage is a black chalkboard, on which has been placed a map of the world, with a red line connecting Russia and the United States. On either side of the map are handwritten equations, two of which resemble the charting of the swing of a pendulum on an x – y axis. Flanking this central panel are more collages. The right side is titled 'The East', and contains images from Russian and Soviet popular culture: Neznaika,[8] the phrase 'Not by bread alone' (*Ni khlebom edinym zhiv chelovek*), and the Lenin Mausoleum. The left side is 'The West', and places Donald Duck opposite Neznaika, the McDonald's logo opposite 'Not by bread alone' and a picture of the Taj Mahal to complement the Lenin Mausoleum.

In front of the image is a common frictionless pendulum, which is known for its regular movement. The bob for the pendulum in both pieces is also a relic of the Soviet Union – a

Figure 5.5: Sergei Bugaev (Afrika) and Sergei Anufriev. Performance at the Vera Mukhina statue *Worker and Collective Farm Woman,* Moscow, 1990. Courtesy of the artist.

piece of sheet metal taken from the Vera Mukhina statue *Worker and Kolkhoz Farmer* (1937), which the artist, together with Sergei Anufriev, stole in 1990. The pendulum swings in an even, regular movement between East and West, between Soviet and American culture, between symbols of communism and capitalism. Afrika created this work just months before the ultimate break-up of the Soviet Union, when the binaries of East versus West, communism and capitalism, were still firmly in place, though beginning to crumble. The regular movement of the pendulum reflected the relative order that still existed, at least for the artist, while the Soviet Union still did. Afrika mentioned the fact that he began working with stochastic pendula only after the collapse of the Soviet Union, when the times became more chaotic than they had been. He commented that 'the creation of a stochastic pendulum coincided with the rise of a most unstable situation in our country which came out of the disintegration of the complex structure known as the USSR. This disintegration caused chaotic processes to occur in geographical, social, economic, political and aesthetic spheres of our territory' (Afrika and Mazin 1994a: 23). The movement of this type of pendulum is an accurate depiction of the turmoil of these times.

The chaotic processes that Afrika referred to in his statement involved the geographical breakdown of borders, which to this day, in some places of the former Soviet Union, have yet to be resolved;[9] social effects such as the loss of Soviet identity that came with the end of the Soviet Union; economic and political changes, such as the transformation from a socialist to capitalist market economy, and from communism to democracy; not to mention the artistic changes as the system shifted from a restricted one (Socialist Realism) to free and open. These changes did not happen overnight, nor were they smooth transitions. In many ways, most of the former Soviet countries are still in a state of flux, rebuilding the infrastructure along with the nation. The stochastic pendulum expounded the current state of affairs in Russia at the time that it was exhibited (1995). What could not be conveyed in words was perfectly illustrated by the regular irregularity of the movement of the stochastic pendulum.

While in the 1980s, the orientation of Afrika's artistic and personal compass was oriented stridently towards the West, after the dissolution of the Soviet Union the artist, like many of his cohorts, changed direction entirely. Realizing that the Soviet past was now simply a legacy that could either fade from memory or be preserved for nostalgic or other purposes, Afrika began to explore the relevance of this past to him as an artist and citizen, as well as to his compatriots. He looked both to the language of the Russian avant-garde, as well as that of Socialist Realism, in order to develop and discover his own new artistic lexicon for the new Russian Federation.

Mamyshev-Monroe

While Afrika's project involved the incorporation of elements from both Soviet and western culture into his work, Mamyshev-Monroe literally embodies East and West through his use of costume and disguise. In adopting a variety of guises in his artistic work, he often changes gender and global orientation. Using make-up and costume, he tries on different personae, exploring role play and the ironic possibility of sporting new identities from the East and the West as a way to negotiate the changing circumstances of post-Soviet Russia.

When he first introduced himself to the public as Mamyshev-Monroe in 1989, a cross-dresser and performance artist, he caused a media sensation. His appearance at the Women in Art opening, dressed in drag, was a scandal on television and in the mass media, and

Figure 5.6: Vladislav Mamyshev-Monroe. Personal diary from the 1980s; property of Sergei Bugaev (Afrika). Photograph taken by the author in Afrika's studio, 2009.

even resulted in death threats to the artist. Mamyshev's obsession with Marilyn Monroe predates that event, however. His personal diary and journal from his high school days demonstrates his interest in the American icon's image, with doodles of her countenance throughout (see Figure 5.6). The artist himself states that he had 'come down with Marilyn Monroe' (in Hoptman and Pospiszyl 2002: 236) around 1986–87, when *Some Like it Hot* (Billy Wilder, 1959) began appearing in Soviet cinemas. The film not only features Marilyn Monroe as Sugar Kane Kowalczyk, the lead singer and ukulele player in an all-girl band, but Tony Curtis and Jack Lemmon as Josephine and Daphne, two male musicians who use cross-dressing to procure parts in the same all-girl band, all to escape being killed by the mob for having witnessed one of their hits.

Mamyshev's obsession with Marilyn, however, was not sexual. Rather, he has stated that 'sometimes I thought that she was my mother, sometimes that she was my god' (Mamyshev, in Hoptman and Pospiszyl 2002: 236). After being drafted into the Soviet Army in 1987, he continued his pursuit of her. As he described it: 'soldier Mamyshev found some old rags in his military pose as artist and director of a drama circle at a children's club, ripped all the hair from little blonde dolls, and reproduced on himself that unique image. I was Marilyn Monroe!' (in Hoptman and Pospiszyl 2002: 237). A friend photographed the transformation, the photographs were later discovered, and 'Soldier Mamyshev' was duly dismissed from the military in 1989, after having spent time in the military psychiatric clinic.

While in the West the fascination with Marilyn Monroe as a pop icon was cultivated by Andy Warhol, Mamyshev's interest in her is distinct from that trajectory. Warhol was interested in fame and celebrity status, believing that in the future everyone would have their 15 minutes in the spotlight. Warhol's focus on the imagery of popular icons is an exploration of the human fascination with celebrity and mass culture, mainly in response to the hyper-consumer culture that began to flourish after World War II when people themselves began to be marketed as commodities. Mamyshev, however, shared Afrika's attraction to the West as the forbidden fruit that was inaccessible to him as an artist. The artist was part of Afrika's and Timur Novikov's cohort, and thus had similar contacts with the West during the 1980s. Nevertheless, he appropriates not Warhol's image of Marilyn Monroe, but Marilyn herself, as an actress in *Some Like it Hot*.[10] In embodying Marilyn, Mamyshev becomes part of the West, participating both in the cult of personality surrounding pop icons, as well as the art historical tradition of appropriating Marilyn Monroe's image.[11]

In 1996 Mamyshev-Monroe had his first solo exhibition in Moscow, where he introduced other instantiations of his multiple personalities, presenting photographs of himself living out 'The Lives of Remarkable People', as the exhibition was titled. Here he appeared as Peter I, Lenin, Hitler, Sherlock Holmes and Catherine II, to name but a few. These multiple transformations reflect the manner in which Mamyshev's 'basic principle of […] subjectivism is maintained: stable mobility (or mobile stability)' (Mamyshev-Monroe, in Hoptman and Pospiszyl 2002: 239), to use his words. Thus it is an identity that combines both sides of the binary: fixed/in flux, single unassailable identity versus mutable and multivalent, as well as eastern and western. Like the bob of Afrika's stochastic pendulum, Mamyshev's costume changes represent regular, chaotic movement. They also reflect the peculiar character of all of the post-Soviet nations at this time, which were forced to balance and assimilate several identities at once, both past and present, East and West.

One cannot help but think of Mamyshev-Monroe's art of disguise in relation to the photography of American artist Cindy Sherman,[12] who also took on a variety of roles throughout her career. While in her *Untitled Film Stills* series (1977) she played an anonymous woman, in her *History Portraits*, from the late-1980s and early 1990s, artist became subject as she took on the roles of iconic images throughout the history of art. As Douglas Crimp has stated about her work, 'her photographs reverse the terms of art and autobiography. They use art not to reveal the artist's true self, but to show the self as an imaginary construct' (Crimp 1980: 10). Conversely, following the loss of his Soviet identity, Monroe commandeers disguise in order to reconstitute himself, amalgamating into his 'self' personalities from both sides of the East-West divide. His characters oscillate between East and West, much in the way that Afrika's banners do. Because he changes character so often, Mamyshev refuses to rest on either side, yet remains content in swaying between the two, like the bob of a pendulum.

As Russian art historian Oleysa Turkina has written, 'identification with one or the other personage may be perceived as the personality's defensive mechanism at the moment when the collective or personal identity is lost, as a peculiar therapy of possible multiple-personality disorder' (Turkina 1998). Mamyshev's 'personality disorder', much like Afrika's depression, is the result of the collapse of the Soviet Union, and his role-playing reflective of his search for a new sense of self in a new Russia.[13] Turkina emphasizes that despite all of Mamyshev's cross-dressing, this 'did not bring him to change his sexual identity (in one of the photographs that portrays Marilyn Monroe wearing a skirt lifted up by a gust of wind, the artist showed his penis). It is characteristic of the artist that he does not lose his personal identity, and the combination within himself of many historical heroes, leaders – sources of collective identification' (Turkina 1998). The artist himself described his strategy as an attempt 'to embody mankind in all its variety, experience all these destinies myself, take on myself all these countless sins, neutralise these countless good deeds, eliminate sexual, national, social and other differences and remain myself in this singular variety' (in Hoptman and Pospiszyl: 234–35). In the same way that Afrika amalgamates signs and symbols from East and West in his banners, so, too, does Mamyshev, although he incorporates these aspects into his very being.

Just as Afrika attempted to resurrect Soviet objects and symbols from the past, Mamyshev recreated one of the most beloved films from the Stalin era, *Volga-Volga* (Grigorii Aleksandrov, 1938), wherein the artist took on not the male lead, but Orlova's starring role as 'Strelka' Petrova. The entire film remains the same, except that Orlova's character is now played by Mamyshev, who disembodies his head and places it on the awaiting body of Orlova's in the film, literalizing his split personality. As the artist reads her lines and sings her songs in his strained falsetto, a light-hearted film from a darker period in Russian history is infused with humour and irony, in a similar way that Afrika's banners are.

While in the West appropriation has been identified as indicative of the crisis of representation in art, in the East it offers new opportunities for representation. Craig Owens has noted how Cindy Sherman's photographs signal a shift from the self-critical mode of modernism to the self-reflexivity of postmodernism (Owens 1984: 235). With both Sherman and Sherrie Levine, the meaning of the artwork becomes about meaning itself. In Crimp's words, referencing Levine's work, 'we are not in search of sources or origins, but of structures of signification: underneath each picture there is always another picture' (Crimp 1979: 87).

Conversely, the appropriations of Afrika and Monroe appear not as the result of a crisis in representation, but as a strategy of reconnecting and rebuilding, owing to the protracted period of modernism that Russia underwent in the twentieth century.[14] In the East, the development of modernism was interrupted – or continued, as Boris Groys (1992) would argue – with the adoption of the method of Socialist Realism in 1932. Thus, while Afrika's work does lay bare the structures of sign systems, more significant is the fact that his re-working of Lissitzky enables the artist to reconnect with his art-historical past; here appropriation serves as a bridge, a conduit by which Afrika can continue the developments begun by the historical avant-garde. Similarly, Mamyshev's engagement with Pop Art icon Marilyn Monroe links him with that tradition in the West, allowing the artist to participate in the shift from western modernism to postmodernism, as he moves from his instantiations of the 1950s film star to other characters, in the manner of Cindy Sherman. Both artists combine this engagement of Russian and western avant-garde traditions with a resurrection of the Soviet past. In uniting these elements, past and present, East and West, the artists manage to restart their interrupted history, reconnect with western art history, yet also arrive at new developments of their own.

Boym has described a cinematic image of nostalgia as 'a double exposure, or a superimposition of two images – of home and abroad, past and present, dream and everyday life' (Boym 2001: xiv). In fact, this is an apt description of the appropriations witnessed in both Mamyshev-Monroe's and Afrika's works. While both grew to maturity in Soviet Russia, their connections with the West during their formative years, in the 1980s, make them as much a product of the West as of the East, and their work reflects this liminality. While Afrika's appropriations of Soviet-era banners attempt to combine the forces of communist eastern and capitalist western iconography to produce a new signs and symbols for post-Soviet Russian, Mamyshev-Monroe's performances embody the schizophrenia that is characteristic of that period and reflect a search for an individual, integrated identity. Both artists use appropriation not only to access a lost or previously inaccessible past and reclaim the Soviet one, but also to incorporate those histories into their futures.

Works cited

Afrika, S.B. (sic) (1995), 'Ethics and Ethology of the Artist', in Peter Noever (ed.), *Crimania: Icons, Monuments, Mazàfaka,* Ostfildern: Cantz, pp. 61–71.

Afrika, S.B. and Viktor Mazin (1994a), 'The Reflection of the Rebus and Stochastic Oscillations', in S.B. Afrika, *Sergei Bugaev Afrika – Rebus,* New York: Paul Judelson Arts, pp. 17–25.

———— (1994b), 'Within the Spheres of Interimagery', in S.B. Afrika, *Sergei Bugaev Afrika – Rebus,* New York: Paul Judelson Arts, pp. 5–15.

Bowlt, John (1988) (ed.), *Russian Art of the Avant-Garde: Theory and Criticism, 1902–1934,* New York: Thames and Hudson.

Boym, Svetlana (2001), *The Future of Nostalgia,* New York: Basic Books.

Bryzgel, Amy (2013), *Performing the East: Performance Art in Russia, Latvia and Poland since 1980,* London: I.B. Tauris.

Crimp, Douglas (1979), 'Pictures', *October* 8 (Spring), pp. 75–88.

———— (1980), 'The Photographic Activity of Postmodernism', *October* 15 (Winter), pp. 91–101.

Erjavec, Ales (ed.) (2003), *Postmodernism and the Postsocialist Condition: Politicized Art under Late Socialism*, Berkeley: University of California Press.

——— (2008), *Postmodernism, Postsocialism and Beyond*, Newcastle: Cambridge Scholars Publishing.

Erofeev, Andrei (1995), 'Nonofficial art: Soviet Art of the 1960s', in Hoptman and Pospiszyl 2002: 37–52.

Groys, Boris (1992), *The Total Art of Stalinism*, Princeton: Princeton University Press.

——— (2008), *The Total Enlightenment: Conceptual Art in Moscow 1960–1990*, Ostfildern: HatjeCantz.

Hoptman, Laura and Tomas Pospiszyl (eds.) (2002), *Primary Documents: A Sourcebook for Eastern and Central European Art Since the 1950s*, Boston: MIT Press.

Lawton, Anna (2004), *Before the Fall: Soviet Cinema in the Gorbachev Years*, Washington, DC: New Academia Publishing, LLC.

Malevich, K. (1915), 'From Cubism and Futurism to Suprematism: The New Realism in Painting', in J. Bowlt (ed.), *Russian Art of the Avant-Garde: Theory and Criticism 1902–1934*, New York: Thames and Hudson, 1988, pp. 116–135.

Mamyshev-Monroe, Vladislav (1993), 'Where the Heck Am I? Where Are my Things?', in L. Hoptman and T. Pospiszyl (eds.), *Primary Documents: A Sourcebook for Eastern and Central European Art Since the 1950s*, Boston: MIT Press, 2002, pp. 234–242.

Mazin, Viktor (1995), 'Afrasia', in Noever 1995: 21–45.

Noever, Peter (ed.) (1995), *Crimania: Icons, Monuments, Mazàfaka*, Ostfildern: Cantz.

Owens, Craig (1984), 'The Allegorical Impulse', in B. Wallis (ed.), *Art After Modernism: Rethinking Representation*, New York: New Museum of Contemporary Art, pp. 203–235.

Ryklin, Mikhail (1995), 'The Artist in the Collection and the World', in Noever 1995: 15–20.

Solomon, Andrew (1991), *The Irony Tower: Soviet Artists in a Time of Glasnost*, New York: Alfred A. Knopf.

Turkina, Oleysa [sic] (1998), 'Russia in Search of New Identity; Art Identifies Conflict', in Conference Papers, *Swedish Joint Committee for Literary and Artistic Professionals World Conference on Culture*, Stockholm, Sweden, 31 March-2 April, http://www.klys.se/worldconference/papers/Oleysa_Turkina.htm. Accessed 10 May 2011.

Notes

At the time that this book went to press, Vladislav Mamyshev-Monroe died tragically in an accident in Bali, where he had lived since 2006. He died as dramatically as he lived, and his inimitable spirit will be missed in the artistic community.

1   Shortly after the artist's arrival in Leningrad (he was born in Novorossiisk), he acquired the nickname 'Afrika' from one of his mentors, Boris Grebenshchikov, a singer and songwriter in the Russian underground music group Akvarium. Bugaev developed an interested in reggae music and all things 'African' as a result of Grebenshchikov's influence, and the musician eventually named one of his albums, 'Radio Afrika' (1983), as well as one of its songs, 'Captain Afrika', after Bugaev.

2   It should be noted that, although by the 1970s and 1980s many artists in Soviet Russia were aware of the work of their avant-garde precursors, this work was not *officially* part of standard art history. Rather, artists learnt of this work in a more haphazard way. In Afrika's case, his association with Timur Novikov most likely provided a link with the past, as Novikov worked in the Russian Museum, and had access to the work of the avant-garde, which was tucked away in the basement.

3   It is also important to note the fact that much of the filming of *ASSA* took place in Crimea, as well as the art-historical significance of Crimea for not only Afrika, but also for art history. It was here that German artist Joseph Beuys' plane is said to have crashed in 1944, his rescue by Tatars marking the moment of his rebirth.

4   For an in-depth discussion of this performance, see Bryzgel (2013, chapter 1).

5   During the Soviet period, these banners were given as prizes of achievement, for example, to a collective farm with the greatest harvest.

6   Ilya Prigogine was a Belgian physicist and mathematician of Russian origin who was known for his work on dissipative structures (chaotic structures that are far from equilibrium). This work and his ideas inspired Afrika in his creation of the pendulum, also based on chaos and disorder.

7   As confirmed by Afrika in a conversation with the author, March 2006, as well as by Dr. Ron Rusay, Professor of Chemistry at Diablo Valley College in California.

8   Neznaika (roughly translated as Dunno or Know-Nothing) is the anti-hero created by children's writer Nikolai Nosov.

9   A border agreement between Russia and Latvia, for example, was only just signed in 2006, and the border between Estonia and Russia is still being disputed.

10   Andrew Solomon has commented on the distinction between the reception of Warhol's prints in Russia, in the 1970s, and the critical reception thereof in the West, noting that Soviet artists were more interested in the fact that the artist had created the prints using photo-silk screen technique, which they had never seen before (Solomon 1991: 37).

11   Mamyshev-Monroe also played her in an episode of 'The Lives of Remarkable People', which was part of Pirate TV, founded by Mamyshev, Novikov and Iurii Lesnikov in 1989. In this episode, Mamyshev appears as Marilyn, talking on the phone with John F. Kennedy, just prior to her suicide.

12   Furthermore, it is interesting to juxtapose his use of costume and disguise with that of Japanese artist Yasumasa Morimura, an artist from the East who inserts himself into canonical images from western art history, also using costume and disguise.

13   The issues of the Russian identity in the post-Soviet era are convoluted and complex, for a variety of reasons, namely, the fact that the Russia was the seat and centre of the Soviet Union meant that it promoted a Soviet identity at the expense of a Russian one.

14   See, for example, Groys (1992, 2008), Erjavec (2003, 2008) for more discussion on the meaning of 'postmodernism' for the East.

Chapter 6

Military Dandyism, Cosmism and Eurasian Imper-Art

Maria Engström

A distinctive feature of the artistic process of the last decade, not only in a conservative but also in a liberal environment, is the reassessment of the Soviet era, forging a new view on the recent Soviet past from the present day perspective shaped by the total domination of a market economy and mass culture. If in the 1990s and the early 2000s art opposed institutions of authority, above all the official ecclesiasticism, patriotism and nostalgia for power, then in recent years the personalized search of liberal nonconformists have been replaced by a drive for a new generality, where the unique experience of the collective is considered in the context of the history of the orthodox church and in the Soviet experience. The modern situation in Russian art is characterized even more often (and with the various feelings) as 'new patriotism', 'new conservatism' and 'progressive nostalgia'. A book titled *Progressive Nostalgia: The Modern Art of the Countries of the Former USSR* was published in 2007 by the editor-in-chief of the art journal *Khudozhestvennyi zhurnal/Art Journal*, the most authoritative publication of the Russian art community, and one of the main inspirers of the Moscow Art Biennale, the art-critic Victor Miziano. In an interview to *Nezavisimaia gazeta/Independent Gazette* he remarked that the nostalgia for the Soviet past does not suggest an aspiration to return to totalitarianism, but that it represents resistance against the glamour that has come to replace the Soviet system:

> Why is nostalgia for Soviet civilisation so important in my project? Because right now, a certain resistance to the mainstream is emerging. And the anti-glamour resistance searches a background, a tradition; it needs to lean on something. And modern culture finds support in the Soviet space, because Soviet civilization rested on the cult of innovation, on the utopian cult of a drive towards the future. Therefore, for artists with 'left' and 'right' political sympathies, even at an unconscious level, the Soviet aesthetic resource is indispensable: the resisting Soviet resource is brought up to date. The emptiness of glamour and its hopelessness gains an alternative repulse from the Soviet past. This is not about the reanimation of the totalitarian political system, but about aesthetics.
>
> (Kutlovskaia 2008)

However, the latest aesthetic and ideological searches of the former conceptualists in terms of tradition, belief and the Soviet past are driven by market demands rather than a struggle against them. The conservative turn in arts has begun much earlier than the second term of Vladimir Putin's presidency, namely in the early 1980s in the counterculture, the underground and marginal intellectual circles of the two capitals. The aversion against Soviet officialdom and against the emerging liberal market attitudes laid the foundation for an interest in conservative traditions and imperial aesthetics. The temptation of glamour and the power of mass culture had to be opposed by something more powerful and gripping: the conservative, imperial idea. While in Moscow the temptation of the empire was derived from traditionalism and from the principle of the Absolute and Authority, in Petersburg the imperial dreams were born by the city itself, its architecture, palaces and myths, which were directly connected to the traditions of dandyism and the Empire style.

Imper-art

At present there is no standard term that would adequately describe the phenomenon discussed below: of imperial metaphysics in art. In a few critical works devoted to the search of new aesthetics in the framework of radical conservatism, the following concepts are often used as synonyms: 'reactionary avant-gardism', 'right-wing postmodernism', 'punk-conservatism' or 'imperial avant-garde'. I suggest to call the new imperial style 'imperial sots-art', or 'imper-art'. In its attitude to power, imper-art is close to traditional, archaic cultures where authority expresses a certain and specific ontological status, while a requirement for wielding power is the ability to act, the presence of will, desire, force and energy. This kind of art visualizes the metaphysics of power and shows the spectator its magic foundation, its sacral quality and its *sensus numinous*.[1]

Imper-art is interested not so much in the phenomenon of empire in its historical hypostasis, but in empires as *imperium*, the sacral dimension of power and force. The concept of *imperium* must be distinguished from the concept of 'empire' as a state system. The modern Russian imperial discourse is a discourse not of empire, but *imperium*; a discourse of the legitimacy of power and its sacral nature.[2] Julius Evola (1897–1974), one of the most important authors for Russian neo-conservatives, has written in his book *Men Among the Ruins*:

> For instance, the ancient Roman notion *of imperium* essentially belonged to the domain of the sacred. This notion, in its specific meaning, even before expressing a system of territorial, supernational hegemony, designated the pure power of command, the almost mystical power and *auctoritas* inherent in the one who had [the] function and quality of Leader [...] A power and authority that are not absolute, are not real authority or real power.

> (Evola 2002: 122–23; emphasis in the original)

Like sots-art, imper-art admires its object: the totalitarian, hierarchical system. While the basic approaches of postmodernist poetics (irony, distancing, double reading, the combination of marginality with mainstream, etc.) remain, the axiology changes. There is no contradiction here, because – as Slavoj Žižek remarks – distancing is today inherent in any ideology, whether liberal or not, and the presence of irony, laughter or the carnivalesque alone does not yet speak of anti-totalitarian deconstruction (Žižek 1989: 27–28). As a phenomenon of the postmodern era, imper-art is a liminal and inconsistent phenomenon where the power of Utopia is combined with sober, sad and cold alienation. Unlike examples from both totalitarian art and sots-art, imper-art – with its combination of imperialism and avant-garde – is very quiet, looking at the Russia of the past and future with a metaphysical, almost otherworldly point of view, combining positive pathos and emotional distance. In imper-art ideological enthusiasm is combined with emotional disengagement and coldness, unlike sots-art, where the ideological alienation from the represented object is accompanied by an emotional involvement in the critical project. Totalitarian art is dominated by a third correlation: ideological enthusiasm is matched by full emotional involvement. This specific 'cold' style, required for an art which is a paradigm of traditionalism, is described by Evola in his book *Ride the Tiger* (1961). Evola calls the style that reflects a traditional outlook, where individualization is burnt out by transcendence and personality as understood in bourgeois society is replaced by type, 'magical realism' (117), or 'metaphysical typification'. This style, characterized by simplicity and even some asceticism and poverty, can help 'the new free man' to find a line of conduct and creativity in the modern world, which is, according to traditionalists, at the point of decline and disintegration. Evola remarks that the 'new objectivity' (*Neue Sachlichkeit*) and the new 'classicism' are closest to the required 'active anonymity':

> The essential traits of the new attitude were well described as distance, otherness, loftiness, monumentality, a laconic quality, and the revulsion against all that is warm proximity, humanity, effusiveness, expressionism; the line of objectivity in figures, of coolness and grandeur in forms.
>
> (Evola 2003: 116)

An example of imper-art in the modern Russian art scene is the well-known Moscow artist, winner of the 2008 Kandinsky Prize (a non-state national competition in the field of modern art), Aleksei Beliaev-Gintovt, who is the leader of the Eurasian movement since 2002. Beliaev-Gintovt (b. 1965) is an associate and colleague of the chief ideologist of the Eurasian *imperium*, Aleksandr Dugin, and of the founder of the 'new academism', Timur Novikov. The poetics of art of the new imperium, which Beliaev-Gintovt develops in his work, is a distanced, impersonal and cold eclecticism of archetypes of Russo-Soviet civilization. In the artist's opinion, only the heroic Grand Style (*Grand Manière*), which reflects the traditionalist principle of 'active anonymity', corresponds to the metaphysics of an Absolute state:

> The Grand Style is at the core of imperium. Looking back, we see the general features of the Grand Project of Russian and Soviet power [...] The anonymous will, collectivism, selfless work for the benefit of the next generations when it is clear that the declared aims will not be achieved during one's lifetime. The project assumes self-rejection and

dreaming [...] The basic concepts of the Grand Style are hierarchy, canon, command. The signs of the style are usefulness, durability, beauty. Apollo is with us.

(Beliaev-Gintovt 2004)

Classicism and empire depend on each other as demonstrations of the Apollonian beginnings:

The prosperity of the Russian State is inevitably connected with a celebration of classicism. Classicism is the art of the Sun, the art of creation and of fullness, the art of our Victory. On the one hand, this system of views and implementations is clear for everyone without comments; on the other hand, it is an aristocratic anti-bourgeois phenomenon where one can find today battle attributes of an offensive nature. Not pacification and conformism, but an attacking, heroic, military style.

(Kovalev 2004)

Eurasian imper-art visualizes the affinity of the ideology of Eurasianism and the German conservative revolution (on the latter, see Rutkevich 2006). Beliaev-Gintovt openly declares that his work has a 'conservative-revolutionary character' (Beliaev-Gintovt 2002) and gives new models for the *gestalt* of the 'worker', a cold 'passionary', the builder of the Eurasian empire. For these aesthetics the 'worker' is an archetype that overcomes in synthesis both the individualism of the elite and the mechanism of mass. War, work and sports are the central themes of the conservative revolution, comparable to the sensuality of mechanisms that release energy. In a war, at work and at sports the 'new man' is born, while bourgeoisie and femininity perish. In the projects *Polius/The Pole* (2002) and *Rodina-doch'/Motherland-Daughter* (2008) we see the utopia of the body, a steel form, hypertrophied masculinity, a body-mechanism 'on the other side of pain'. The severity of these sculptures is a sign of typification rather than individualization. Ernst Jünger (1895–1998), one of the leaders of the conservative revolution, wrote:

What the liberal world understood by a 'good' man was, actually, a refined man: nervous, mobile, changeable and open to various influences and stimuli. A disciplined man, on the contrary, is closed; he has a firm view and is monotonous, materially-driven and stark.

(Iunger 2002: 496–97)

The best-known project of the group *FSB: Front Spokoinogo Blagodenstviia/FSB: Front of Quiet Prosperity*³ of Beliaev-Gintovt, Andrei Molodkin and Gleb Kosorukov is 'NovoNovosibirsk' (2001), which resonated widely in the artistic community. It consists of a series of large canvasses of neo-classical sculptures drawn with a ball pen for the new capital of the Eurasian empire, NovoNovosibirsk (New Novosibirsk). According to the artists' idea, the city of Novosibirsk would set up 24 huge monuments, among them a building-cum-statue to Apollo-Pantokrator with rockets in his quiver, a huge swan and the colossus of colossi.

Figure 6.1: Aleksei Beliaev-Gintovt and Andrei Molodkin, 'Apollo's Dam' (NovoNovosibirsk, 2000). Courtesy of Aleksei Beliaev-Gintovt

This is a cold Utopia of the new capital of the Eurasian empire, close to the North Pole, in the 'geometrical centre of Eurasia'. The dark blue, deathly and icy colours enhance the lifelessness and solitariness of the new utopian space. Made with ball pens, the work reflects the main principle of the Neo-Academicians: painstaking manual skills. Their revival is characteristic for this movement and represents a revolt against the 'spirit of time', against the specialization in humanities and arts, against the loss of an all-embracing outlook and the ability to create total works of art. Jünger frequently mentioned the increase of fragmentariness, specialization and localness as signs of an epoch of 'nihilism':

> We may consider as a related sign the growing propensity to specialization: division and detailed elaboration. It is evident both in the humanities, where synoptic talent almost disappears, and in professional life, where the manual craft requiring special qualifications has disappeared completely. Specialization has gone so far that the individual needs to develop only a personal idea, and carry out only one operation on the conveyor belt.
>
> (Iunger 2009)

On the other hand, the obvious discrepancy of the material and the scale of the project *NovoNovosibirsk* lay bare the essence of imper-art poetics: the simultaneous rapprochement to and repulsion of totalitarian aesthetics, which emphasizes the utopianism and deliberate monumentalism of the project and introduces a playful element of 'flickering aesthetics'. The school colour of the dark blue ball pen can be interpreted as a 'trace' of the little man, as the dream of a boy drawing a magic world during a dull lesson. The name alone of the new capital NovoNovosibirsk is a kind of echo of this direction (neo-academism equals neo-neo-classicism); critics argue whether this is ironical or not. Obviously, the joking quality of imper-art is sometimes accompanied by extremely serious comments of the artist. At other times, on the contrary, the gravity of the image is commented upon in an ambiguous manner. The overall objective of such a 'flickering aesthetics' is to force the spectator or reader to formulate an opinion and 'define' his own position.

The art-critic Aleksandr Borovskii emphasized the difference of style of the group FSB and the project *NovoNovosibirsk* both from postmodernist and official, pro-Putin art:

> [S]omething could be felt deeper than the carefree young postmodernist *steb* [...] which, as a rule, is level and seeks its source within itself. Yet here things are different [...] Moreover, the project started before the publication of our domestic political innovations. It is terrible to say this, but it anticipated something, it is externalised (*ovneshnit'*, to use Bakhtin's term) what had only just started, what had gelled in our new post-Soviet air [...] The authors really groped around and hit something vital for the psychology of the modern establishment. Namely: an eclecticism which lies not even in ideology (that, it seems, remains unexplicated), but in the need for this ideology [...] The authors came upon a most interesting, atavistic substance that is embedded in the psychologies of the Russian elites: a version of imperial neoclassicism.
>
> (Borovskii 2008; emphasis added)[4]

Although in Neo-Eurasian ideology the 'supporters of the idea of Petersburg are enemies of Eurasianism', *NovoNovosibirsk* is created on antique models, which involuntarily reminds us of the most consistently classicist city and the most successful Grand Project of Russian history. Therefore the neo-imperial discourse with its Byzantinism, Eurasianism and Third-Rome mythology is connected exclusively with Moscow only at first sight. Genetically the shift to imper-art represents the realization of the Petersburg text of Russian culture and, following Vladimir Toporov, can be considered as the 'peak of Apollonianism', which has accompanied each new century of Russian culture since 1700 (see Toporov 2003). However, we see here not a pure return of classicism, but a mimicry, an eclectic reference to these aesthetics through the prism of the avant-garde and Stalinist art on the one hand, and of Russian symbolism on the other hand, as well as an attempt to revive the trends that unite these two directions of Dionysian and Apollonian discourse. Imper-art deliberately formulates an alternative to the mainstream of the 1990s, denying the horizontal, shapeless and style-less Moscow postmodernism and emphasizing instead the vertical, super-human and timeless character of classicism as Apollonian art.[5]

In the cold style the total light exposure and logic readability of art disappears. Paradoxically, behind the clear, precise, simple form which assumes no interpretational shifts, something impenetrable is hidden that appeals to another dimension in art. The spectator, left alone with this harsh and cold form, is compelled to breathe used-up air. He may experience the irritating feeling of spiritual bankruptcy and discomfort. The images of the new classics contain no trepidation of life. Rather, the new form appeals to images of death, or more precisely to borders, but maybe through this coldness that is so alien to the 'spirit of the present' something that has been forgotten can return, or something unknown can emerge in modern culture.

(Bobrinskaia 2004)

The melancholy for hierarchy is expressed through nostalgia for the active male beginning, through the enchantment with the trained male body doomed to death – in the army, in uniform and in parades. The new imperial aesthetics is an expression and simultaneously an overcoming of the 'eternal female' in Russian culture. In the works of Beliaev-Gintovt power and its attributes are above all objects of an aesthetic and mystical experience, as in Vasilii Rozanov's description of the feeling numenosity during a casual meeting with the cavalry that we find in the book *The War of 1914 and Russia's Revival*:

I shyly looked at this endless chain of heavy horsemen, each of whom was so enormous compared to me! I was taken more and more by a sense of my own depression. I felt embraced by a strange strength, so huge that my 'I' seemed to be carried away like a tiny flake in the whirlwind of this grandeur and size [...] When I suddenly felt that I was not only 'afraid', but actually fascinated by them, captivated by the strange charm which I experienced only this one time in my life. Something strange happened: the exaggerated courage of the force before me seemed to change the structure of my organization, and rejected and overturned it into a female one. I felt an unusual tenderness, languor and drowsiness in all my being [...] My heart fell – with love [...] I wanted them to be even larger, I wanted for them to be even more [...] This colossus of physiology, a colossus of life should be the source of life; this created in me a purely female sensation of weak will, humility and an insatiable desire 'to be closer' and to see without lowering the eye [...] Strength – that is beauty in the world [...] Strength is what subdues: people fall before it, pray to it [...] In strength lies the secret of the world.

(Rozanov 1915: 230–33)

Imper-art certainly contains Rozanov's 'gender' concept of strength as fullness of life, might, source of power and energy, which is shared between the beholder of strength/power and his subjects, whose ontological status is characterized, in turn, by weakness, shortage, decline and inferiority. Strength is visualized as a subject that presents, awards and shares its mystical force, making the spectator an object that accepts, thanks, reveres and serves.

Military dandyism

Central for an understanding and adequate evaluation of imper-art and Neo-Eurasianism as a whole is, in my opinion, the concept of 'romantic irony'. The principle of romantic irony has found its clearest embodiment in the lifestyle and behaviour of the dandy. I invoke here the classical definition of dandyism given by Charles Baudelaire (1863):

> Dandyism appears especially in those periods of transition when democracy has not yet become all-powerful, and when aristocracy is only partially weakened and discredited. In the confusion of such times, a certain number of men, disenchanted and leisured 'outsiders', but all of them richly endowed with native energy, may conceive the idea of establishing

Figure 6.2: Aleksei Beliaev Gintovt, *Cosmoparade,* or *The Victory Parade of 2937*(2010). Courtesy of Aleksei Beliaev-Gintovt

a new kind of aristocracy, all the more difficult to break down because established on the most precious, the most indestructible faculties, on the divine gifts that neither work nor money can give. Dandyism is the last flicker of heroism in decadent ages.

Thus, the dandy is not so much a man of fashion, but a cultural type who positions himself against the social current purely relying on his self and a certain aesthetic taste.[6] This aesthetic taste is characterized by distance, duality, ambivalence, a combination of tradition with revolution, creation with destruction, Dionysius and Apollo. Dandyism is close to conservative romanticism, as it is a form of demonstrating the presence of personality, of uniqueness and singularity against the background of mass culture, shapeless mass clothes, the unification of gender (unisex) and behaviour (political correctness). The dandy takes the position of a sober observer and perceives the world as a performance; he displays a predilection for metamorphoses and masking, as well as provocative behaviour. Dandyism is a contradictory combination of engagement and dispassionateness, narcissism and self-parody, the position of the last hero, the image of vanishing, victorious courage. The dandy underlines his love for the artificial, his contemptuous attitude to women and nature; he is self-sufficient, narcissistic and lonely. If we turn to philosophical or historiosophical predilections of the Moscow traditionalists or the Petersburg Neo-Academicians, the most important and most quoted authors are aesthetes and dandies, loners and critics of the bourgeois European elitism and mediocrity, adventurers and military men: Konstantin Leont'ev, Julius Evola, Ernst Jünger, Nikolai Gumilev. Coldness, orderliness and frequently immoral aestheticism are the key concepts both for dandyism and imper-art. Aleksandr Dugin notes the distancing as the basic attribute of the hero's behaviour:

> By definition, the hero should be 'cold'. If he does not stand apart from the surroundings, if he does not freeze in himself his warm energy of daily human life, he will not be up to the level of completing the Impossible, i.e. at a level of what makes a hero heroic. The hero must be apart from the people. But behind the social cosiness there storm the penetrating winds of an objective reality, severe and inhumane. The earth and the stones rise against fauna and flora. An aggressive flora corrodes minerals, and wild animals ruthlessly trample down obstinate weeds. The elements beyond society know no leniency. The world itself is a triumphal feast of substance, whose bottom layer is merged with blocks of cosmic ice. The hero is cold, because he is objective, because he accepts from the world the relay baton of spontaneous power, wild and bad.
>
> (Dugin 1997)

Julius Evola in his book *Ride the Tiger* discusses the concept of Apollo and Dionysius in Nietzsche, and writes in detail about 'Dionysian Apollonism' as a style of behaviour of traditional man in the modern world. The Dionysian experience, which Evola interprets as a necessary level of tension in life and a way to mystery, should be stabilized through

'Apollonism'. The result of the synthesis is the removal of the contradiction between 'spirit' and 'feelings':

> Detachment coexists with a fully lived experience; a calm 'being' is constantly wedded to the substance of life. The consequence of this union, existentially speaking, is a most particular kind of lucid inebriation, one might almost say intellectualized and magnetic, which is the absolute opposite of what comes from the ecstatic opening to the world of elementary forces, instinct, and 'nature'.
>
> (Evola 2003: 66)

In neo-conservative circles Otto Mann's essay 'Dandyism as Conservative Lifestyle' (*Dandysmus als konservative Lebensform*, 1925), first published in Russian in the almanac *Volshebnaia gora/Magic Mountain*, enjoys great popularity. Using the example of the story of the well-known dandies Jules Amédée Barbey d'Aurevilly and Joris-Karl Huysmans, Mann traces the path from dandyism to religious conservatism. He relates the dandy to Stefan George and Ernst Jünger, emphasizing that dandyism lies not so much in fashion than in behaviour and an intellectual position. Mann pays special attention to the image of the dandy in Jünger's novel *Heliopolis* (1949) and writes:

> For Jünger the dandy is not only a literary hero, which is proven by his shape and by the fact that he singles out and welcomes men in this position in his works: greatness and aristocratic distance, personified by his hero, the position of the sober (cold) spectator, the experience of the world as performance, the predilection for masks and masking, the desire to provoke – i.e. behaviour typical for the dandy.
>
> (Mann n.d.)

Military Dandyism and imper-art are inseparable from the notions of hierarchy and elitism and simultaneously from patriotism, surmising the death of the best. The researcher of dandy culture Filip Khor has emphasized the connection between dandyism and military craft, especially tangible during the First and Second World Wars; he writes about 'the existence of an esoteric, non-generic link, the histories of mutual influence and an attraction, the paradoxical tension between [...] eccentricity and drill, open decadence and patriotic practicality' (Khor 2008: 12). Military dandyism and imper-art share the presence of beauty and power, youth and death, a certain shrill desire of absolute order in the face of chaos. The American artist Marsden Hartley left a comment in his diaries of 1914–15, giving the following worrying and bitter description of German soldier as theophany:

> [T]he Pariser Platz was packed jammed to the stoops and windows with those huge cuirassiers of the Kaiser's special guard – all in white – white leather breeches skin tight – high plain enamel boots – those gleaming blinding medieval breast plates of silver and brass – making the eye go black when the sun glanced like a spear as the bodies moved.

There were the inspiring helmets with the imperial eagle and the white manes hanging down – there was six foot of youth under all this garniture –everyone on a horse – and every horse white – that is how I got it – and it went into an abstract picture of soldiers riding into the sun, a fact to take place so not long after – for all of these went out into the sun and never came back.

(Ryan 1997: 90)

Figure 6.3: Aleksei Beliaev-Gintovt, *Cosmoparade,* or *The Victory Parade of 2937* (2010). Courtesy of Aleksei Beliaev-Gintovt

The dandy aesthetics and the distanced position of the observer are also evident in the words of Beliaev-Gintovt after his visit to Tskhinvali, the zone of military actions during the Russian-Georgian conflict in August 2008, when speaking of Ossetian soldiers:

> At last the South of Russia looks as it should do. Seeing such a number of young (and not so young) armed men, each of whom could be mould into a statue [...] A man in body armour, with a wide leather belt, a garland of grenades for the launcher, holding a knife, a pistol and a machine gun is worthy of a sculpture.
>
> (Kanishchev 2008)

The artist constantly returns to the theme of sports and military parades, this staged mystery display that most piercingly shows the union of the Dionysian tension of life forces and Apollonian organization, the struggle and interdependence of order and chaos. From 27 May until 15 June 2010 the Moscow gallery Triumph showed a new exhibition of the works of Beliaev-Gintovt, titled *The Victory Parade of 2937*. According to the author, the prototype for this series of pictures was the parade of athletes of 1937 (Karpekina 2010).

The parade of 2937 (see Figure 6.4) in a sun-drenched New Moscow, the capital of the Eurasian empire, is the dream of the neo-conservatives concerning the total mobilization of the 'victors of chaos'. People and zoomorphs in scaly armour march shoulder to shoulder across an archeo-futuristic Red Square; battle-mammoths trod along and red star-ships fly over. The entire herbal world is united in a struggle against death and distemper: technology, people and animals, buildings, squares and streets of a flawlessly organized city:

> I see communism with an inhuman face. That is why people, animals, birds and angels walk in one line in the parade, symbolizing the catholicity and universality of the big Eurasian Victory Parade. A parade of a victory over chaos, a victory of centripetal processes over centrifugal ones.
>
> (Tikhonov n.d.)

But not only nature and technology are united with man in the parade of the victory over chaos. History participates too, the revived forces of the most organized empires and katechon-empires:[7] Egypt, Greater Mongolia, India, Rome, Byzantium and the Soviet Union.

The name of the capital of the Eurasian empire of the future, New Moscow, refers to Aleksandr Medvedkin's film of the same title from 1938. The film is well known for an episode where the protagonist presents a 'living' model of the new Soviet Moscow, of what it should become according to Stalin's grand plan for the reconstruction of the capital. The New Moscow of 2937 in Beliaev-Gintovt's version has undergone a general Eurasian reconstruction. Red Square can be recognized by the Kremlin, the Mausoleum and St Basil's Cathedral, but in all other aspects the Eurasian metropolis has been reconstructed: we see pyramids, high-rises, a new Palace of Soviets topped this time by a statue of Apollo instead of Lenin. The Eurasian civilization project is one of alter-globalization, which is signalled both

Figure 6.4: Aleksei Beliaev-Gintovt, *Cosmoparade,* or *The Victory Parade of 2937* (2010). Courtesy of Aleksei Beliaev-Gintovt

by the high-rises and the statue of Responsibility, an alternative to the New York Statue of Liberty. The city centre is occupied by the Ministry of Cosmic Space, the Ministry of Truth, the Ministry of Struggle against Chaos, the Ministry of Love. The project is distinguished by its futurism and apocalypse, its revolutionism and neo-archaism. Technology does not remove the spell from the world of the Eurasian empire, but mythologizes it afresh: the mammoths can keep their step while carrying spaceships, and people are covered by impregnable scales.

Cosmism

The dream of interosculation of man and nature, nature and technology, man and technology is characteristic both for conservative revolution movement (in particular Spengler and Jünger) and for the Russian philosophy of totality (*vseedinstvo*), for Russian cosmism engaged in the spiritual-technical problem of a victory over death. The stages on the path of science to mastering the secret of immortality are the re-creation of the physical world and of the human body whose organs become tools, while the 'external' organism, i.e., nature, returns to man, giving him the means for overcoming death. If the artist perceived NovoNovosibirsk as capital of Eurasia-Hyperborea and created it in a deathly dark blue colour, then New Moscow is in flames and shines with 'red' meaning. The style of both projects is distinguished by an active anonymity, a combination of the impersonal and maximally individual which is reflected in the artistic technique. In the project *NovoNovosibirsk* the monumental pictures were drawn with a ball pen, while Victory Parade was made with handprints of the artist with red typographical paint and leaf gold. Beliaev-Gintovt speaks about a new tactility, where prints of the palm are a component of the image created in the painting, and about the new objectivity connecting dispassionateness and photographic objectivity with maximal involvement: 'The objective of the photo-camera and the extreme subjectivity of the author meet in a new paradoxical manner' (Guintovt 2010).

However, according to the artist the chosen technique also has another purpose, namely, to leave skin particles in the paint, sufficient for a future revival.[8] Nikolai Fedorov (1829–1903), the chief theorist of Russian cosmism, derives the principle of imperium and supreme power from man's aspiration for victory over death. In his article 'Autocracy' (*Samoderzhavie*) Fedorov writes about the necessity for a strong, centralized state for the 'common cause', while the image of the supreme ruler is connected to the archaic image of the tsar-priest:

> Autocracy in the original sense is a dictatorship created by danger not from other people like yourself, but from a blind force, which threatens everyone without exception with death. Autocracy [...] emerged immediately after the death of the first father, uniting everyone through a single will and uniform desire caused by loss and death.
>
> (Kozhevnikov and Peterson 1906: 375)

In his novel *Gospodin Geksogen/Mister Hexogen* (2002) Aleksandr Prokhanov draws a similar parallel and reduces the meaning of the Soviet project to the main task of all imperia: the revival of the dead and overcoming death; the idea is voiced in the novel by the Doctor of the Dead:

> 'The red sense' [...] consists in one single point: overcoming death. The ancient Egyptians, who professed the revival of Osiris, were 'red'. The Indian pantheists, believing in the resettlement of the soul and the non-eradicability of life, were 'red'. Jesus, who 'with his death conquered death and gave life to the dead' was 'red'. Nikolai Fedorov, who preached the revival from dead, challenging mankind to unite and revive the dead ancestors, to settle them on planets of the galaxy by means of Tsiolkovsky's rockets, was 'red'. The Soviet Union was an enormous laboratory, where 300 million people, having studied letters and sciences, mastering nuclear energy and constructing a rocket fleet, prepared for an exit into the Universe.
>
> (Prokhanov 2002: 309)

The revival of the 'red sense' has occurred in the Victory Parade of 2937, and at the head of the mystery procession walks Lenin, resurrected and covered in scales (see Figure 6.5).

Thus, the imperial theme in modern art – if seen as continuation, on the one hand, of the traditions of military dandyism, and on the other of the ideas and figurativeness of Russian

Figure 6.5: Aleksei Beliaev-Gintovt, *Cosmoparade,* or *The Victory Parade of 2937* (2010). Courtesy of Aleksei Beliaev-Gintovt

cosmism – develops not in the context of real politics, but in the sphere of meta-politics and metaphysics. It is indissolubly connected with the theme of victory over chaos and death, with the search for images of a new collectivity and a new 'common cause'. Beliaev-Gintovt, already recognized as 'one of our own' in the contemporary art scene, deliberately breaks all its taboos: the interdiction of a bent for meta-narratives, of ideocracy, of a reduction to irony, the interdiction of the lack of critical reflection, making the only avant-garde and provocative gesture in the context of modern art. On the other hand, the reference to archaic models and the search for a 'common cause' as some alternative to the deadlock atomization and fragmentation is undoubtedly in demand in post-secular Europe and Russia. In this duality, the simultaneous fear of and desire for new meta-narratives, lies the reason for Beliaev-Gintovt's ambiguous status in the system of current Russian art and for the discrepancy in the evaluation of his creativity by critics and researchers, and the unconditional commercial success of his project.

Translated by Birgit Beumers

Works cited

Beliaev-Gintovt, Aleksei (2002), 'Iarche tysiachi solnts', *Zavtra* 15, http://zavtra.ru/cgi/veil/data/zavtra/02/438/81.html and also on Aleksei Beliaev's website http://www.doctrine.ru/vchera/interview/zavtra/. Accessed 15 October 2011.

——— (2004), 'My. Oni nemy', *Khudozhestvennyi zhurnal* 54, http://xz.gif.ru/numbers/54/my-oni-nemy/. Accessed 15 October 2011.

Bobrinskaia, Ekaterina (2004), 'Somnitel'naia sushchnost' iskusstva', *Khudozhestvennyi zhurnal* 54, http://xz.gif.ru/numbers/54/somnitelnaya/. Accessed 15 October 2011.

Baudelaire, Charles (1863), 'The Dandy', from *The Painter of Modern Life*, transl. by P.E. Charvet, http://www.dandyism.net/baudelaires-the-dandy/. Accessed 20 July 2012.

Borovskii, Aleksandr [2008], 'Etaticheskii estetizm', (on *Rodina-doch*'), http://www.doctrine.ru/vchera/rodina-doch/03/. Accessed 15 October 2011.

Dugin, Aleksandr (1997) 'Orion ili zagovor geroev', *Arktogeiia*, December http://arcto.ru/modules.php?name=News&file=article&sid=96. Accessed 15 October 2011.

Evola, Julius (2002), *Men Among the Ruins*, translation by Guido Stucco, Rochester: Inner Traditions, http://www.juliusevola.com/site/MenAmongtheRuins..pdf. Accessed 27 July 2012.

Evola, Julius (2003), *Ride the Tiger*, translation by Guido Stucco, Rochester: Inner Traditions, http://www.kathodos.com/ridethetiger..pdf. Accessed 31 July 2012.

Guintovt, Alexey [sic] (2010), 'Interv'iu Novomu Muzeiu', *YouTube*, 3 August http://www.youtube.com/watch?v=7EEkYQ0FERM. Accessed 15 October 2011.

Iunger, Ernst [Ernst Jünger] (2002), *Rabochii. Gospodstvo i geshtal't. Total'naia mobilizatsiia. O boli*, (Der Arbeiter, Herrschaft und Gestalt, 1932; Die totale Mobilmachung, 1931; Über den Schmerz, 1934), Sankt Petersburg: Nauka.

——— (2009), 'Cherez liniiu' (Über die Linie, 1950), *Politicheskaia kontseptologiia* 2, pp. 251–279. http://politconcept.sfedu.ru/2009.2/13.pdf. Accessed 15 October 2011.

Kanishchev, Pavel (2008), 'Ia videl absoliutno geroicheskuiu real'nost'', Interview with Aleksei Beliaev-Gintovt, *Evraziiskii soiuz molodezhi*, http://www.rossia3.ru/culture/gintovtosetinte?PHPSESSID=9b53ad8. Accessed 15 October 2011.

Karpekina, Tat'iana (2010) 'Boevye slony Beliaeva-Gintovta', *Golos Rossii*, 1 June, http://rus.ruvr.ru/2010/06/01/8879227.html and http://doctrine.ru/zavtra/victory/004/. Accessed 15 October 2011.

Khor, Filip (2008), '"Mne nravitsia muzhchina v forme": chest' mundira v predstavlenii dendi', *Teoriia mody* 7.

Kovalev, Andrei (2004), 'Zvezda vo lbu', *Russkii zhurnal* 19 February http://old.russ.ru/columns/pictures/20040219_kov.html. Accessed 15 October 2011.

Kozhevnikov, Vladimir and Nikolai Peterson (eds) (1906), *Filosofiia obshchego dela. Stat'i, mysli i pis'ma Nikolaia Fedorovicha Fedorova*, vol. 1, Vernyi: n.p.

Kutlovskaia, Elena (2008), 'Made in SSSR. Miziano protiv meinstrima' [review of Viktor Miziano's book *Progressive Nostalgia*], *Nezavisimaia gazeta* 12 September, http://antrakt.ng.ru/theme/2008-09-12/21_ussr.html. Accessed 15 October 2011.

Mann, Otto (n.d. [1925]), 'Dendizm kak konservativnaia forma zhizni', *Volshebnaia gora*, http://www.metakultura.ru/vgora/kulturol/ot_mann.htm. Accessed 15 October 2011.

Otto, Rudol'f (2008), *Sviashchennoe. Ob irratsional'nom v idée bozhestvennogo i ego sootnoshenii s ratsional'nym*, [Das Heilige. Über das Irrationale in der Idee des Göttlichen und sein Verhältnis zum Rationalen (1917)], transl. by A. Rutkevich, St. Petersburg: Izdatel'stvo Sankt-Peterburgskogo universiteta.

Prokhanov, Aleksandr (2002), *Gospodin Geksogen*, AdMarginem.

Rozanov, Vasilii (1915), *Voina 1914-go goda i russkoe vozrozhdenie*, Petrograd.

Rutkevich, Aleksei (2006), *Konservatory XX veka*, Moscow: RUDN.

Ryan, Susan Elizabeth (ed.) (1997), *Somehow a Past: The Autobiography of Marsden Hartley*, Boston: MIT Press.

Tikhonov, Andrei (n.d.), 'Mne viditsia kommunizm s nechelovecheskom litsom', Interview with Aleksei Beliaev-Gintovt, *Evraziiskii soiuz molodezhi* http://rossia3.ru/smi/nechelovechesko. Accessed 15 October 2011.

Toporov, Vladimir (2003), *Peterburgskii tekst russkoi literatury*, Sankt-Peterburg: Iskusstvo.

Vainshtein, Ol'ga (2006), *Dendi. Moda, literatura, stil' zhizni*, Moscow: Novoe literaturnoe obozrenie.

Voloshin, Maksimilian (1988), 'Apollon i mysh'', *Liki tvorchestva* Leningrad: Nauka.

Žižek, Slavoj (1989), *The Sublime Object of Ideology* London: Verso.

Notes

1 The numinous, i.e., a feeling of simultaneous awe, fear and trembling, is a term of Rudolf Otto (2008).

2 The word *imperium* designates 'complete power' and is formed from the Latin verb 'imperare' – to command. An empire is the territory to which the action of holding *imperium* applies. Initially the concept of *imperium* designated full executive (military, legal and administrative) power of magistrates (consuls, praetors and – in extreme circumstances – dictators) during the time of the Roman republic. After the fall of the republic the emperor received at his enthronement the highest degree of power to command: *summum imperium*, which included military and other powers that were bestowed on him for life and applied to all state territories. The symbols of the *imperium* were *fasces*, i.e., bundles of birch rods held together with red leather ribbon and with a bronze axe protruding from the centre. In ancient Rome *fasces* were used in processions and carried by twelve lictors who accompanied the magistrates. The axes were removed inside the town (*pomerium*), but were displayed outside the town's boundaries, because only there the lictors were entitled to execute Roman citizens. The axe symbolizes power over life and death of Roman citizens of the magistrate who holds *imperium*. Although today the term fasces is associated exclusively with fascism and national socialism, but we should note that fasces appear as ornaments in the military and administrative symbolism of a number of modern democratic states, including America, France, and Sweden.

3 FSB also stands for the Federal Security Bureau (*Federal'naia sluzhba bezopasnosti*)

4 *Steb* (also *styob*) is a term used in cultural studies for a mocking, derisory attitude that borders on provocation.

5   On the connection between Apollo and the idea of time see Voloshin 1988: 96–112.
6   About various types of dandyism see Vainshtein (2006).
7   In the ideology of Eurasianism space dominates over time, and historical time loses its force. Neo-Eurasianism inherits the historiosophical concept of the Christian empire of the Romans as *katechon* (Greek: that what/the one who withholds), protecting the ecumeny (*oikoumene*) in a situation of general apostasy from the triumph of the Anti-Christ. For the Byzantines the empire is an earthly icon of the heavenly order, keeping at bay the forces of chaos. It has no single and permanent spatial-temporal characteristic, and can change its geographical position and transform in the territories of different states (*translatio imperii romani*). In the orthodox tradition, Russian statehood inherits the messianic katechonic meaning of the Byzantine Empire.
8   Before us we have not only the materialisation of the metaphor 'the artist lives in his art', but also a reflection of one of the maxims of cosmism, the theory of *sphragis* (Greek: seal, signet). According to the doctrine of Grigory Nissky, the body bears an imprint of the soul, hence the Christian reverence of remains, of icons, relics and burial places of saints.

Chapter 7

Sweet Dreams: Retro Imagery on Chocolate Packaging in Post-Soviet Russia

Bettina Jungen

The past 20 years have seen a search for adequate visual and verbal expression of the mood of post-Soviet society in all areas of life. One prominent place for the exploration of new imagery was the packaging of chocolate and pralines, or toffees (*konfety*), which were regarded as a product of national culture. My observations and deliberations regarding the design of post-Soviet chocolate wrapping paper touch on various factors which determine the success of packaging design, ranging from the history of Russia's chocolate production to the post-Soviet economic situation and specifically the chocolate market, from global marketing regulations to specific examples of design. These examples are drawn from online collections, which became rather fashionable and widespread in the 1990s, thus reflecting and supporting the popularity of the object under investigation here.[1]

History

In the nineteenth century, the major chocolate- and toffee-producing companies were led by Ferdinand Theodor von Einem (since 1922 Krasnyi Oktiabr' Factory); Aleksei Ivanovich Abrikosov (since 1922 Babaev Factory); and the Lenov family (since 1931 Rot-Front Factory), which leveraged chocolate and *konfety* in Russia. Packaged chocolates, however, such as chocolate bars and truffle boxes, were a luxury good for most households and would, until after World War I, only be consumed on special occasions. After the slumps of the war, the Civil War, the short economic upturn during the New Economic Policy (NEP, 1921–28) and the forced collectivization of the late 1920s, chocolate experienced a revival in Soviet Russia in the 1930s. Anastas Mikoyan, Commissar of Foreign Trade and responsible for food industries from 1926–49, himself fostered the increase of the quality and variety of the chocolate production and supported particularly Krasnyi Oktiabr' 'which as early as 1937 produced well over 500 different types of candies and chocolate' (Gronow 2003: 43). The production, distribution and advertisement corresponded to Socialist Realism in the arts, delivering the message of the 'happy and abundant socialist way of life' (Gronow 2003: 14). With regard to the promise of a happy life, Soviet advertising did not differ much from its western counterpart, where the function of design has been described as 'absorbing insecurity and conveying faith in the world' (Bolz 1999: 32): that is precisely what Socialist Realism did. In contrast to the West, however, Soviet advertisement stood in for the advertised goods, which were not accessible for most Soviet citizens (Goscilo 2009: 55).

In the 1930s chocolate was associated with elitist luxury brought to the masses by the Soviets; as Gronow puts it: '[t]he new luxuries were symbolic of a lifestyle lived by the Russian elite of the nineteenth century, or rather a life which the Bolsheviks had read about in Tolstoy, Chekhov and Gogol' (Gronow 2003: 33).

This ambition for a new lifestyle while pining for the past is captured in Konstantin Vaginov's novel *Bambochada* (1931), where he describes the vanishing of pre-Soviet life and culture. Indeed, chocolate wrappers play an important role in the lives of two characters, members of a group deciding to found a society to preserve ephemeral everyday objects, including soap wrappers, chocolate wrappers, cigarette boxes and so on. For the chocolate wrappers, a collection already exists. The engineer Toropulo collects wrappers in a drawer and from time to time he takes them out to reflect on the changes of motifs and implicitly of Russian culture at large. A striking observation, relevant again in post-Soviet times, is that in Toropulo's younger days the ingredient coffee was represented by a serving (seductive) female figure, while in Soviet times it is represented by some floating chairs and a table, suggesting a café. In this way not only gender issues, but also sensuousness have vanished, making way for stark imagery. The other chocolate-related character is Ermilov, who mourns for his daughter, a ballerina, and bewails that she died too young. 'He was sad that Varenka never experienced real fame; that the image of herself in a tutu would never appear on a perfume bottle, on a bar of soap, on pralines, on candies, and that no bronze medal would ever be made in her honour' (Vaginov 1991: 276, translation of the author). Perfume and chocolates appear in this sentence on the same level as medals, appropriate to commemorate heroes and cultural values. Notwithstanding the irony, the text describes the mental state of Russian people and their values in the early twentieth century. Actual wrappers from pre-Soviet times show indeed motifs related to high-culture and achievements, including the victory over Napoleon, characters from Dostoevsky's *The Brothers Karamazov* and Flaubert's *Salammbô*, along with light-hearted dance motifs. All of these images belonged to the cultural sphere of an intellectual elite, which can be defined as the consumers of chocolate, since any imagery on packaging has to reflect common knowledge and values of the target consumer.

Themes

Due to their popularity and rootedness in Russian everyday culture, chocolate and *konfety* could potentially project Russianness after the collapse of the USSR. Contemporary identification propositions called upon the same Russian elite as did the chocolate campaign of the 1930s. Now, however, it was not the participation in consuming a luxury formerly reserved for the elites, which was in the centre of attention, but the actual imagery on the packaging, which evoked the noble world of Russia's past. The new compositions often combined in an eclectic way a variety of pre-Soviet elements, thus evoking a pseudo-Russian world. The new creations appeared as part of the 'post-Soviet [...] display of Russian cultural myths, a jumble of old and new conceptions of prestige and cultural hierarchies' (Boym 1994: 274).

A general survey of the designs that appeared in the first two post-Soviet decades reveals several trends, tying in more or less with the aesthetics of past eras: flowers were a popular subject-matter already in pre-Revolutionary times; less frequently bows would appear on boxes and chocolate bars that were meant to be gifts. Thus, the designs for the pralines Osennyi val's and Palitra included golden autumn leaves and petals and buds to evoke positive connotations. Images from visual arts and literature, which were widespread before the Revolution and during NEP, were not revived in the 1990s. Most important, however, for the immediate rendering of Russianness were symbols of national power (Rathmayr and Schimpfössl 2005: 230). They included historical personalities and sites as well as Russian types, such as peasant and noblewomen. Chocolates with sounding names such as Sudarushka (Rossiia), the friendly and endearing form of *sudarynia*, meaning lady, or Gvardeiskii (Babaev), a member of the 'troops close to the sovereign, dressed like a dandy and paid with privileges' (Dal' 1996), as well as the Tretiakov art series (Krasnyi Oktiabr') and Vechernii Zvon [Evening Bells] (Rot Front) verbally and visually communicated a grandness of the Russian past, which was implicitly imposed upon the present. This identification proposition made sense only for those generations that could link the images to the Russian culture of past centuries, descriptions of which could be found in Russian literature. Hence, the erudition of Soviet citizens was indispensable for the success of historical motifs on post-Soviet chocolate wrappers.

Serguei Oushakine justifiably points out that 'the old form is evoked not in order to express its old meaning. Rather it reveals the inability of existing forms to communicate a relevant content' (Oushakine 2007: 453). The old form is used to construct a trajectory from the remote past to the post-Soviet present; eluding the immediate past, the imperial past serves as a basis for the construction of a Russian tradition and identity. This practice reminds of the Silver Age and its interest in the pre-Petrine cultural heritage. 'By the turn of the twentieth century, many among Russia's cultural elite considered the high art of the Russian Academy not to be the locus of national identity but rather looked to the icon, decorative arts, and the broadsheet' (Sharp 2006: 6). The belief that these art forms 'have remained uninfluenced by Western culture' (Sharp 2006: 7) made them particularly attractive. In (re-)discovering the own cultural origins artists, scholars and their audiences enjoyed the strange, yet popular – not refined and elevated by the academic canon – object that they could use to express their experience of Russian identity and continuity. The Academy of the nineteenth century had its twentieth-century equivalent in the Soviet bureaucracy, which steered everything, including design: 'The administration of everyday mass culture was just as centralized, bureaucratic, and institutional as that of high culture – and was assessed, recognized, and disseminated by essentially the same ideologically correct criteria' (Groys 2010: 84). Russian retro-design, therefore, aimed to avoid Soviet imagery by referring to a long-gone culture.

While Soviet reminiscences were unloved in most spheres of life, some kept their place in the chocolate market. For example the brand Alenka, released in 1965, drawn after a photograph of the artist Aleksandr Gerinas' daughter and named after the daughter of cosmonaut Valentina Tereshkova, the first woman in space, continues to be a best seller. Another still very popular brand, Mishka Kosolapyi, dates back to Tsarist times – the praline was created in the factory of Ferdinand von Einem and its wrapping design draws on a reproduction of Shishkin's 'Morning in the Pine Forest' (1889/1890); its success at the turn of the twenty-first century was due to both its pre-Revolutionary imagery and its popularity during Soviet times. For those generations of Russians who grew up during the Soviet period such designs were able to provide personal childhood reminiscences and thus a feeling of continuity and comfort. In this way they absorbed the ubiquitous uncertainty, a quality which – along with the capability of conveying faith in the world – has been described as the main function of packaging design and advertisement (Bolz 1999: 32). Hence, following the notion of comfort food, I call *konfety* or chocolate bars with such design 'comfort chocolate'.

Market

The transition from a centralized to a free market economy in the 1990s stimulated new forms of distribution. While self-service supermarkets came from the United States to Europe after the Second World War, many of Russia's shops preserved traditional distribution over the counter well into the first decade of the twenty-first century. Moreover, the Russian customer often relied on the vendor's opinion and advice when buying products. This habit dates back to the distribution system before 1917 when the merchant's choice outweighed the significance of individual brands (Rathmayr 2004: 210). The form of distribution – not only available variety – is crucial to the design, which is either accompanied by the words of the vendor or has to speak for itself in the shelf of the supermarket.

The increase of supermarkets towards the end of the first post-Soviet decade went hand in hand with a rapidly growing Russian chocolate production. *Konfety* continued to be most popular with consumers, and – sold by weight – took approximately half of the market during the post-Soviet era. They tended to be purchased for own consumption and cost about half the price of chocolates in boxes, usually bought as a gift and supposedly of better quality (Anon. 2006). New brands entered the market, including the domestic Russkii Shokolad (Russian Chocolate) in 1998, where the name and the addition 'made in Russia' evokes national pride, and Korkunov in 1999. In 2000 Nestlé successfully introduced the brand Rossiia – Shchedraia Dusha (Russia, the Generous Soul). In 2001 Konfael' joined the market with its eccentric chocolate products, including chocolates cast in the shape of pets or portraits.

Interestingly, the high-end brands Korkunov and Konfael' did not flirt with Russia's past, while high-end restaurants such as Cafe Pushkin, which opened in Moscow in 1999 featuring a neo-Russian style, or the restaurant Russkii Ampir, which opened in 2004 in the completely renovated (rather than restored) premises of a St Petersburg palace, attract well-to-do customers with the exoticism of Russia's past.

Identification proposition

Packaging is a text, featuring multiple codes, functions and genres (Rathmayr 2004a: 261). In conjunction with advertising it offers an identification proposition consisting of immaterial values such as prestige, comfort, pleasure, soothing of the conscience (Doebeli 1988: 130) and sensual qualities such as size, material, sound upon touch, colour, surface texture and others.

The importance of the material qualities is evident in the failure of the *konfeta* brand Derzhava, launched by Mars in Russia in 2000. The *konfeta* was to be sold by weight, i.e. in the lower-price segment. The design options were carefully explored and finally several series were created, titled Strany mira (Countries of the World), Geroi skazok (Heroes of Fairy Tales), Rossiiskie imperatory (Russian Emperors), providing a variety of identification propositions for a broad range of consumers. This related to Mars' declared goal to create a brand that would be popular throughout all Russia. Hence, the problem with Derzhava was neither the message nor the design, but that the product was made according to American safety standards. These required that the product is completely sealed from the time of its production to the moment when the user opens the packaging, a feature not applicable to the Russian *konfeta*. In order to meet the standards, the wrapped *konfeta*, which potentially could be unwrapped and rewrapped, had to be sold in boxes, which were expected to contain expensive chocolates. Derzhava, however, was conceived as affordable product and did not meet the expectations regarding the quality of boxed chocolates. After three years of unsuccessful attempts to make the product suitable for the Russian market, it was discontinued (Anon. 2006).

A similar case happened in the chocolate country Switzerland. In 2006 Cailler (owned by Nestlé) launched a new plastic packaging, designed by acclaimed architect Jean Nouvel. It was accompanied by an advertising campaign invoking a vibrant urban mindset. An informal survey showed that architects loved the campaign, but the large mass of consumers rejected this packaging, and the company soon went back to the previous paper-and-foil wrapper, featuring the old design. This example might explain why the design of post-Soviet *konfety* never refers to the art of the avant-garde, although it has the potential to convey Russianness. The intellectual forms of the avant-garde catered already in the early twentieth century only to a small circle and were, as history showed, suppressed in favour of floral and similar patterns within the aesthetic comfort zone of the masses (Gillen 2001, 217–28). Both stories illustrate the delicacy of material culture with regard to packaging.

The chocolate Liuks (Luxury) may be used as a case study for the ways in which packaging design developed during the transitional period of the 1990s and into the new millennium. My interest in the design of this particular brand stems from the fact that the name Luxury does not refer to an *a priori* motif, which makes it open to visual experiments and options to capture the essence of the name. According to Babaev's product catalogue, the recipe dates back to 1939,[2] which means that it was introduced during Mikoyan's chocolate campaign,

Figure 7.1: Liuks in 1993.

promulgating happiness and abundance. Beginning with the early 1990s chocolate producers created new designs, aiming for a style that resonated with the cultural background of contemporary consumers. Not always did they follow the design rule that

> in order to be received the message of advertisement must tie in with existing socio-cultural concepts, fashion tendencies, traditions or secret dreams. Advertisement of food can intensify and move preferences of taste in certain directions, but it can not create completely new norms.
>
> (Nast 1996: 163, translation by the author)

The successful designer, however, paid heed to the above rule. In 1993 Babaev's design of Liuks featured a dark blue, wallpaper-like background with the name Liuks in a typeface that imitated a somewhat exalted handwriting with a silver contour. Despite the luscious lines of the handwriting and the silver sparks, the overall design appears austere and is reminiscent of the pattern on Soviet wrapping papers for earlier versions of Liuks (see Figure 7.1).

A few years later a new design was presented, which referred to Russia's aristocratic past: a purple background sported two trumpeting golden angels, flanking a medallion with the chocolate's name and a squiggled smaller medallion with a B for Babaev (see Figure 7.2). It borrowed the gold and the shape of the angel's wings from the Russian Empire Style of the early nineteenth century, while the trumpeting angel is a baroque motif. Although this version was soon abandoned, the visual allusion to a noble past was pursued further in the final iteration of the design, which was in the market by 1999. This time the composition included a variety of elements: the notion of luxury was addressed with a large deal of gold colour; the past appeared in the medallion, featuring the building at the corner of Malaia Krasnosel'skaia and Proezzhaia streets

Figure 7.2: Liuks in 1996.

in Moscow, where the factory's founder Aleksei Abrikosov lived in the early twentieth century (see Figure 7.3). Over the next decade the image of the building underwent several variations, and its size and dominance in the composition increased. This suggests that the identification proposition with the pre-Revolutionary era held its significance. As a new element lace was added to the background of the script. Lace appeared at that time on multiple brands, always in a noble or at least elegant context. While fine lace – a precious and expensive fabric – was used in wealthy, potentially aristocratic and cultivated society, it also ties in with Soviet *kul'turnost'* as Adele Barker describes it: 'This *kul'turnost'* to which the new Soviet man and woman were busily aspiring was anything but high class. For example, peasants and workers desiring to be kul'turnyi accumulated everything form doilies to pink lampshades to collections of cut glass and figurines' (Barker 1999: 26, emphasis in the original). I argue, therefore, that lace as an element of design connected the pre-Soviet with the Soviet past as a status symbol inherent in both cultures. Hence, the wrapper design of Liuks offered the notion of remote nobility combined with a hint of continuity from the close past.

In the early 2000s all three major producers of chocolate, Babaev, Krasnyi Oktiabr' and Rot Front, had a chocolate bar named Liuks on the market. While Babaev's classic design for 100g chocolate bars of Liuks remained as described above, in 2000 the brand featured golden silhouettes of figures in historical dress – two groups of adults, children and a dog, suggesting a noble family – on a red and green background for the smaller bars of Liuks. It appears to have been an attempt to add to the identification proposition by inserting a narrative layer into the design. In 2001 Krasnyi Oktiabr' produced two chocolate bars under the name Liuks, experimenting for the wrapping design with similar visual elements as Babaev, yet very different in character. The dominant motif on one chocolate wrapper was a couple performing a Latin American dance in fancy red-and-black costumes. The 'floor' consisted of a gigantic red rose, while the background was gold and white. The notion of luxury seemed to overlap here with seduction and physical attractiveness. The other design appeared much less sophisticated; while the typeface imitated handwriting, investing the item with a personal touch, the two medals demonstrate objective quality; they are reminiscences

Figure 7.3: Liuks in 2012.

from the nineteenth century when medals awarded at national and international fairs served as a reliable sign of high standard. The blue ribbon adds a festive element; the bow, however, seems too modest for a luxurious present. Rot Front's Liuks was produced in 2001 as chocolate bar. The design differed from the competing brands by its simplicity; the background was divided into two halves, the upper black and the lower half red. The name Liuks appeared in a simple serif typeface in gold, where the embossed letters and the gold ornament on a ribbon stood out. Instead of a medal, the year 1826, when the company was founded under the name Trading House G.A. and E.S. Lenov, appeared in a medallion. The design can still be found today on praline packaging, which is a sign of its timeless quality.

Comparing the five designs – two by Babaev, two by Krasnyi Oktiabr' and one by Rot Front – the bright red appears as an eye-catching common denominator, except for Babaev's green on the small version of Liuks. Babaev's classic Liuks takes a special place, since it also features red; however, a much darker brown-red, which – compared to the others – bears a resemblance of royal purple. The typeface has seen little variation: only two typefaces appear in different combinations: baroque letters, alluding to handwriting and rather stark serif fonts in upper case. Luxury, so it seems, was connoted with red, handwriting and serif fonts in the early 2000s. Despite the symbolic presence of red in Russian culture, spanning from decorative arts and the icon to avant-garde art, it obviously did not appeal to consumers at the turn of the millennium. The lasting presence in the market of Babaev's classic design suggests that a less flashy appearance lasts longer.

Beyond 2010

Towards 2010 design and product lines adopted more and more Western standards. The number of brands, in particular of *konfety*, was slightly reduced, while the variety within one brand was increased by adding, for example, nuts, raisins or other ingredients. *Konfety*, originally sold in bulk, were now offered in boxes, aspiring to a higher price segment. They still evoked the past, yet not explicitly Russian tsarist culture, but the European turn of the twentieth century. The already mentioned chocolate bar Sudarushka used to display golden lace and a medallion with the bust of a noblewoman from old Russia with a kokoshnik and pearls around her neck on a purple wrapping paper. Purple, gold and lace were also used during the transformation of the design of the brand Liuks. In the mid-2000s a new type of woman was introduced as embodiment of the Sudarushka: the self-conscious beauty from the Belle Epoque.

The return to the fin de siècle, here exemplified in the image of the women, closes the circle: after the First World War the imagery on chocolate wrappers dismissed the rendering of seductive women, which were a typical chocolate-related subject at the turn of the century, based on the perception of chocolate as highly sensual. Even in the 1930s chocolate retained its connotations with luxury, rooted in the reality of the time before the First World War. In the early 1990s designers went much deeper into the past, back to old Russian architecture and eighteenth- and nineteenth-century nobility. Today, after a 20-year search for new symbols to visualize Russia's identity, the images refer to the fin de siècle. They do not emphasize their exclusive Russianness, but relate the Russian product to the chic, which was prevalent in all European cultures at the time. Although these new designs might not appeal to a Western customer in the same way they do to Russian buyers, they communicate a more relaxed attitude with regard to visualizing Russianness, and their target audience is probably a generation that has spent only half of their lives in the Soviet past.

Works cited

Anon. (2006), 'Istoriia padeniia "Derzhavy"', *Vedomosti* 8 (December), http://www.vedomostivuz.ru/article.shtml?2006/12/01/3487. Accessed 31 January, 2012.

Barker, Adele M. (1999), 'The Culture Factory: Theorizing the Popular in the Old and New Russia' in Barker (ed.), *Consuming Russia. Popular Culture, Sex, and Society since Gorbachev*, Durham, London: Duke University Press, pp. 12–45.

Bolz, Norbert(1999), 'Design als Sensemaking', in Matthias Götz (ed.), *Der Tabasco-Effekt. Wirkung der Form, Formen der Wirkung. Beiträge zum Design des Designs*, Basel: Schwabe, pp. 29–36.

Boym, Svetlana (1994), *Common places: Mythologies of everyday life in Russia*. Cambridge MA: Harvard University Press.

Dal', Vladimir (1996), *Tolkovyi slovar' zhivogo velikorusskogo iazyka*, Sankt-Peterburg: Diamant. (First published 1880.)

Doebeli, Hans P. (1988), 'Konsumenten zwischen Verpackungs-Convenience und Umweltpolitik', *Schweizer Verpackungskatalog*, Laufenburg: Binkert, pp.129–130.

Gillen, Eckhart (2001), 'Übergang zum Sozialistischen Realismus', in: Wilhelm Hornbostel, Karlheinz Kopanski, Thomas Rudi (eds), *Mit voller Kraft. Russische Avantgarde 1910–1934*, Bönnigheim: Wachter, pp. 217–228.

Goscilo, Helena (2009), 'Luxuriating in Lack: Plenitude and Consuming Happiness in Soviet Paintings and Posters, 1930s–1953', in M. Balina and E. Dobrenko (eds), *Petrified Utopia. Happiness Soviet Style*, London, New York: Anthem Press, pp. 53–78.

Gronow, Jukka (2003), *Caviar with Champagne. Common Luxury and the Ideals of the Good Life in Stalin's Russia*, Oxford, New York: Berg.

Groys, Boris (2010), 'Communist Conceptual Art', in Boris Groys, *History Becomes Form. Moscow Conceptualism*, Cambridge, London: The MIT Press, pp. 79–86.

Nast, Matthias (1996), *Die stummen Verkäufer: Lebensmittelverpackungen im Zeitalter der Konsumgesellschaft (1950er Jahre bis heute): umwelthistorische Untersuchung über die Entwicklung der Lebensmittelverpackungen und den Wandel der Einkaufsgewohnheiten*, Bern: Peter Lang.

Oushakine, Serguei A. (2007), '"We're nostalgic but we're not crazy": Retrofitting the Past in Russia', *The Russian Review* 66, pp. 451–482.

Rathmayr, Renate (2004), 'Produktnamen als wesentlicher Bestandteil der Textsorte Lebensmittelverpackungen', in Marion Krause, Christian Sappok (eds), *Slavistische Linguistik 2002*, München: Otto Sagner, pp. 201–234.

——— (2004a), 'Tekstovoe prostranstvo upakovki pishchevykh produktov: esteticheskii aspekt', in N. Arutiunova (ed.), *Logicheskii analiz iazyka. Iazyki estetiki: semanticheskie polia prekrasnogo i bezobraznogo*, Moskva: Indrik, pp. 260–282.

Rathmayr, Renate and Schimpfössl, Elisabeth (2005), 'Lebensmittelnamen als Spiegel oder Zerrspiegel der Kultur. Parallelen und Unterschiede bei motivierten und nicht motivierten Lebensmittelnamen am Beispiel des Russischen und Deutschen', in Sebastian Kempgen (ed.), *Slavistische Linguistik 2003*, München: Otto Sagner, pp. 223–244.

Sharp, Jane A. (2006), *Russian modernism between East and West: Natal'ia Goncharova and the Moscow Avant-garde*, Cambridge, New York: Cambridge University Press.

Vaginov, Konstantin (1991), 'Bambochada' in *Kozlinnaia pesn': Romany*, Moskva: Sovremenik, pp. 262–370.

Notes

1   See, for example, the collection of old chocolate wrappers by Viktor Kudriavtsev, http://www.kudvic.ru, or Martin Mihál's international chocolate wrapper museum http://www.chocolatewrappers.info; or http://shokolader.ru/.

2   See the joint website for Babaev, RotFront and Krasnyi Oktiabr' at http://www.uniconf.ru. Accessed 31 January 2012.

Chapter 8

Victory Day: Rituals and Practices of War Commemoration in Russia

Nataliya Danilova

Introduction

Victory Day (V-Day) on 9 May is one of the most popular holidays in Russia. This holiday appeals to older and younger generations, politicians and ordinary people, veterans, service personnel and those who have never been in the military. This chapter explores V-Day by focusing on popular practices of its celebration. The main research objective is to discuss the public perception of V-Day and its social functions in establishing commitments between the nation-state, the military and society.

War commemoration is a complex phenomenon – embodied in representations and practices, mediated by cultural institutions, and drawing upon past and present traditions of commemoration (Ashplant, Dawson and Roper 2000; Misztal 2003; Nora 1998; Olick 2007; Winter 1995). Following Amitai Etzioni's point that 'holidays provide one major and relatively accessible source of global data about the beliefs and other attributes of a giving society' (Etzioni 2000: 46), the chapter explores popular practices of celebration by juxtaposing them with the social and cultural context of post-Soviet Russia. I suggest that the modern form of V-Day celebration reproduces some features of postmodern commemoration described by Pierre Nora, such as particularism and diversity, commodification and entertainment in dealing with war memory, and declining social commitments to the nation-state or the armed forces.

The chapter proceeds as follows. First, I discuss the public importance of V-Day and popular practices of its celebration. Further, I examine different components of celebration, such as a military parade in Moscow, the expression of gratitude to the fallen and veterans of the Second World War. The third part is concerned with a recently 'invented tradition' of wearing a St. George ribbon, discussing also ongoing commodification and entertainment of V-Day celebrations. In conclusion, I raise questions about the social and political function of V-Day in contemporary Russia.

War commemoration in Russia: a theoretical discussion

Without doubt contemporary memory study is a truly interdisciplinary field of enquiry (Kansteiner 2002). Some scholars argue that this 'nonparadigmatic, transdisciplinary, centreless enterprise' might be productive, yet a systematic reconsideration is beneficial (Olick and Robbins 1998). I do not propose here a systematization in collective memory studies as a whole; instead, I take for granted the methodological diversity. However, the chapter seeks to unfold and challenge established theoretical conventions in studying the experience of a particular country. I put forward the argument that two approaches dominate the study of Soviet and post-Soviet war commemoration: a state-centred and a social agency approach.

A state-centred approach explores war commemoration as a political phenomenon, 'a key element in the symbolic repertoire of the nation-states' (Ashplant et al. 2000: 7). It analyses how western European societies were established by means of new national rituals and 'invented traditions' from the late eighteenth to the middle of the twentieth century (Anderson 1983, Gillis 1994, Hobsbawm and Ranger 1983, Mosse 1990). In contemporary collective memory studies, a state-centred approach is often criticized, because it oversimplifies the possibility of constructing the past from above and at will (Schudson 1992; Schwartz 1982, 2000; Zelizer 1995). As a result, this approach lacks methodological capacities to capture a particularistic nature of war commemoration in modern democratic societies where different agencies and social groups are involved in this process. On the contrary, it is assumed to be perfectly suitable 'for the exploration of commemorations and rituals imposed by authoritarian regimes' (Misztal 2003: 127). Drawing upon this view, war commemoration in the Soviet Union or post-Soviet Russia tends to be studied from the perspective of the state or its representatives. This angle of research overlooks popular perceptions and practices as they appear to be less important or not even visible to researchers.

The social-agency approach examines war commemoration in terms of survivors' experience and a response of civil society or communities to the tragedies of war. It describes a commemorative process as 'the outcome of agency, the product of individuals and groups who come together, not at the behest of the state or any of its subsidiary organisations, but because they have to speak out' (Winter and Sivan 1999: 9). This approach is often applied in studies of collective memory in democratic and pluralistic societies. In recent years, the social-agency approach became popular among scholars of Soviet and post-Soviet societies. However, their take on the cornerstone ideas of the social-agency approach is different. They examine 'suppressed' or 'cruelly damaged' *private* memories of Soviet people, contrasting them with the politics of the state (Adler 2001; Hosking 1989, 2002; Ignatieff 1988; Khazanov 2008; Merridale 1999, 2000; Rondewald 2008). The critical comments towards the social-agency approach as a whole are its abstraction, its departure from the particular social and historical context, its subjectification and universalization of personal traumatic experience (Ashlant et al. 2000; Radstone 2005, 2008). It might be suggested that these shortcomings are present in the study of Soviet or post-Soviet experience.

Therefore, both approaches establish a 'totalitarian-democratic' dichotomy where the state imposes a dominant narrative and suppresses *private* memories or practices of remembrance. I suggest here an alternative approach in studying war commemoration.

First, I consider war commemoration as a dynamic social institution, which incorporates past rituals and practices of commemoration, yet reconfigures them under the pressure of political, social and cultural demands. This analytical concept draws upon the *dialogical approach* proposed by Jeffrey Olick in his study of the 8 May 1945 commemoration in Germany

(1999, 2007). Olick considers collective memory as 'a distinct set of mnemonic practices situated in various social rites and sites' (Olick and Robbins 1998: 112). He thinks that this process, while embedded in historical, political and social contexts, is also driven by its own memory of past celebrations and debates. For this reason, post-Soviet war commemoration should demonstrate a mixture of practices that come from the Soviet past and 20 years of post-Soviet celebration.

Second, as Christel Lane notices in her study of Soviet holidays, during the 1980s V-Day had 'generally less developed, less standardized and more decentralised' ritual which 'united officially devised ritual sequences and some evolved by the people themselves' (Lane 1981: 152). In other words, V-Day celebration during the heyday of Soviet commemoration presented a mixture of practices, introduced from above by the state, coming from below. This happened not only because of mass involvement of the civilian population in the Second World War but because of the constant changeability in the official traditions of celebration. For example, from 1947 (when the 'people's war' was re-conceptualized in terms of 'Stalin's great victory'), V-Day was demoted to a workday and marked only by fireworks and informal gatherings of veterans (Zubkova 1998: 28). Only in 1965 V-Day received the status of a national holiday and was marked with new 'invented' traditions such as a Minute of Silence, and a pilgrimage of politicians to the Tomb of the Unknown Soldier, unveiled in 1967. By means of V-Day celebration, 'the new leaders [led by Leonid Brezhnev], bureaucrats par excellence, set about trying to orchestrate a vast program of public displays of loyalty, expecting, no doubt, that these would somehow lead to real popular sentiments of devotion to the regime, its values, and its goals' (Tumarkin 1994: 132, see also Weiner 1996, 2001). This political re-use of V-Day had been overlapping with earlier established public practices of marking the victory. These practices could easily include such activities as the pilgrimage to the tombs of the 'sacred dead' or family gatherings and trips to the countryside. In this sense, V-Day exhibited the complexity of life in the Soviet Union where 'living socialism to them [Soviet people] often meant something quite different from the official interpretations provided by state rhetoric' (Yurchak 2006: 8).

Third, I place the celebration of V-Day in the context of contemporary changes in collective memory of modern societies. According to Nora (1984–92/1996–98), the approaching era of commemoration means a transition from classical national commemoration with hierarchy, epic and order towards patrimonial, multiple-layered and cultural commemoration. This is a result of a series of transformations of nation states, social structure and civil society in Europe, and the increased influence of the mass media, consumer and entertainment cultures. Applying this point to post-Soviet society, it can be argued that the 1990s led to a soaring particularization in war commemoration and opened the country to the influence of global media, consumer and entertainment cultures (Barker 1999; Oushakine 2000; Zvereva 2010). This resulted in the commodification of war memory and limitations in the potential of V-Day to impose social commitments to larger entities, such as the nation state or the military.

Fourth, V-Day celebration as a public holiday has social functions. Following the classification of holidays proposed by Etzioni (2000), V-Day exhibits a mixture of both types he identifies: recommitment and tension management. It declares to be a recommitment holiday which 'by means of narratives, drama and ceremonies to directly enforce commitments to shared beliefs' (Etzioni 2000: 47), but in practice functions more as a tension-management holiday. Its recommitment function assumes that V-Day establishes national unity and a sense of belonging to post-Soviet Russia (Gudkov 2005, 2006). However, as Etzioni explains, the complexity of modern society means there is a divergence in the integrative appeal of modern recommitment holidays. They unite varied social groups involved in the process of celebration to a different degree, appealing to large entities, such as nations, or smaller social groups such as friends and family. In the same way celebrations – while calling for national unity – can cause contestation and political protests. Therefore, V-Day in post-Soviet Russia has multiple functions: strong potential establishing social commitments, but also political protests and leisure activities.

V-Day as a popular holiday

In the 1990s Tumarkin predicted the decline of the 'national heroic myth', observing the changes in celebrations, yet it seems V-Day has survived the times of political turbulence and reestablished itself as a popular holiday in post-Soviet Russia (Tumarkin 1994). The heyday of war commemoration in Russia starts from the last week of April and continues to the second week of May. The focal point of celebration is 9 May, Victory Day. According to public opinion surveys, V-Day is one of the most popular holidays in contemporary Russia. Furthermore, as Table 8.1 demonstrates, it is the only holiday in a list of ten, which introduces shared national beliefs and commitments (Gudkov 2006; Klimov 2003a and b).

Considering V-Day in the context of other holidays, it can be suggested that this is also the only holiday that has a broader public appeal. Its celebration assumes a belonging to

Table 8.1. Question: Which holidays do you normally celebrate? (Any number of responses allowed) (FOM: Russian Holidays 2006).

Popular holidays	Percentage of choices
1. New Year	93%
2. My Birthday	83%
3. Easter	78%
4. Women's Day (8 March)	71%
5. Victory Day (9 May)	71%
6. The Birthdays of Adult Family Members	60%
7. Christmas	58%
8. Children's Birthdays	57%
9. Defender of the Fatherland Day (Feb 23)	49%
10. 1 May (Labour Day)	36%

something more than a personal or family connection, professional or religious communities, and gender identifications. For example, over the late Soviet and, especially, post-Soviet periods, the original meaning of 8 March and the Day of the Defender of the Fatherland have been transforming into a Women's Day (Karpova and Iarskaia-Smirnova 2003) and a Men's Day (Klimov 2003a). Both days assume the congratulations of women or men on the pure ground of their gender with loose or without any special commitments to be mother or father, or even perform other duties such as a service in the armed forces. In this context of a continuous privatization of post-Soviet holidays, V-Day plays a formative role in 'national and civil identities' of Russians (Klimov 2003b). Furthermore, as data from surveys show, there is a trend towards a growing popularity of V-Day throughout the 2000s. According to different agencies, its popularity ranges from 74 per cent to 76 per cent of supporters (i.e., Savel'ev for Levada Centre, 2009) to 92 per cent (FOM 2006 a and b) and 94 per cent (VTsIOM 2010). This difference in public support can be explained by different systems of measurement of public opinion. However, undeniably V-Day is a popular public holiday in contemporary Russia.

The next important question concerns popular practices of V-Day celebration. Secondary data from public opinion surveys in 2005–06 give us some preliminary answers. As illustrated in Table 8.2, a significant range of activities may be planned and performed on this day.

Table 8.2: Question: Do you plan to celebrate Victory Day on May 9? If so, how will you celebrate it? (Any number of responses allowed per card) (FOM: Russian Holidays 2006).

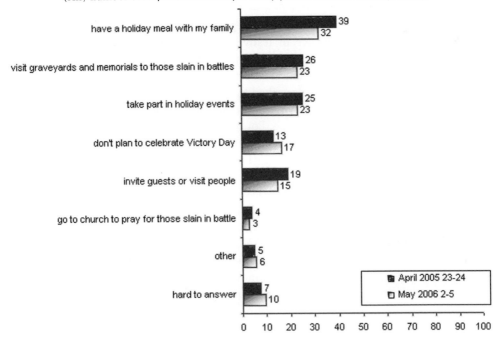

According to Table 8.2, the most popular planned activity for V-Day is a festive meal with the family (32 per cent and 39 per cent in 2005 and 2006 respectively). This option can merge with another socializing option in the list of popular activities: to have guests or visiting friends, selected by 15 per cent and 19 per cent of respondents. Activities directly related to war remembrance include visits to graveyards and war memorials (26 per cent/ 23 per cent respectively) and participation in holiday events (25 per cent/23 per cent respectively). The practical implementation of the second option can include diverse activities, from participation in street performances, observing a military parade or a march of veterans, enjoyment of fireworks in the evening or spending time with friends in the city centre. Also, Table 8.2 shows that only 4 per cent and 3 per cent respectively include visits to church. Hence there is an increasing influence of the Russian Orthodox Church in contemporary Russia (Knox 2005, Shlapentokh 2006), yet V-Day continues to be a secular holiday as it was established in the Soviet times. Thus, the distribution of popular practices represents two types of activities: festive-related (or *sacred* in terms of Durkheim's methodology; see Durkheim 2001) and directly unrelated to the significance of V-Day (or *profane* time-spending). The contribution of the second type of practices to social commitments towards the large entities such as nation state, the armed forces or welfare of Second World War veterans is minimal. Drawing upon Etzioni's comment on the varied integrative effect of 'recommitment holidays', it can be said that V-Day seems to be to a large degree a privatized holiday in modern Russia. While imposing certain shared beliefs, it functions effectively as a day of re-establishing social commitments within smaller entities, such as family and friends.

The public opinion surveys on activities performed during V-Day disclose other popular, yet unarticulated practice of festive time-spending: watching television and gardening, with trips to the countryside (FOM: V-Day 2004). It might be suggested that the nature of these practice sets them in a section of routine or everyday practices such as reading, sleeping or walking as described by Michel de Certeau (1984). Although it is often difficult to consider these activities as significant in themselves, they may form a significant proportion of time-spending. For example, Russians like watching television on V-Day (FOM: Between May 1–9 2006), but in modern Russia watching television is the second popular activity after 'sleeping' (Dondurei 2009). TV programmes on V-Day include Soviet and post-Soviet war films (FOM 1996, 2004, 2005). The cultural and social importance of war films is beyond the scope of this investigation. With regard to popular practices, both watching television and visits to the countryside contribute to social cohesion of varied entities, from the nation state through shared media representations to small social groups. The potential of these activities to establish national values is an issue that needs additional research; at this point we can only conclude that passive leisure activities occupy a significant amount of time on V-Day, functioning as tension management and stress relief. This is important, bearing in mind the popularity of this passive time-spending. The next part examines the activities of those who have decided to join the crowds on V-Day.

The military parade: legacy and post-Soviet controversies

In the Soviet Union soldiers marched through Red Square twice a year: on the day of the October Revolution (7 November) and on V-Day (9 May). After the collapse of the Soviet Union, the October parade went into history without regrets or comebacks. In contrast with this silent change, a V-Day military parade has returned to Red Square after a short period of suspension.

As Kathleen Smith explains, a strong association of military parades with the Soviet past burdened the decision of post-Soviet leaders whether to hold them or not. First, in 1992 the first president of the Russian Federation, Boris Yeltsin, replaced the military parade with a ceremony of wreath-laying at the Tomb of the Unknown Soldier. As Smith suggests, in doing this 'Yeltsin paid homage to the ordinary fighting man and elevated the status of informal, popular celebrations' (Smith 2002: 86). This interpretation sounds interesting, yet questionable: the Tomb of the Unknown Soldier is a relatively new component of the V-Day celebration in Russia. It was constructed by authorities during the heyday of state-led commemorations in the late 1960s. Consequently, it has more connections with political ritual of celebration than informal practices of marking V-Day. In this sense, it could be right to suggest that Yeltsin sought to change the Soviet political ritual of V-Day celebration by paying respect to those fallen during the Great Patriotic War.

The cancellation of the parade, together with the political uncertainty of the early 1990s, brought demonstrations and protest marches to V-Day. In 1992 the democrats in support of the president's idea organized a 'civilian' parade on the outskirts of Red Square, as communists – joined by groups of Second World War veterans – held an alternative celebration in a different part of Moscow (Krylova 2004). During the 1990s, pro-communist groups of veterans of the Second World War protested during V-Day at meetings held near Theatre Square or Poklonnaia Gora. However, as surveys show, the public was reserved in its support for the veterans' political activism. For instance, in 1995 almost 43 per cent of respondents did not support separate marches of veterans. The public was more willing to accept veterans marching though Red Square or sitting in a lounge of honoured guests (21 per cent of respondents) than to see them as participants of opposition protest (only 12 per cent sympathizers) (Migdisova et al. 1995).

The ethnographic observation of a veterans' march in St Petersburg in 2010 shows that today the public is also reserved in its support for the veterans' political activism. During the march the public loudly expressed its gratitude to the veterans with applause and cheers. Which ceased instantly when, following a group of veterans representing the fronts of the Second World War, there came veterans associated with political parties. Their political identity was expressed by waving communist banners, red flags and portraits of Lenin and Stalin. The public responded to this demonstration with silence and a declining interest in the march. To put it simple, people stopped clapping and moved to the shops, pubs and cafes. The same effect produced the participation of veterans of the Soviet Afghan War or other post-Soviet conflicts in the march. Therefore, on V-Day the public was ready to pay tribute to veterans of the Second World War, but not willing to discuss current political issues or paying the same respect to veterans of post-1945 wars and conflicts. First and foremost, V-Day is a day of celebrating the shared past rather than the political or military present. However, it is important to stress that for Second World War veterans as participants of late Soviet and post-Soviet conflicts V-Day is a rare opportunity to declare their presence in the social and political life of the country.

Back in 1995 public dissatisfaction with a reduced version of official ritual brought back the military parade as well as the red banner to the armed forces. The problem of the first 'democratic' parade was its reminiscent, Soviet, quality: 'the ceremonies were now too Soviet' (Smith 2002: 90). Whereas Soviet-*ness* was expressed through the form of celebration, it had a strong post-Soviet connotation. The parade has incorporated what seemed to be conflicting symbols, such as the three-colour and the red banner, the red star and double-headed eagle, the cadets and service personnel in military uniform from different historical epochs. These symbols, alluding to different historical times, have established 'continuity with a suitable historical past' (Hobsbawm and Ranger 1983: 1), by joining the glory of Russian Empire, the Soviet Union and post-Soviet Russia. This has produced a fragile narrative of historical continuity which – while legitimating the past – has established post-Soviet Russia as a successor to both empires.

The economic and political stabilization of the 2000s has influence the appearance of the V-Day military parade. The first parade on a larger scale was held in 2005 on the 60th anniversary of the victory, when it became more sophisticated and representative internationally. The invitation of heads of foreign governments caused confusion among new members of European Union, as it was perceived as an expression of power pressing towards them (Onken 2007).

Although politicians and experts are concerned with a broader political resonance of the parade, these issues do not concern the general population. According to public opinion surveys, only 3 per cent of respondents were interested in the international resonance of the parade and of the V-Day celebration as a whole. On the contrary, the public liked this celebration because of the attention to veterans (21 per cent of choices), the atmosphere of festivities (16 per cent), proper organization of the celebration (15 per cent), and good organization of some of events as the military parade, street performances and fireworks (14 per cent) (FOM: Celebration of 60th Anniversary 2005). In other words, while for outsiders the military parade was a concentrated political message, the public perceived this event as a demonstration of the government's commitment to the welfare of veterans a 'brighter, colourful and more interesting' performance, enjoyed by over 70 per cent of the population (FOM 2005). The public opinion surveys in 2009 and 2010 demonstrate consistency in the attitude to the parade (Savel'ev for Levada-Centre 2009, (VTsIOM 2010). As in 2005, in 2010 the international importance of the parade concerned only 5 per cent of the respondents. The parade continues to be considered as a tribute to veterans of the Second World War (39 per cent of the respondents) and also a reminder to younger generations about the victorious past (29 per cent) (VTsIOM 2010). In this sense, the public considers veterans and young people as the main target audience of the parade.

Television broadcasting of the military parade in 2005 has projected 'a quintessential Russianness to an imagined community otherwise dispersed across this still disparate nation'

(Hutchings and Rulyova 2009: 138). This 'Russianness' is written according to the Soviet canon, but re-adapted to post-Soviet reality by means of new tactics of commenting the festivities. These tactics include the over-identification of the performers [journalists] with the symbols of the Soviet past, and the repetitive usage of *steb* which researchers consider as evidence of the fragility of Russian national identity, 'which is deconstructed at the moment of being constituted' (Hutchings and Rulyova 2009: 139). However, the parade has also been a relatively successful instrument of building national identity. This identity assumes a demonstration of tributes to veterans of the Second World War while also lecturing the young generation about the shared historical past. In many senses, described public perceptions overlap with the government politics of re-using the memory of the Second World War to legitimize the present political course (Weiner 2001, Wertsch 2008). This intersection of state politics and public perception is important, yet it does not eliminate the multi-vocality of post-Soviet military parade (Kertzer 1988). The parade can be read in a various ways: older generations could see in this exaggerated, Soviet, appearance of V-Day parade a demonstration of government commitments to veteran welfare or an attempt 'to restore ruined national pride', as younger generations may consider the parade as cultural kitsch which reminds them about the shared glorious past, packed in a recognizable form of contemporary consumer and entertainment culture (Lipovetsky 2004; Sabonis-Chafee 1999; Zvereva 2010).

In regard to popular practices, the most important quality of the military parade in Moscow is its exclusivity.[1] The parade is only for a few invited guests, while for the vast majority of the population in Russia it is purely a TV experience. This is not entirely true for the parades or marches in other regions of Russia; in some cities the wider public can attend the parade without restrictions but this depends on the local authorities. In many cases the personal experience of V-Day is connected with other sets of popular, sacred, practices: visiting military cemeteries and paying tribute to the veterans of the Second World War.

Flowers for the dead and flowers for the living

My personal childhood experience of V-Day celebrations in the 1980s is connected with trips to the largest military cemetery in Perm in the Urals. My grandfather had fought in the Great Patriotic War as a mine-finder. He came back in 1946 but soon died, spending only months with his family. Sometimes, instead of visiting his grave on V-Day, we visited the graves of unrelated, fallen soldiers of the Second World War. My family ritual did not differ from visits to a civilian cemetery on other occasions. We used to bring some food and flowers to the cemetery. We ate, talked and just sat quietly by the grave of someone who died during the Second World War.

As a researcher, I struggle to fit this experience in the canon of Soviet propaganda war commemoration. The pilgrimage to military cemeteries and war memorials with laying flowers and wreaths had been part of the official ritual of commemoration since the late 1950s. Furthermore, local authorities, schoolchildren and members of the Young Communist

League (Komsomol) used to be responsible for the maintenance and clean-up activities of local war memorials and military cemeteries (Jones 1985: 152). However, state-organized encouragement in war remembrance coexisted with commemorative traditions of paying tribute to the dead long before the Soviet regime (Merridale 1999, 2000). Developing this point, the popularity of this practice seems to fluctuate according to the state politics of memory, but its fundamental change could happen only with major shifts in funeral and commemorative practices (Cook and Walter 2005).

Figure 8.1: Piskarevskoe cemetery, St Petersburg on 9 May 2010 (Photo courtesy of Yuliia Egereva).

As ethnographic observations at Piskarevskoe military cemetery and Serafimovskoe memorial cemetery in St Petersburg in May 2010 show, this form of tribute is still popular (see Figure 8.1). People from varied social backgrounds with or without personal connections to the fallen bring flower tributes to the cemeteries and war memorials. A visitor to the military cemetery might encounter red or white dianthuses. In the Soviet Union red dianthuses had a special symbolic meaning, as they are a flower of the revolution (*Bolshaia Sovetskaia Entsiklopedia* 1978). Consequently, it became associated with V-Day as a day of sacrifice and victory. However, in post-Soviet Russia these ritualistic conventions are flexible in terms of the type of flowers or their colour. This form of public tribute to the fallen of the Second World War is democratic and inclusive. It is performed by politicians at memorials of national importance as well as ordinary people at memorials or cemeteries. This form of tribute overcomes the barriers of national, local and personal memories; it joins these threads of memories in a simple ritualistic act of dealing with death and loss.

Flowers on V-Day are not only tributes to the dead. They can also be presented to war veterans as a sign of gratitude and appreciation. As a journalist from *Nezavisimaia gazeta*

Figure 8.2: March of veterans, Nevsky Prospect, St Petersburg on 9 May 2010 (Photo by the author).

has commented, 'veterans were often surprised by this extensive attention and flower tributes from unknown people presented to them on the streets of Moscow' (Smirnov 2010). These flower tributes can have a two-fold interpretation. On the one hand, they establish a short-term personal contact between a veteran as an 'embodied symbol of the past' and a representative of contemporary society. The act of giving flowers functions as an integrative social mechanism which creates experiential ties between generations. On the other hand, this act is often accompanied by an act of verification. Many flower-givers have asked permission to take a photo with veterans. In this sense, the photos with veterans as 'embodied symbols of the past' (Winter 2006) construct not only a sense of belonging to a shared past, but gained symbolic capital and additional social prestige to the flower-giver. In other words, applying Pierre Bourdieu's analysis of the social functions of photography, photos with veterans have produced recognizable and legitimate memories of V-Day attendance (Bourdieu 1996). These floral tributes to the dead or veterans of the Second World War tell us more about the strong desire of the public to belong to and share a historical past than about the interests of veterans. For them, these fragile tributes on V-Day are often the only tokens of public gratitude and emotional support.

St. George Ribbon: 'I remember, I am proud' and 'It looks cool'

The St. George Ribbon as a symbol of V-Day appeared in 2005. This is a clear-cut case of an 'invented' tradition in terms of Hobsbawm's typology (1983). Officially, this tradition was introduced by a group of journalists from the news agency *RIA Novosti* and supported by the Moscow government and other government organizations (St. George Ribbon Campaign 2011). The media background provided the organizers with the resources of speedy popularization of this tradition and its transfer from Moscow to other parts of the country. Government support legitimized this initiative, while also covering the costs of the production of the ribbons. From the start, the St. George ribbons were meant to be distributed free of charge. Consequently, although this tradition was fashioned according to the Poppy Appeal in the United Kingdom and other similar traditions of First World War remembrance (RIA Novosti 2005), it is not connected with the welfare of war veterans. The official website of the campaign encourages sponsors to support hospitals for veterans of the Second World War, but this is a voluntary act. War veterans themselves are not the main target audience of this campaign. In the Russian version of the Poppy Appeal, the position of veterans or service personnel is replaced by the 'invented symbol' itself. The practical value of the ribbons is purely symbolic, clearly articulated in the official motto of the campaign: 'I remember, I am proud'. In this sense, the main and only function of the ribbon is as a symbol of national belonging and identification.

The St. George Ribbon (*Georgievskaia lenta*) is a black narrow ribbon with yellow stripes. In the eighteen century it was a part of the Order of St. George introduced by Catherine the Great. In the twentieth century the ribbon was incorporated in the Order of Glory by

Stalin during the Second World War. This historical legacy of the ribbon makes it a symbol which perfectly matches other symbols of post-Soviet national identity (Tolz 2001). By alluding to the military successes in the eighteen, nineteenth and twentieth centuries, the St. George ribbon restores historical continuity, positioning post-Soviet society as a legitimate successor of the past. However, this seeming conception has an interesting quality, as in the past a ribbon was a part of distinguished military honours while in the present it is a priceless symbol for everyone. Serving as a symbol of national identification, the St. George ribbon does not assume any commitments other than remembering the past and being proud of being a Russian citizen. In a sense, the ribbon is a truly postmodern symbol with loose, or without any, social commitments.

In 2005 sceptics predicted a failure of this tradition. These predictions turned out to be wrong. According to a survey in 2007, 76 per cent of the population supported this initiative (FOM: St. George Ribbon 2007). In 2010 the ribbons were everywhere, from the streets of St Petersburg to TV shows or official meetings of government representatives. This success demonstrates that the public in Russia was 'ready to tune in' as Hobsbawm put it (Hobsbawm and Ranger 1983: 263). According to his view, this readiness is one of the most important factors in 'the business of inventing traditions'.

The popularity of the St. George ribbon does not assume strict rules of wearing it. According to the website of the campaign, the ribbons should be attached to a car, clothes, or the handle of a handbag or tied to the wrist. The ribbons can be a fashion accessory, a hair decoration, a belt or even shoe laces or the lead for a dog (Anon. 2009). This treatment of a national memory symbol illustrates its complacence with the consumer and entertainment culture of contemporary Russia. This apparent flexibility does not destroy the potential of the ribbons to be a source of 'a banal nationalism' (Billig 1995) during and after V-Day.

Ribbons are one of the many symbols of remembrance which can be purchased in the streets. In modern Russia V-Day is a day of souvenirs, flying flags and signs associated with the Second World War or the Soviet military. This commodification of national and military symbols is aggressive in its appeal to potential consumers. It calls to buy and bring home a piece of shared war memory. V-Day celebration is accompanied with developed facilities to satisfy this thirst for consumption, such as street cafes, fast-foods and pubs.

V-Day celebration in modern Russia is joyful and entertaining. The local authorities in every city or village across the country organize street performances. In St Petersburg in 2010 these street performances, concentrated in the heart of the city, along Nevsky Prospect, include Second World War songs or dances in historical military uniform. In this sense, V-Day celebration confirms a tendency of post-Soviet society 'to escape to the Soviet past in search of entertainment' (Novikova 2010: 294).

This commemoration does not dwell on the sufferings of millions of people. The presenters would mention the huge human losses of the Soviet Union in the Second World War before a staged Minute of Silence. However, as this ritual is set in an entertainment context, its committing appeal is weak. Some people could choose to keep the silence in memory of

Figure 8.3: Nevsky Prospect, St Petersburg on 9 May 2010 (Photo by the author).

the deceased while others continue socializing with friends. This illustrates a complexity of V-Day celebration which, while introducing a strong national identification, is also a great tension-management occasion.

Conclusion

War commemoration has a profound historical legacy in Russia. Military victories were the focal point of the unification of the public with its leaders. For a very long time the remembrance of the Second World War was also a part of family history or a traumatic personal experience. However, as this analysis demonstrates, in contemporary Russia broader societal changes, combined with a decreasing number of veterans, have had an impact on the popular practices of celebration. V-Day has become a day for dances, songs, brightness and kitsch in the military parade, flowers and photos with veterans, and the waving of flags and St. George ribbons in an atmosphere of overall enjoyment. This is an emotional day. The participation in its festivities assumes positive and appreciative attitudes towards veterans of the Second World War. This overwhelming public response is touching but short-lived. It does not assume public contributions to welfare for veterans or support for the armed forces.

Considering this appearance of V-Day, we can speculate about its contribution to the contract between the military and society. The position of the military in modern Russia is a peculiar one. The population places the military amongst the most trusted social institutions, but in practice there are few who want join the army (Gudkov 2006: 55–6, Gudkov 2012, VTsIOM 2010). This trend is juxtaposed with the widespread criticism of brutality in the army, a lack of public support for reforms of the armed forces, and problems with the low prestige of the military as a profession (Baev 2002; Golts and Putnam 2004; Taylor 2001, 2003). The existing gap between the cultural and institutional images of the military in Russia can explain this paradox. The images of the military do not coincide or overlap with each other. The promotion of war remembrance enhances the bonds of national belonging, but it is hardly an effective instrument of military mobilization. V-Day in its present state transforms military objects into commodified symbols of consumption and entertainment, demonstrating much more a cultural demilitarization of society than its readiness to join the military or fight for national interests.

The postmodern appearance of V-Day celebration could hardly contribute to a military reform or lead to a serious debate about late Soviet and post-Soviet conflicts. Furthermore, V-Day celebration lacks the potential to discuss the Second World War, establishing a void 'where neither trauma nor responsibility matters anymore' (Lipovetsky 2004: 359). However, I would suggest that the practices of V-Day celebration could tell us more about society and its search to deal with the military past. Perhaps, in the long run these practices could bring the re-evaluation of Second World War memory as well as a contract between the government, the military and Russian society.

Works cited

Adler, Nanci (2001), 'In Search of Identity: the Collapse of the Soviet Union and the Recreation of Russia', in Alexandra Barahona De Brito, Carmen Gonzalez Enriquez, Paloma Aguilar (eds), *The Politics of Memory: Transitional Justice in Democratizing Societies*, Oxford: Oxford University Press, pp. 275–302.

Anderson, Benedict (1983), *Imagined Communities. Reflections on the Origin and Spread of Nationalism*, London: Verso.

Anon. (2009), 'Simvol pobedy prevrashchaetsia v udobnye shnurki', *BaltInfo* 4 May, http://www.baltinfo.ru/tops/Simvol-pobedy-kak-udobnye-shnurki. Accessed 2 June 2011.

Ashplant, Timothy, Dawson, Graham and Roper, Michael (2000), 'The Politics of War Memory and Commemoration: Contexts, Structures and Dynamics', in Ashplant, Dawson and Roper (eds), *The Politics of War Memory and Commemoration*, London, New York: Routledge, pp. 3–85

Baev, Pavel (2002), 'The Plight of the Russian Military: Shallow Identity and Self-Defeating Culture', *Armed Forces and Society* 29.1, pp. 129–146.

Barker, Adele (ed.) (1999), *Consuming Russia. Popular Culture, Sex and Society since Gorbachev*, Durham NC: Duke University Press.

Billig, Michael (1995), *Banal Nationalism*. London: Sage Publication.

Bolshaia Sovetskaia Entsiklopediia (1969–78), Moscow: Sovetskaia Entsiklopediia, http://slovari.yandex.ru/~книги/БСЭ/Гвоздика/. Accessed 25 June 2011.

Bourdieu, Pierre (ed.) (1996), *Photography: A Middle-Brow Art*, London: Polity Press.

Cook, Guy and Walter, Tony (2005), 'Rewritten rites: Language and Social Relations in Traditional and Contemporary Funerals', *Discourse&Society* 16.3, pp. 365–391.

de Certeau, Michel (1984), *The Practice of Everyday Life*, Berkeley: University of California Press.

Dondurei, Daniil (2009) 'Kinopatriotizm – eto glamur v Den' Pobedy', interview with Natal'ia Davletshina, *Russkii zhurnal* 7 May, http://www.russ.ru/pole/Kinopatriotizm-eto-glamur. Accessed 2 July 2011.

Durkheim, Emile (2001), *The Elementary Forms of Religious Life*, Oxford: Oxford University Press.

Etzioni, Amitai (2000), 'Toward a Theory of Public Ritual', *Sociological Theory*, 18.1, pp. 44–59.

FOM (1996), 'ORT vybiraet voennye fil'my i vyigryvaet', http://bd.fom.ru/report/map/of19960905. Accessed 2 July 2011.

FOM (2004), 'V-Day – Den' Pobedy i pamiat' o voine', http://bd.fom.ru/report/map/d041911. Accessed 2 July 2011.

FOM (2005), 'Celebration of 60th Anniversary of the Victory: General Comments', 19 May, http://bd.fom.ru/report/map/dd052022. Accessed 2 July 2011.

FOM (2006a), 'Between May 1–9', Dominants in a Range of Opinions. http://bd.fom.ru/report/map/dominant/dominan2006/dom0619/dtb061910. Accessed 2 July 2011.

FOM, (2006b), 'Russian Holidays: Monitoring', *Dominants in a Range of Opinions*, 17–18 May, http://bd.fom.ru/report/map/dominant/dominan2006/dom0618/dd061824#d061815. Accessed 2 July 2011.

FOM, (2007), 'St. George Ribbon (*Georgievskaia Lenta*)', http://bd.fom.ru/report/cat/hist_ro/world_war_2/d072022. Accessed 2 March 2011.

Golts, Alexander, Putnam, Tonya (2004), 'State Militarism and Its Legacies. Why Military Reform Has Failed in Russia', *International Security* 29.2, pp. 121–158.

Gillis, John (1994), 'Memory and Identity: The History of a Relationship', in Gillis (ed.), *Commemorations. The Politics of National Identity*, Princeton, New Jersey: Princeton University Press, pp. 3–24.

Gudkov, Lev (2005), 'Pamiat' o voine i massovaia identichnost' rossian', *Neprikosnovennyi zapas*, 40–41, http://magazines.russ.ru/nz/2005/gu5-pr.html. Accessed 1 July 2011.

—— (2006), 'The Army as an Institutional Model', in S. Webber, J. Mathers (eds.) *Military and Society in post-Soviet Russia*, Manchester, New York: Manchester University Press, pp. 39–60.

—— (2012), 'Drugikh pobed u nas net', Interview with Iuliia Burmistrova, *Chastnyi Korrespondent*, 22 June, http://www.chaskor.ru/p.php?id=7698. Accessed 20 August 2012.

Hobsbawm, Eric and Ranger, Terence (eds) (1983), *The Invention of Tradition*, Cambridge: Cambridge University Press.

Hosking, Geoffrey (1989), 'Memory in a Totalitarian Society: the Case of the Soviet Union', in T. Butler (ed.), *Memory: History, Culture and the Mind*, Oxford: Basil Blackwell, pp. 97–114.

—— (2002), 'The Second World War and Russian National Consciousness', *The Past and Present Society* 175.1, pp. 162–187.

Hutchings, Stephen and Rulyova, Natalya (2009), 'Commemorating the Past/Performing the Present: Television Coverage of the Second World War Victory Celebrations and the Reconstruction of Russian Nationhood', in B. Beumers, S. Hutchings and N. Rulyova (eds), *The Post-Soviet Russian Media: Conflicting Signals*, London: Routledge, pp. 137–156.

Ignatieff, Michael (1988), 'Soviet War Memorials', *History Workshop Journal*, 17, pp.157–163.

Jones, Ellen (1985), *Red Army and Society. A Sociology of the Soviet Military*, Boston: Allen&Unwin.

Kansteiner, Wulf (2002), 'Finding Meaning in Memory: A Methodological Critique of Collective Memory Studies', *History and Theory* 41, pp. 179–197.

Karpova, G., Iarskaia-Smirnova E. (2003), 'Simvolicheskii repertuar gosudarstvennoi politiki: Mezhdunarodnyi zhenskii den' v rossiiskoi presse, 1920–2001', in N. Pushkareva (ed.), *Sotsial'naia istoriia. Ezhegodnik. Zhenskaia i gendernaia istoria*, Moscow: Rosspen, pp. 488–509.

Kertzer, David (1988), *Ritual, Politics and Power*, New Haven: Yale University Press.

Khazanov, Anatoly (2008), 'Whom to Mourn and Whom to Forget? (Re)Constructing Collective Memory in Contemporary Russia', *Totalitarian Movements and Political Religions* 9.2–3, pp. 293–310.

Klimov, I. (2003a), 'Prazdnik sotsial'noi identichnosti i gendernoi prinadlezhnosti', *FOM: Determinanty. Pole Mnenii*, 7, http://bd.fom.ru/report/map/dominant/dominant2003/698_471/dd030730. Accessed 29 June 2011.

—— (2003b), '9 maia. Den' pobedy, kak on by lot nas dalek...', *Determinanty. Pole Mnenii*, 17, http://bd.fom.ru/report/map/dominant/dominant2003/810_42/dd031724 . Accessed 26 June 2011.

Knox, Zoe (2005), *Russian Society and the Orthodox Church*, Abingdon and New York: Routledge.

Krylova, Anna (2004), '"Dancing on the graves of the dead", or building a WWII memorial in Post–Soviet Russia', in D. Walkawitz and L. Knauer (eds.), *Memory and the Impact of Political Transition in Public Space*, Durham, NC: Duke University Press, pp. 83–97.

Lane, Christel (1981), *The Rites of Rules. Ritual in Industrial Society – the Soviet Case*. Cambridge: Cambridge University Press.

Lipovetsky, Mark (2004), 'Post-Sots: Transformations of Socialist Realism in the popular Culture of the Recent Period', *The Slavic and East European Journal* 48.3, pp. 356–377.

Merridale, Catherine (1999), 'War, Death, and Remembrance in Soviet Russia', in J. Winter and E. Sivan (eds), *War and Remembrance in the Twentieth Century*, Cambridge: Cambridge University Press, pp. 61–83.

——— (2000), *Night of Stone. Death and Memory in Russia*, London: Granta Books.

Migdisova S., Petrenko E., Zecharova T, Vorontsova, A., Chubukov D. (1995), 'Odobrenie uchastiia veteranov v torzhestvakh organizovannykh pravitel'stvom', *FOM*, http://bd.fom.ru/report/cat/job_and_leis/lei/_vict_day/of19952002. Accessed 3 July 2011.

Misztal, Barbara (2003), *Theories of Social Remembering*, Maidenhead, Philadelphia: Open University Press.

Mosse, George (1990), *Fallen Soldiers. Reshaping the Memory of the World Wars*, Oxford: Oxford University Press.

Nora, P. (ed.) (1996–1998/1984–1986), *Les Lieux de Memoire. Realms of Memory: the Construction of the French Past*, vols 1–3, New York: Columbia University Press.

Novikova, Anna (2010), 'Myths about Soviet Values and Contemporary Russian Television', *Russian Journal of Communication* 3.3–4, pp. 281–295.

Olick, Jeffrey (1999), 'Genre Memories and Memory Genres: A Dialogical Analysis of May 8, 1945 Commemorations in the Federal Republic of Germany', *American Sociological Review* 64.3, pp. 381–402.

——— (2007), *The Politics of Regret: On Collective Memory and Historical Responsibility*, London, New York: Routledge.

Olick, Jeffrey and J. Robbins (1998), 'Social Memory Studies: From 'Collective Memory' to the Historical Sociology of Mnemonic Practices', *Annual Review of Sociology* 24, pp. 105–140.

Onken Eva-Clarita (2007), 'The Baltic State and Moscow's 9 May Commemoration: Analyzing Memory Politics in Europe', *Europe-Asia Studies* 59.1, pp. 23–46.

Oushakine, Serguei (2000), 'In the State of Post-Soviet Aphasia: Symbolic Development in Contemporary Russia', *Europe-Asia Studies* 52.6, pp. 991–1016.

Radstone, Susannah (2005), 'Re conceiving Binaries: the Limits of Memory', *History Workshop Journal* 59, pp. 134–150.

——— (2008), 'Memory Studies: For and Against', *Memory Studies* 1.31, pp. 31–39.

RIA Novosti (2005), 'Poviazhi georgievskuui lentochku. Itogi i bodushchee aktsii', Online Conference, 13 May, http://rian.ru/online/20050513/39979664.html. Accessed 2 July 2011.

Rondewald, Stefan (2008), 'Post-Soviet Remembrance of the Holocaust and National Memories of the Second World War in Russia, Ukraine and Lithuania', *Forum for Modern Languages Studies* 44.2, pp. 173–184.

Sabonis-Chafee, Teresa (1999), 'Communism as kitsch: Soviet symbols in Post-Soviet Society', in A. Barker (ed.), *Consuming Russia. Popular Culture, Sex, and Society Since Gorbachev*, Durham NC: Duke University Press, pp. 363–383.

Savel'ev, Oleg (2009), 'Prazdnovaniia 9 maia', *Levada-Centre* 6 May, http://www.levada.ru/press/2009050604.html. Accessed 24 February 2011.

Schudson, Michael (1992) *Watergate in American Memory: How We Remember, Forget and Reconstruct the Past*. New York: Basic Books.

Schwartz, Barry (1982), 'The Social Context of Commemoration: A Study in Collective Memory', *Social Forces* 61.2, pp. 374–402.

—— (2000), *Abraham Lincoln and the Forge of National Memory*, Chicago, London: The University of Chicago Press.

Shlapentokh, Vladimir (2006), 'Trust in Public Institutions in Russia: The Lowest in the World', *Communist and Post-Communist Studies* 39.2, pp. 153–174.

Smirnov, Roman (2010), 'Voennyi parad: do vstrechi cherez piat' let', *Nezavisimaia Gazeta*, 14 May, http://nvo.ng.ru/notes/2010–05–14/16_parade65.html. Accessed 20 August 2012.

Smith, Kathleen (2002), *Mythmaking in the New Russia. Politics and Memory during the Yeltsin Era*, Ithaca, London: Cornell University Press.

St. George Ribbon (2012), http://gl.9may.ru/. Accessed 2 June 2012.

Taylor, Brian (2001), 'Russia's Passive Army: Rethinking Military Coups', *Armed Forces and Society* 34.8, pp. 924–952.

—— (2003), *Politics and the Russian Army: Civil-Military Relations, 1689-2000*. Cambridge: Cambridge University Press.

Tolz, Vera (2001), *Russia: Inventing the Nation*, London: Hodder Arnold.

Tumarkin, Nina (1994), *The Living and the Dead: The Rise and Fall of the Cult of World War II in Russia*, New York: Basic Books.

Webber, Stephen and Jenny Mathers (eds) (2006), *Military and Society in post-Soviet Russia*. Manchester, New York: Manchester University Press.

Weiner, Amir (1996), 'The Making of a Dominant Myth: The Second World War and the Construction of Political Identities within Soviet Polity', *Russian Review* 55, pp. 638–660.

—— (2001), *Making Sense of War: the Second World War and the Fate of the Bolshevik Revolution*, Princeton: Princeton University Press.

Wertsch, James (2008), 'Blank Spots in Collective Memory: A Case Study of Russia', *The ANNALS of the American Academy of Political and Social Science* 617, pp. 58–71.

Winter, Jay (1995), *Sites of Memory, Sites of Mourning. The Great War in European Cultural History*, Cambridge: Cambridge University Press.

—— (2006), *Remembering War: The Great War between History and Memory in the 20th Century*, New Haven: Yale University Press.

Winter, Jay and Sivan, E. (eds) (1999), *War and Remembrance in the Twentieth Century*, Cambridge: Cambridge University Press.

VTsIOM (2010) 'Voina narodnaia – voina velikaia, 27 April http://wciom.ru/index.php?id=459&uid=13446. Accessed 2 July 2011.

Yurchak, Alexei (2006), *Everything Was Forever, Until It Was No More: The Last Soviet Generation*, Princeton: Princeton University Press.

Zelizer, Barbie (1995), 'Reading the Past against the Grain: the Shape of Memory Studies', *Critical Studies in Mass Communication* 12, pp. 214–239.

Zvereva, Vera (2010), 'Lifestyle Programs on Russian Television', *Russian Journal of Communication* 3.3–4, pp. 266–280.

Zubkova, Elena (1998), *Russia after the War: Hopes, Illusions and Disappointments, 1945–1957*, Armonk, NY: M.E. Sharpe.

Note

1   The military parade in St Petersburg has the same exclusive status. It is held at 10 a.m. at Palace Square (*Dvortsovaia ploshchad'*). However, the public can attend the second march of the veterans on Nevsky Prospect at 4 or 5 p.m.

PART III

Cinematic Culture

Chapter 9

A Kiss for the KGB: Putin as Cinematic Hero

Stephen M. Norris

On Valentine's Day 2008, the first-ever straight-to-DVD movie in Russia became available throughout the country. Billed as the perfect gift, *Potselyi ne dlia pressy/ A Kiss Not for the Press* was a love story, a 'film for everyone', as the publicity for the film stated.

A Kiss Not for the Press is a love story that spans the 1970s Soviet Union to present-day Russia. The film's protagonist, Aleksandr Platov, has a secret job that his wife, Tat'iana, never truly knows about. She meets him in Leningrad in the 1970s while she worked as a flight attendant. On their first date, he secures hard-to-get tickets to a performance of the comic Arkadii Raikin. He speaks German. He practices martial arts. His work sends him in the 1980s to East Germany. They have two daughters. He returns home to the newly renamed city of St Petersburg after the collapse of communism to work for the region's governor. Eventually his work takes him to Moscow. As his wife meets him in a lavish hotel suite there, she asks: 'So, this is the Presidential suite?' Platov walks out into a press conference as President Platov. The film presents a fairy tale where men are men and need a good woman to back them up without asking about their work. What matters is that Tat'iana has a man like Andrei: hard-working, sober, manly and a completely positive hero.

Clearly, *A Kiss Not for the Press* is about Vladimir Putin. Yet the film-makers attempted to deny it. Olga Zhulina, the director, stated that her film was not about Putin, but someone like him, commenting that 'it would be strange to assign actors the task of playing a concrete person' (quoted in Kishkovsky 2008). She claimed that 'I did not begin to read the Putin family biography before I started filming' (Perova 2008). The producer, Anatolii Voropaev, claimed that the film is 'a collective image' of what a heroic Russian President should act like. He suggested that people might view Platov as Putin because Andrei Panin, the actor who played him, has blond hair (Kishkovsky 2008). As a final 'defence', both Zhulina and Voropaev stated that they had started the film in 2003, before Putin's biography was so well known, and finished it in 2004. It was not released until February 2008 because Voropaev became a government employee in 2003, eventually serving as vice-governor in two regions. When he resigned in December 2007, he allowed the film to be released and commented that 'It's a film on family values – and we want families to watch it at home together'. To make this wish come true he put it out on DVD so that it could 'reach people across the country, where movie theaters do not exist, not just in the cities' (quoted in Zarakhovich 2008).

Leaving aside the ridiculousness of these claims, Voropaev's and Zhulina's views express the desire for someone like Putin, if not Putin himself, that existed before the actual

Figure 9.1: Poster for *A Kiss: Not for the Press* with Aleksandr Platov/Putin (Andrei Panin) and his wife, Tat'iana/Liudmila Putina (Dar'ia Mikhailova).

politician's meteoric rise. If *Kiss*'s makers could claim that their story of Putin was not a story about Putin at all, then we can look at other cinematic stories similarly. This chapter analyses Putin's presidency by taking a look at movies about Putin that are not about Putin on the surface.

What these films reveal are the links between cinematic heroes, cultural desires and redefined masculinity in Russia. As Barbara Evans Clements has argued, masculinity and the attempts to define it are central to understanding Russia's history: 'Tsarist bureaucrats, Stalinist economic planners, intellectuals and social reformers from the eighteenth to the twentieth century understood that they could not change Russia unless and until they changed Russian men. Fundamental to this task was defining what Russian men were and what they should become' (Clements 2002: 12). *A Kiss Not for the Press* and the host of patriotic 'Putin films' that cast new heroes attempt to recapture what it means to be a Russian man. The star of these productions was a man like Putin.

First person: A hero for our time

The desire for a man like Putin had in many ways been first articulated by Nikita Mikhalkov in his speech to the Russian Filmmakers' Union in 1998. Mikhalkov asked Russian film-makers to create new heroes for Russian audiences; for, as Mikhalkov thundered, 'man cannot exist without a hero. He has to have a model, a symbol' (Mikhalkov 1999: 50–51).

While not scripted by Mikhalkov, the story of Putin's rise reads like one of his movies. His appearance on the political and public scene in August 1999 prompted a host of questions about who this 'Mr. Putin' was (see Tolstaya 2003: 227–39). When Boris Yeltsin resigned on 31 December 1999 and appointed Putin as the Acting President, the clamour for information about the young, serious politician grew. To meet the demand, a trio of journalists published *Pervoe litso/First Person* early in 2000 (Putin 2000: xv). The publication became a bestseller in Russia and was soon translated into several languages: it helped to provide the basic outlines of Putin's life to Russian citizens. It also – however much they denied it – provided *Kiss*'s film-makers with a script. Putin, as he famously stated, was depicted as 'a pure and utterly successful product of Soviet patriotic education' (Putin 2000: 41–42). When the state he served collapsed, he claimed that he 'regretted that the Soviet Union had lost its position in Europe, although intellectually I understood that a position built on walls and dividers cannot last'. He 'wanted something different to rise in its place. That's what hurt' (Putin 2000: 80).

Just two weeks before Putin was elected as President in March 2000 and as he was sitting down with the *First Person* interviewers, the venerable Russian historian Roy Medvedev compared Putin to an actor and the 'Putin phenomenon' to theatre:

Politics is frequently, and not without reason, compared with the theatre, where one speaks about scenes and masks, directors and rehearsals, roles and prompts. In the life of the theatre there are cases when a famous actor unexpectedly fell ill and could not go to perform a scene in an already full public hall. In order not to ruin the spectacle, it is necessary for the director and his assistants to turn over the main role to an unknown understudy. But, surprisingly to both the director and to the spectators, the understudy fulfilled the difficult role even better than his lead performer, and this immediately made him famous. This plot is common in Hollywood musical dramas, but this plot is encountered, perhaps, for the first time on the Russian political scene.

(Medvedev 2000)

Dismissing the early criticisms that Putin was a puppet for some hidden master working behind the scenes, Medvedev instead argues that Putin's sudden popularity stemmed from his abilities and his clear judgement. Russia, Medvedev posits, needed a new hero who provided order and the aura of a strong leader (Medvedev 2000). Medvedev views Putin's rise through the lens of personality and cultural desires:

When public needs and national interests cannot be satisfied without the appearance of a hero, i.e., of a person capable of seeing further than others, wanting to be stronger than others, and to make sure that more and more people are better than others, this person usually appears. But this occurs not automatically. The necessary person can and does not always appear in the necessary time and in the necessary place.

(Medvedev 2000)

What the country needed, Medvedev implied in language that echoed Mikhalkov's call for new heroes, was a man like Putin, a hero for this time.[1]

As his popularity grew, historical serials retrofitted this new hero's biography to literary classics. Mikhail Lermontov's novel *A Hero of Our Time* (*Geroi nashego vremeni*, 1840) certainly lent this process of historicizing the Putin phenomenon a catchy title. The problem, however, was that Pechorin, the novel's protagonist, embodied nineteenth-century literary concerns. As a man of the 1830s, Pechorin is bored, selfish, egotistical, alienated and a womanizer.

The First Channel, which aired the six-part series in June 2007, took Lermontov's idea that Pechorin should represent the men of his generation seriously. Their Pechorin, while inhabiting 1837 on-screen, was a hero for 2007. Aleksandr Kott, who filmed the series and cast Igor' Petrenko as the lead character, stated that he 'tried to preserve the mood of Lermontov's novel' in the series. He expanded:

We decided to move beyond these stereotypes [of Pechorin], to make a hero of our time, i.e., a living man, a man who lives pleasurably, who breathes completely and fully each minute. We left that strange history behind. Our Pechorin is a man who handles himself easily, he does what he wants to do, he speaks his mind, and therefore he causes discomfort in many.

(Kott 2007)[2]

The present-day Pechorin projected onto the past retains some of his nineteenth-century characteristics but is less of a melancholic hero.[3]

The idea of a 'hero for our times' as a suitable marketing strategy for new Russian serials had been used before Kott's series aired. The Russian television channel billed its 2003 crime series *Instructor* as one that contained 'a hero of our time'. It promoted the series in the following way:

> The hero of Lermontov's time, as the author himself wrote, embodied the sins of a generation. A hero of the twenty-first century, however, is made of virtues. He doesn't roam the countryside aimlessly, seducing women as he goes. A modern hero busies himself with something socially useful: he restores old books, teaches the younger generation martial arts or struggles against organized crime. Although [...] on the subject of women [...] we wouldn't say they're completely absent here! On that score, perhaps, all heroes of all times *are* the same; the same difference between our hero and Pechorin, however, is that ours doesn't leave women with a broken heart. He genuinely loves them.
>
> (quoted in MacFadyen 2008: 34–35)

The two films both represented an attempt to articulate how a contemporary should act. What matters in both cases is how both filmmakers retrofitted Pechorin-like heroes with contemporary values. Pechorin today, in other words, would be a man like Putin.

Liquidating the past

When asked by his interviewers for *First Person* about how he became a KGB agent, Putin replied that he developed an interest in security forces from popular culture: 'books and spy movies such as *Shchit i mech/The Sword and the Shield* (1968, dir. Vladimir Basov) took hold of my imagination. What amazed me most of all was how one man's effort could achieve what whole armies could not. One spy could decide the fate of thousands of people. At least, that's the way I understood it' (Putin 2000: 22).

When Putin was a student at Leningrad State University studying law, he and several million of his countrymen watched the television series *Sem'nadtsat' mgnovenii vesny/ 17 Moments of Spring* (1973, dir. Tat'iana Lioznova). Based on a novel by Iurii Semenov and backed by KGB Chief Iurii Andropov, the series depicted a Soviet mole within the Nazi hierarchy. The spy, Maksim Isaev (played by Viacheslav Tikhonov), works under the name Max Otto von Stirlitz. He attempts to forestall secret negotiations between SS General Karl Wolff (representing Heinrich Himmler) and Allen Dulles (then working in wartime intelligence, later head of central intelligence). The series depicts a completely positive hero who has sacrificed everything for his Motherland. For Soviet officials such as Brezhnev (who once drunkenly told Tikhonov that he would 'award Comrade Stirlitz a Hero of Socialist Labor'), Stirlitz embodied the patriotism and sacrifice they wanted from their citizens (Prokhorova 2003a: 108). At the same time, the series struck a chord with Soviet viewers after it aired in 1973. Electricity usage spiked when it was on television and street crime dropped (Prokhorova 2003a: 82). For viewers, Isaev's ability to become someone else, to blend into another society, proved to be a powerful characterization. In the words of a critic, Stirlitz embodied 'the idea that one can cheat, deceive history, the state, and your own fate' (quoted in Prokhorova 2003a: 91). The wartime spy acted as an important imaginary agent in the Brezhnev era: he is an individual who survives within a totalitarian society; he preserves his inner voice while outwardly conforming (Prokhorova 2003a: 91). Stirlitz became a folk hero, the subject of numerous anecdotes and even had a statue built in his 'hometown' of Gorokhovets.[4] He also represented an embodiment of Soviet masculinity, a man who exhibited 'self-control, hard work, study, submission to superiors, patriotism, and the individual success that all this dutiful behavior brought' (Gilmour and Evans Clements 2002: 221).

The Brezhnev years provided a host of extraordinarily popular television serials that offered interesting heroes for viewers. Spy series and crime series dominated the genre. Stanislav Govorukhin's *Mesto vstrechi izmenit' nel'zia/The Meeting Place Cannot be Changed* (1979) in many ways engaged in an unofficial competition with *17 Moments* for the title of 'most popular Soviet series ever'. Set in post-war Odessa, the series, 'established an entirely new paradigm in representing the police' (Prokhorova 2003b: 515). It starred Vladimir Konkin as Sharapov, an officer who is sent to Odessa by the Moscow Department for Fighting Banditry to end criminality there. He teams up with the homicide detective Gleb Zheglov, played by Vladimir Vysotsky. Together they infiltrate and eliminate the group Black Cat, which had been responsible for murders and mayhem in the post-war years. The main drama of the series, however, revolves around the clash between Sharapov and Zheglov. Sharapov, a representative of official Soviet security forces, trusts the rule of law. By contrast, Zheglov believes in justice: in the most-repeated line from the film, he tells Sharapov, 'a thief belongs in jail; the public couldn't care less how I put him there'. *The Meeting Place*, like *17 Moments*, prompted interesting questions. Did one root for Sharapov's ideals and humanism, even though he was a Moscow security officer? Or did you pull for Zheglov's streetwise, Robin-Hood like personality, even though he favoured an emotional, extralegal idea of justice? In the end, Zheglov kills a gangster who had once been in Sharapov's military unit but was sent to a penal battalion after his capture. After the deed he states, 'I have killed a gangster'; Sharapov replies, 'you have killed a person'. Their conflict is never resolved (Prokhorova 2003a: 154–76).

The on-screen world of *Sword and Shield*, *17 Moments* and *Meeting Place* is the cultural world that Putin inhabited as a young man. Spies were heroic and interesting, sacrificing their personal desires for the good of the country. Crime needed to be cleaned up by the same sort of heroic person. It is not a stretch to state that Putin became Putin because of this cultural world – he admitted that reading Semenov and watching movies made him want to be a heroic spy. Soviet popular culture therefore acted as a construction site of sorts, one that provided young Putin with the blueprints for building his life (see Lahusen 1997: 5).

Putin's last year of his first tenure as President (2007) saw a host of spy serials appear on Russian television. The one that got the most press was Sergei Ursuliak's *Liquidation*, which premiered on 2 December 2007 (Prokhorova 2008). The show garnered 43.4 per cent of the TV audience (Dolgopolov 2008). It is set in 1946 Odessa, which is depicted as a den of thieves. Wartime crime and wartime chaos is still rampant a year after the end and Marshal Zhukov arrives to deal with it. The main hero is the head of the Department for Fighting Banditism, lieutenant colonel David Markovich Gotsman (Vladimir Mashkov). Gotsman and his department have to take care of thieves, counterfeiters, a Chekist turned mobster, and numerous Nazi collaborators. Gotsman eventually realizes that one of his own men, an MGB officer, is the ringleader of a host of baddies who want to overthrow the re-established Soviet government and take control of Odessa. If this was not bad enough, Gotsman also clashes with Zhukov over the General's order to get rid of all Odessa crime 'by whatever means necessary'. Ultimately, though, the city is cleansed of criminals, largely through a Counterintelligence plan where elite forces dress as easy targets to lure the real criminals. When the thieves take the bait, they are 'liquidated'.

Ursuliak, when not busy lamely denying that his series was not a remake of Govorukhin's *Meeting Place* (even the television channel advertised it as such), also commented that he was not trying 'to make an historical, documentary film' (Al'perina 2007). Instead, he wanted to capture the 'spirit' of the era and offer a 'prototype' of an officer such as Gotsman (Al'perina 2007). What he wanted, he claims, was to create a composite character, a retrofitted hero whose actions and beliefs can serve as a model for present-day viewers looking for cinematic heroes.

Figure 9.2: The Prototype of an Intelligence Officer: Gotsman (Vladimir Mashkov) cleanses Odessa in Sergei Ursuliak's hit serial *Liquidation* (2007).

Likvidatsiia/Liquidation and the other spy serials that appeared in 2007 favoured action, murder and chaos over the psychologically nuanced serials from the 1970s. They offer a reworked biography of the wartime special agent. Gone are Stirlitz's analytic struggles to win the war through his mind. Gone are Sharapov's humanism and his support for the rule of law over justice that act as a counterweight to Zheglov's views. By the end, Gotsman accepts that vengeance can be just and eventually adopts the methods employed by counter intelligence. He has become a conglomerate of both Sharapov and Zheglov. He wears the same hat and clothes as Zheglov, but eventually comes around to Sharapov's thinking. This time, however, the forces of law believe that the ends justify the means. He has become a man like Putin.

In December 2008, the FSB held its annual award show for 'the best works that honour the security services.' The main victor of the evening was *Liquidation*: Ursuliak won for best director, the serial for best television or film drama, Mashkov for best actor, and Mikhail Porechenkov for supporting actor (he played the MGB officer gone bad). In the words of FSB General Viacheslav Ushakov, who handed out the award, *Liquidation* 'is the most talented and fullest movie and illuminated the specific features of the operative's profession' (Borisov 2008).

The film critic Iurii Bogomolov offered the best summary of *Liquidation*'s significance: it provided 'new songs, new fairy tales, new myths about the most important.' The series, he concludes, proved to be as big a ratings hit as *17 Moments* and *The Meeting Place* but did not so much update these classics as 'argue with them' and provide 'a new national hero' in Gotsman (Bogomolov 2008). Without having to say it explicitly, Bogomolov implicitly views the new hero as a man like Putin.

The KGB in Dinner Jackets

Putin's actual career as a KGB agent spanned the late Brezhnev era and Gorbachev's revolution. In his Dresden work, Putin insists he only took part in 'normal intelligence work' and did not participate in any high-level spy games or running KGB operatives in the German Democratic Republic (GDR) or the Federal Republic of Germany (FRG). In *First Person*, Putin makes his KGB career seem rather boring – a lot of paperwork and information gathering.

Television series could hardly make KGB agents zeroes and expect good ratings. Instead, several were set in the years Putin served as an agent and turned Brezhnev-era zeroes into contemporary heroes. Putin's years as a KGB agent are the same years covered in Oleg Fomin's REN-TV series, *KGB v smokinge/The KGB in Dinner Jackets* (2005). As a writer for *Komsomol'skaia pravda* described the drama:

> The events of the series take place in 1977. Once upon a time Valentina Mal'tseva, journalist at a Komsomol publication, introduced herself in a misguided phone conversation as 'one of Andropov's people'. She was immediately visited by all manner of people with those

well-known ID cards in red covers. After an unsuccessful trip for the KGB to Argentina, she ends up connected to the CIA and after that Israel's Mossad also takes an interest in this female Soviet journalist. One woman drives three of the world's great spies crazy. The CIA agent Eugene will fall in love with her, and for KGB agent Viktor Mishin, Mal'tseva will always be his first, schoolboy love.

(Anon. 2005)

The villains of the serial are Andropov and his number two, Matvei Topolov, who manipulate Mishin and Mal'tseva. Brezhnev, who is not seen in the serial, is referred to as 'a wind-up doll' by the CIA; the person pulling the strings in the Soviet Union is Andropov (MacFadyen 2008: 73–74).

The same sort of message is at the heart of the series *Red Square*, which aired on the Russia Channel in 2004. This time the spy series is set in 1982 and explores the mysterious death of KGB Deputy Chairman Semen Tsvigun in January of that year. Tsvigun, who was married to Brezhnev's sister, reportedly died of natural causes, but rumours circulated that he had either committed suicide to avoid exposure for corruption or had been assassinated by fellow KGB agents acting on orders from Andropov. The hero of the series is a prosecutor

Figure 9.3: The Sword and Shield Revisited: Still from the opening sequence of Oleg Fomin's serial *The KGB in Dinner Jackets* (2006).

named Shamraev, who finds himself caught in the middle of high political games. He has to walk a tightrope between the Party hierarchy and the KGB chiefs, both of whom do not want Tsvigun's death explored. Shamraev maintains his professionalism and his idealism, which allow him to survive the 1982 game.

Viacheslav Shalevich, who played the General Procurator in the series (he had played Allen Dulles in *17 Moments*), saw his heroic role and that of Shamraev's as a product of late Soviet subjectivity. Men who worked for the KGB at that time, he commented, 'were made up of three parts. The first was their professional security duty. The second was their Party Card. The third consisted of their conscience, their personal thoughts, their reflections' (Serafimov 2004). They were, in Shalevich's words, 'normal, living human beings' and all had 'a biography', a personal history. Late Soviet people, the actor stated, were men like Stirlitz, who had to balance the three aspects of their personality, the demands the state placed on them and their own personal consciences. The heroes of today can be like them: they can be from any profession, but cannot be 'a total saint like Pavel Korchagin, absolutely correct, for no one will believe them'. Instead, the 'new hero must be vulnerable, bright, ironic, and wicked' (Serafimov 2004).

The plots of both series, set in 1977 and 1982, respectively, share similar themes. Brezhnev is senile and out of touch. The USSR is run by a cadre of KGB brass led by Andropov himself. Everyday citizens include KGB agents such as Mal'tseva and Mishin or lawyers such as Shamraev; they are regular people caught up in larger intrigues. They are not, however, dissidents, for while they experience moments of disillusionment, they maintain devotion to their country or find solace in Soviet culture. Moreover, both series feature the recent past and the past of the Brezhnev era KGB as 'spy games', a James Bond-like atmosphere where CIA agents and KGB officers could be morally good human beings. Nikolai Troitskii, writing in *Pravda*, concluded that *KGB in Dinner Jackets* succeeds because it 'is made in an attempt to recreate the Soviet reality of the 1970s yet also to 'produce a kind of nostalgia among people who lived in that era' (Troitskii 2005). The late socialist KGB agent dressed in a smashing dinner jacket, in other words, did his duty with élan and with patriotism. He had to balance professional duties with personal honour. He was a 'normal human being' capable of good and bad. He was a man like Putin.

12 men and a Chechen boy

Much ink has been spilled about Putin's KGB past and how he continues to operate as a quasi-Stalinist NKVD agent. The 'former security officer', in other words, always will be a security officer and has surrounded himself with fellow *silovki* (the term comes from *silovye struktury*, or 'force structures', and refers to anyone who worked in the army, law enforcement, or intelligence).[5] Putin's most vociferous critics – both at home and abroad – still see him as a KGB agent.

For Putin supporters, the President's KGB past posed no problems for his abilities to govern. The romantic image of the patriotic and sober intelligence officer that inspired Putin to become a spy still inspires others, no one more than Nikita Mikhalkov. His 2007 film *12* mines the Putin biography as a means to support his beloved President.

Based on Sidney Lumet's *12 Angry Men* (1957), the film casts Mikhalkov as an artist named Nikolai who is placed on a jury with 11 other men. The case they hear involves a Chechen boy accused of murdering his Russian stepfather. Lumet's film reaffirmed the judicial principle of reasonable doubt. Mikhalkov's film casts the other jurors as symbolic representatives of the post-Soviet Russian nation. The director dissects how xenophobes, democrats, rich New Russians, and a neurotic performer, among others, do not know what is right and what is best for Russia. The jury is unconcerned with reasonable doubt; instead they set out to find the real murderer and discover that a criminal group murdered the Russian man because he refused to give up his apartment. The jury then votes to acquit the boy, only for Mikhalkov's character to vote against because he believes the Chechen will be safer in prison. He asks each of the jurors if they will take the boy in and protect him. All of them say no. Nikolai, by contrast, agrees to take him in, revealing that he is not an artist after all but a 'former officer' of the KGB (Graham 2008).

The film is, as the director has claimed, 'about Russia and for Russia' (quoted in Kichin 2007). Mikhalkov expanded: 'our film is about the fact that a Russian person cannot live according to the law. It seemed to me that this is a good time to talk about this [...]. It is important. Why? Because it is boring to live according to the law. The law is without personal relations and a Russian person without personal relations is like a barren flower' (Anon. 2007). Nikolai follows his creator's principles, subverting court justice for his own godlike benevolence, thereby bringing 'personal relations' into Russian law (Smorodinska 2010). Russia does not need courts and laws, in other words, it needs the strong hand of a former KGB agent.

Iurii Bogomolov, a critic with *Rossiiskaia gazeta*, clarified the obvious: 'Mikhalkov's hero is a broad hint to Putin: Both are former intelligence officers, both speak foreign languages, both have a burning sense of justice, both feel themselves saviors' (quoted in Rodriguez 2008). Zoia Svetova concurred: 'Certainly, Mikhalkov's character is in no way outwardly similar to Putin. But he is similar in his essence.' Both claim to be 'saviors of the fatherland' (Svetova 2007). In her opinion, *12* is nothing less than 'an apology for Putin'.

Mikhalkov even held a private screening for Putin at the President's residence. Afterwards Putin claimed the film 'brought a tear to the eye' (Isaev 2007). Sometimes it is hard to be a man like Putin.

Saint Vladimir

Putin, therefore, embodied many desires. He had become a hero for our time, a clean KGB agent such as Stirlitz and devoted such as Gotsman. He also, like Mikhalkov's Nikolai, cleaned up the Chechen problem and took 'good' Chechens back into the Russian family. All that remained in this cinematic retrofitting was for someone to attribute the miracle of

Figure 9.4: The Miracles of St. Vladimir: Still from Nikita Mikhalkov's '55'.

a happy childhood to Vladimir Putin. On 7 October 2007, Nikita Mikhalkov's visual vitae, '55', a living hagiography for Saint Vladimir Vladimirovich, aired on television on Channel Russia and did just that.[6] The short film celebrates Putin's miraculous deeds and presents his presidency as an updated life of an Orthodox saint. Reminding his audience that they needed to think about the 'atmosphere' of the 1990s, a time when 'seven bankers' ruled a chaotic and dispirited country and everyone was 'on their knees before them', Mikhalkov intones that 'an absolutely new man came' and had 'a cross placed on his shoulders'. Just eight years later, Mikhalkov claims, the atmosphere has changed completely, for the Russia of 2007 was a prosperous and healthy spiritual nation. Mikhalkov casts his Saint Vladimir as a latter day Saint George, slaying the dragons of poverty, terrorism, and debt that faced his country. These changes, Mikhalkov states, 'did not just happen on their own'; they happened because of Putin.

Mikhalkov had found his hero for our time and his name was Vladimir Putin. Yet the desire for a Putin was not Mikhalkov's alone. In the summer of 2002, the girl group Singing Together – who took their name from the Putin youth group Moving Together – had their first hit. The song was titled 'Someone like Putin'.[7] Its lyrics expressed the desire for a First

Person who was Russian but not like other Russian men. As Eliot Borenstein has argued, the song reveals 'the perceived need not necessarily for Putin himself, but for someone like Putin' that was widespread in Russia by 2000 (Borenstein 2008: 227). Borenstein concludes: 'The Yeltsin years considerably lowered the bar for the country's next leader: Putin's specific policies and actions arguably matter far less than his reassuring symbolic function as a 'real man' who can husband the nation's resources and promise a return to greatness' (Borenstein 2008: 227). Mikhalkov's 1998 speech in many ways should be read similarly: it too expressed a desire for 'someone like Putin' encoded in the desire for new cinematic heroes. That 'someone like Putin' and new cinematic heroes like Putin both appeared less than a year after the speech are not coincidences: they reveal the cultural processes that made Putin's popularity possible.

Let us return to *A Kiss Not for the Press*. Anatolii Voropaev, the film's producer, announced he would hold one public screening at Moscow's Khudozhestvennyi Cinema. The premiere occurred two weeks before the 2 March 2008 presidential elections. National Bolshevik members used the premiere for a protest. Just after Voropaev spoke and before the film screened, they unfurled banners that read 'Putin: Freedom's Hangman' and 'Putin: Beslan's Hangman'. The protestor dropped leaflets condemning Putin and his era. They were scooped up by security (Rostova 2008). Yuri Zarakhovich, who wrote about the premiere for *Time*, commented:

> The audience greeted the film, and the protest, with an indifference typical of today's cynical and worn-out Moscow. Only once during the screening did the audience react with real laughter and applause: when the fictional First Lady told the press that 'Freedom of speech is sacred to us.' I couldn't help laughing either.
>
> (Zarakhovich 2008)

The film failed because it was a poor one, certainly, yet it also told a redundant story. Putin's rise from obscurity certainly sounds like the plot of a bad Hollywood melodrama. *Kiss* proved it.

Putin's story read like a story of Russia's rebirth after the disruptions of the 1990s. Just as Putin had to find his bearings after 1991, re-orienting his career and searching for anchors that could guide him, so too did all Russian citizens. That Putin found his usable past in the form of Russian patriotism and masculine values of self-sacrifice for the nation state also seems appropriate, for many Russians also wanted to feel proud of their past by 1999. Russians wanted a man 'like Putin' before Putin appeared on the scene, and his extraordinary popularity at the time can in part be explained by how much his personal history and his persona embodied deeply felt societal desires. *Kiss* may have shown a silly side to Putin's popularity, but the revising of the past that Putin-era spy serials undertook reveals just how much Putin's story had become accepted. KGB spies were always Russian patriots who played exciting and heroic games. They were also men who embodied societal ideas about masculinity that included sobriety, *kultur'nost'*, and patriotism. Moreover, security agents

Figure 9.5: A Man Like Putin: Still from *A Kiss: Not for the Press.*

and their historical work 'proved' that Russia needs a strong government that can liquidate criminal groups and the oligarchs who lead them. Finally, former KGB agents are best suited for articulating a Russian rule of law where security is more important than legality. Following these guidelines of the past produces a happy paradise where young Muscovites can flirt, talk, walk and consume. All brought to them by Saint Vladimir.

Whether or not we believe Putin's story is irrelevant. What is significant is that most Russians believed his story and saw in it a version of themselves or a version of what they wanted. They also saw the sort of man they wanted. The desire for someone *like* Putin had given way to a desire for someone *such as* Putin.[8]

None of this is to dismiss Putin's brand of 'stealth authoritarianism' or 'managed democracy', nor is it to diminish Putin's reigning in of regional governors and the rule of law. Journalists die at an alarming rate in Russia and, while they probably are not murdered on Putin's orders, the state creates the atmosphere where these crimes take place and remain unsolved. These aspects of Putin and Putinism are widely known, widely reported and widely analysed.[9] They often come with an expression of surprise about Putin's genuine popularity, an implicit (and sometimes explicit) argument that Russians, like their former and new President, are still trapped in Soviet mentalities and therefore unable to create a new system (see, for example, Mendelson and Gerber 2005).

Perhaps these views are too black-and-white. Natal'ia, the fictional stewardess, and Liudmila, the real-life one, both desired a man like Putin: a determined, sober, patriotic, hard-working man. They got their man. During the depths of 1990s cultural overkill and the patriotism of despair, many Russians, from Nikita Mikhalkov to wanna-be pop stars, wanted a determined, sober, patriotic, hard-working man. They got him too. In the early zero years, many Russians wanted their past to be liquidated, re-affirmed as something positive, where heroes from the past were determined, sober, patriotic, and hard-working men.

It is fitting, given the way movies made Putin and the way movies helped to create President Putin, that once his Presidency ended for the first time in 2008 he became the new chairman of the government council on the progress of domestic cinema. Putin, according to the press release, will 'personally supervise government initiatives to support the film industry'. When he appeared at an October 2008 celebration of the 100th anniversary of Russian cinema, Putin remarked that 'cinema has the potential to be a major educational tool and a valuable point of reference for society' (Holdsworth 2008). It had, in other words, the potential to create new heroes for audiences in need of new masculine saints. Putin also used the occasion to promote his new instructional DVD, *Learning Judo with Vladimir Putin* (Walker 2008). No doubt a 16-year old viewer of it, *A Kiss Not for the Press*, *Liquidation* or *12* already has decided to be a man like Putin.

Works cited

Al'perina, Susanna (2007), 'Mesto vstrechi izmenit' mozhno', *Rossiiskaia gazeta* 13 December, http://www.rg.ru/2007/12/13/likvidacia.html. Accessed 4 June 2011.

Anon. (2005), 'Shpionskie igry', *Komsomol'skaia pravda* 27 March, http://www.kp.ru/daily/23484.5/38167/. Accessed 4 June 2011.

—— (2007), 'Nikita Mikhalkov. Interv'iu zhurnalu Time Out Moskva. Sentiabr' 2007', *Time Out* 37, http://www.timeout.ru/journal/feature/1645/. Accessed 4 June 2011.

Bitkina, Svetlana (2006), 'Shtirlitsa uvekovechat v bronze', *Rossiiskaia gazeta* 20 July, http://www.rg.ru/2006/07/20/shtirlic.html. Accessed 4 June 2011.

Bogomolov, Iurii (2008), 'Kartina maslom', *Rossiiskaia gazeta* 20 December, http://www.rg.ru/2007/12/20/a197647.html. Accessed 4 June 2011.

Borenstein, Eliot (2008), *Overkill: Sex and Violence in Contemporary Russia Popular Culture*, Ithaca and London: Cornell University Press.

Borisov, Timofei (2008), 'Lubianka nagrazhdaet', *Rossiiskaia gazeta* 18 December, http://www.rg.ru/2008/12/18/fsb.html. Accessed 4 June 2011.

Bremmer, Ian and Samuel Charap (2006–7), 'The *Silovki* in Putin's Russia: Who They are and What They Want' *Washington Quarterly* 30.1, pp. 83–92.

Clements, Barbara Evans (2002), 'Introduction' to Clements, Rebecca Friedman, and Dan Healey (eds.), *Russian Masculinities in History and Culture*, Basingstoke: Palgrave.

Dolgopolov, Greg (2008), 'Liquidating the Happy End of the Putin-era', *KinoKultura* 21 (July), http://www.kinokultura.com/2008/21-dolgopolov.shtml. Accessed 4 June 2011.

Felshtinsky, Yuri and Vladimir Pribylovsky (2009), *The Corporation: Russia and the KGB in the Age of President Putin*, New York: Encounter Books.

Gamov, Aleksandr and Aleksandr Samozhnev (2003), 'Ottsa Putina zapisali v predateli, a on vzryval fashistskie eshelony', *Komsomol'skaia Pravda* 8 August, http://www.kp.ru/daily/23089/5494/. Accessed 4 June 2011.

Gilmour, Julie and Barbara Evans Clements (2002), '"If You Want to Be Like Me, Train!": the Contradictions of Soviet Masculinity', in B. Evans Clements, Rebecca Friedman, Dan Healey (eds), *Russian Masculinities in History and Culture*, Houndmills: Palgrave, pp. 210–222.

Graham, Seth (2008), 'Review of *Twelve*', *KinoKultura* 19, http://www.kinokultura.com/2008/19r-twelve.shtml. Accessed 4 June 2011.

Hahn, Gordon (2004), 'Managed Democracy? Building Stealth Authoritarianism in St. Petersburg', *Demokratizatsiya* 12.1, pp. 195–231.

Holdsworth, Nick (2008), 'Putin Takes Charge of Local Film Industry', *Variety* 15 December, http://www.variety.com/article/VR1117997388.html. Accessed 4 June 2011.

Isaev, Ruslan (2007), 'V Moskve i Chechne pokazali novyi fil'm Nikity Mikhalkova "12"', *Prague Watchdog* 6 November, http://www.watchdog.cz/?show=000000-000015-000006-000023&lang=2. Accessed 4 June 2011.

Jack, Andrew (2004), *Inside Putin's Russia*, NY: Oxford University Press.

Kichin, Valerii (2007), 'L'vinaia dolia', *Rossiiskaia gazeta*, 10 September, http://www.rg.ru/2007/09/10/veneciya.html. Accessed 4 June 2011.

Kishkovsky, Sophia (2008), 'A Love Letter to Putin (but It's Not Addressed to Him)' *New York Times* 6 February. http://www.nytimes.com/2008/02/06/world/europe/06russia.html. Accessed 4 June 2011.

Kochetkova, Natal'ia (2007), 'Akter Igor' Petrenko: "Ne mogu skazat', chto u menia s geroem Lermontova net nichego obshchego"', *Izvestiia* 13 June, http://www.izvestia.ru/televizor/article3105101/. Accessed 4 June 2011.

Kolesnikov, Andrei (2004a), *Ia Putina videl!*, Moscow: Eksmo.

——— (2004b), *Menia Putin videl!*, Moscow: Eksmo.

Kott, Aleksandr (2007), 'Illiustrirovat' "Geroia nashego vremeni" – zaniatie nablagodarnoe', *russiandvd.com*, 5 March, http://www.russiandvd.com/store/newsreport.asp?id={5C6251D1-9EF1-4FEC-B947-0614F333A11F}. Accessed 4 June 2011.

Lahusen, Thomas (1997), *How Life Writes the Book: Real Socialism and Socialist Realism in Stalin's Russia*, Ithaca: Cornell University Press.

Levine, Steve (2009), *Putin's Labyrinth: Spies, Murder, and the Dark Heart of the New Russia*, NY: Random House.

MacFadyen, David (2008), *Russian Television Today: Primetime Drama and Comedy*, London: Routledge.

Medvedev, Roi (2000), 'Poznanie Putina', *Rossiiskaia gazeta* 11 March, http://www.rg.ru/anons/arc_2000/0311/2.htm. Accessed 4 June 2011.

Mendelson, Sarah and Theodore Gerber (2005), 'Soviet Nostalgia: An Impediment to Russian Democratization', *The Washington Quarterly* 29.1, pp. 83–96.

Mikhalkov, Nikita (1999), 'The Function of a National Cinema' in Birgit Beumers, ed., *Russia on Reels: The Russian Idea in Post-Soviet Cinema*, London: I.B. Tauris, pp. 50–51.

Mosse, George (1996), *The Image of Man: The Creation of Modern Masculinity*, New York: Oxford University Press.

Perova, Irina (2008), 'Ol'ga Zhulina, rezhisser melodramy "Potselyi ne dlia pressy": Snachala Putinym khoteli sdelat' Khabenskogo', *Komsomol'skaia pravda* 25 March, http://www.kp.ru/daily/23484/38146. Accessed 4 June 2011.

Piontkovsky, Andrei (2006), *Another Look into Putin's Soul*, Washington, DC: Hudson Institute.

Politkovskaya, Anna (2004), *Putin's Russia*, London: Harvill Press.

Prokhorova, Elena (2003a), *Fragmented Mythologies: Soviet TV Mini-series of the 1970s*, Ph.D. Dissertation, University of Pittsburgh.

—— (2003b), 'Can the Meeting Place be Changed? Crime and Identity Discourse in Russian Television Series of the 1990s', *Slavic Review* 62.3, pp. XX–YY.

—— (2008), 'Review of *Liquidation*', *KinoKultura* 21 (July), http://www.kinokultura.com/2008/21r-liquidation.shtml. Accessed 4 June 2011.

Putin, Vladimir (2000), *First Person: An Astonishingly Frank Self-Portrait by Russia's President Vladimir Putin*, with Nataliya Gevorkyan, Natalya Timakova, and Andrei Kolesnikov, New York: Public Affairs.

Putina, Vera (2008), 'I Am Ashamed of my Son', *KavkazCenter.com* 7 December, http://www.kavkazcenter.com/eng/content/2008/12/07/10381.shtml. Accessed 4 June 2011.

Rodriguez, Alex (2008), 'Pairing Pop Culture with Propaganda', *Chicago Tribune* 13 (January), http://www.chicagotribune.com/news/opinion/chi-corr_russiajan13,0,7816315.story. Accessed 4 June 2011.

Rostova, Natalia (2008), 'Pervoe litso – na prokat', *Novaya gazeta* 14 February, http://www.novayagazeta.ru/data/2008/11/29.html. Accessed 4 June 2011.

Sakwa, Richard (2004), *Putin: Russia's Choice*, London: Routledge.

Serafimov, Mikhail (2004), 'Viacheslav Shalevich: Emotsii vlast' vsegda schitala priznakom slabosti', *Ogonek* 52, http://www.ogoniok.com/archive/2004/4866/39-28-30/. Accessed 4 June 2011.

Shlapentokh, Vladimir (2007), *Contemporary Russia as a Feudal Society: A New Perspective on the Post-Soviet Era*, Basingstoke: Palgrave.

Smorodinska, Tatiana (2010), 'Rule of Law vs. 'Russian Justice': Mikhalkov's '12'', *Studies in Russian and Soviet Cinema* 4.2, pp. 161–170.

Svetova, Zoia (2007), '"12" kak apologiia Putina', *Ezhednevnyi zhurnal* 19 October, http://www.ej.ru/?a=note&id=7473. Accessed 4 June 2011.

Tolstaya, Tatyana (2003), *Pushkin's Children: Writings on Russia and Russians*, Boston: Houghton Mifflin.

Troitskii, Nikolai (2005), '"KGB v smokinge": Nostal'giruem vsemi fibrami', *Pravda*, 20 July, http://www.pravda.ru/culture/2005/4/7/14/20370_KGBtuxedo.html. Accessed 4 June 2011.

Walker, Shaun (2008), 'Let's Learn Judo with Vladimir Putin', *The Independent* 8 October, http://www.independent.co.uk/news/world/europe/lets-learn-judo-with-vladimir-putin-954578.html. Accessed 4 June 2011.

Weinberg, Kate (2008), 'Could This Woman be Vladimir Putin's Real Mother?' *The Telegraph* 5 December, http://www.telegraph.co.uk/news/worldnews/europe/russia/3568891/Could-this-woman-be-Vladimir-Putins-real-mother.html. Accessed 4 June 2011.

Zarakhovich, Yuri (2008), 'A Movie Valentine for Putin', *Time* 13 February, http://www.time.com/time/arts/article/0,8599,1712848,00.html. Accessed 4 June 2011.

Notes

1   Tolstaya also noted in 2000 that Putin's PR image was already branded as 'a mysterious, steely, decisive, masculine leader' (Tolstaya 2003: 230).
2   See also Kochetkova (2007) for Petrenko's take on his Pechorin versus Lermontov's.
3   For more on changing definitions of manliness, see Mosse (1996).
4   For Stirlitz anecdotes, see the website Shtirlitsiada: http://webideas.com/shtirlits/. For the statue plans, see Bitkina (2006).
5   For the most succinct account of the silovki, see Bremmer and Charap (2006–7: 83–92).
6   The film is available for your viewing displeasure on youtube: http://www.youtube.com/watch?v=yl79JkDF-Lc.
7   You can watch the video at: http://www.youtube.com/watch?v=zk_VszbZa_s&feature=related.
8   Within Russia some resistance to Putin has converged around his saintly history and clean biography as 'one of us'. Internet reports have suggested that Putin's real mother is an 82-year old Georgian who gave up her young son to his father. Putin's parents were really his grandparents in this tale while Putin becomes like Stalin – a man of the borderlands who conquers the Russian heartland. See Weinberg 2008. The story has made the rounds on Russian sites, including Putina (2008) on *KavkazCenter.com*. Other stories suggest that Putin's 'real' father was an NKVD defector who fought in Vlasov's Nazi-collaborating army. See Gamov and Samozhnev (2003) and republished at http://www.compromat.ru/main/putin/vlasovets.htm. Both stories take the central mystery of Putin's saintly life – his birth to two older parents – and find a more 'logical' answer.
9   I tend to follow Richard Sakwa's account of Putin, which stresses his personality, the dilemmas facing Russia in 1999, the practical nature of Putin's solution, his charisma, and the way that Putin's life 'reflected the lives of millions of his fellow citizens' (Sakwa 2004). Another source of inspiration are the two books (2004a and b) by Andrei Kolesnikov (one of the *First Person* interviewers and a correspondent for *Kommersant*): in them, Kolesnikov covers the banalities of modern leadership but also the way Putin's charisma affected ordinary Russians. For more critical approaches on Putin's personality and his KGB past, see Politkovskaya (2004); Felshtinsky and Pribylovsky (2009); and Piontkovsky (2006). Steve Levine (2009) sees Putin as 'an archetypal man from nowhere' who reflects Russian predispositions to authoritarianism. Andrew Jack (2004), another journalist working in Russia, views Putin as a 'man from nowhere' who is building 'liberal authoritarianism'. Gordon Hahn (2004: 195–231) provided Putinologists with two frameworks for understanding his Russia: 'managed democracy' and 'stealth authoritarianism'. Vladimir Shlapentokh (2007) has written scores about Putin's Russia, which he characterizes as a 'feudal society'.

Chapter 10

'Address Your Questions to Dostoevsky': Privatizing Punishment in Russian Cinema

Serguei Alex. Oushakine

Rossiiskaia gazeta, the newspaper of the Russian government, reported in 2009 about a court case in Briansk. A 62-year-old pensioner was sentenced to 11 years of imprisonment for killing three foreign-currency dealers. As the newspaper explained, the pensioner took to the gun in a desperate attempt to defend his own dignity, after the dealers insulted and then beat him up. When asked about the source of his motivation, the pensioner cited *Voroshilovskii strelok/Voroshilov Sniper*, a 1999 film by director Stanislav Govorukhin, in which, similarly, a pensioner turns into a gunfighter in order to make justice right and to punish some juvenile offenders. As the newspaper concludes, the 'locals are still divided about this blood vengeance: some consider the pensioner a murderer, while others share his deadly [*ubiistvennyi*] approach to the notion of "justice"' (Bogdanov 2009).

This case is not the norm, but it is not an exception in today's Russia. In the last decade, the practice of *samosud*, a do-it-yourself version of popular justice, has emerged as a prominent social phenomenon – be it ethnic riots in Kondopoga in 2006 (Anon. 2006) or a smaller-scale murders and punishments throughout Russia (see Gomzikova 2011). In this chapter I will explore only one aspect of this trend: the way the privatization of punishment is represented in Russian cinema. The chapter offers a close reading of two cinematic cases, Andrei Zviagintsev's *Elena* (2011) and Govorukhin's *Voroshilov Sniper*, in order to demonstrate in a reverse engineering move how publically executed punishments of the late 1990s were translated into quiet murders a decade later. This transition from 'punishments outside the law' to 'crimes without punishment', I suggest, is usually linked in Russian cinema to two important trends. First, the impotence of the existing legal system – the inefficiency of the regulatory functions of the state are often counterbalanced by the increasing prominence of networks of reciprocity and forms of loyalty based on family ties. Second, the privatization of punishment, the appropriation of extrajudicial authority is frequently achieved through the aestheticization of violence. The separation of moral issues from the distribution of force allows us to perceive violence as a 'communicative phenomenon', as Birgit Beumers and Mark Lipovetsky aptly put it (2009: 63), that is to say, as an artistic device, as a structural solution which is called upon to restore a necessary (narrative) balance.

Snobs vs slobs: Quiet murders

In September 2011 Russia's prominent film director Andrei Zviagintsev presented his new film *Elena* at the Russian festival Golden Phoenix. In May 2011 *Elena* had received a Special Jury Prize at the Cannes festival in the Certain Regard section; a dozen or so other international awards followed after that. The critical acclaim abroad was amplified by a similarly laudatory reaction of Russian critics. Some even described *Elena* as 'the best film about contemporary Russia' (Galitskaia 2011), reading in it 'an anticipation (*predchuvstivie*) of a possible collapse' (Borisova 2011). In an extensive interview in Smolensk, Zviagintsev outlined the essence of his artistic project in general and of *Elena* in particular:

Andrei Zviagintsev: I might be pathetic, but the time of camp (*steb*) and irony is almost over. It is time for pathos now.

Journalist: More and more films now show to our young generation how to kill ... Our youngsters are not ready for such a solution! They are not ready [to accept] crime without punishment!

Andrei Zviagintsev: Are you blaming me? Do you really think that the object of art is a manual of sorts, an instruction how to kill? This is ignorance! The idea that art should educate was forcefully imposed on Russian culture by Soviet power, which had only one goal – to forge people, as if they were nails. The artist should be telling the truth, not giving [the audience] the gift of positive emotions. You should address your questions to Dostoevsky. […] Unfortunately, quite fearsome murders have become a part of our daily routine. Evil has come into our world. […] the model *Good Defeats Evil* is outdated. Evil sometimes triumphs ... The world is built out of horrible stuff, and therefore neither art nor cinema can take any responsibility for us (Petrakova 2011).

The dismissal of didactic and cathartic qualities of art – getting rid of 'Dostoevsky' – is important, as is Zviagintsev's emphasis of the triumph of Evil. The film, Zviagintsev seems to suggest, creates a possibility for judgement, but it is not a judgement in itself. The responsibility of moral (or aesthetic) evaluation is delegated to the viewer.

With its vaguely religious undertones and minimalist aesthetics, the film clearly managed to touch a social nerve, crystallizing key issues about social inequality, family responsibility, and the line that the individual may (or may not) cross when pursuing his or her view of justice. A story about crime without punishment, *Elena* follows a trend in Russian cinema that envisions the post-Soviet world as a place of moral decay and social anomie. With visual virtuosity, it transmits through a slow-pacing narrative a message that has already been articulated quite vividly in Petr Buslov's *Bummer* (2003): 'Nobody deserves pity. Nobody.'

Certainly the story that Zviagintsev tells us is not new. Vladimir, a successful businessman and a widower in his early seventies, marries Elena, a nurse in her late fifties, whom he met while being hospitalized. The story that preceded the marriage, as well as the two years of family life that preceded the starting point of the film, are never clarified. Yet the film portrays both characters as autonomous units that exist in the same space and even coincide with each other (at breakfasts) but who rarely merge into a couple. Throughout the film, Vladimir and Elena spend most of their time in a luxurious Moscow apartment in self-isolation – in separate rooms in front of their TVs. The proverbial description of the family as the 'nucleus cell of society' is decomposed in the film to its elemental actors. Family here is a form of spatial co-habitation; intimacy and affection are not entirely absent but they are buried under daily routines and personal reservation.

This spatially dispersed conjugality as a metaphor for contemporary family starts looking different when we learn that Elena and Vladimir have children from their previous marriages. Elena's Sergei, a flabby beer-drinker with a wife, two kids and no job, lives in a crummy apartment in a depressing Moscow suburb. Vladimir's Katerina – the 'hedonist', as Vladimir calls her – is caustically smart and physically fit; she does not plan to have kids or any other long-term personal or professional attachments, preferring sex and cocaine instead. Despite their radically different economic and social background, both Sergei and Katerina practice the same structure of relation with their respective parent: without the parent's money, they would not be able to sustain their lives.

Subtly but persistently Zviagintsev demonstrates how money assumes the function of 'shared substance', i.e., the role of the key organizing entity (like blood or sperm in traditional societies) around which all kinship networks – from family to nation – are built. It is the circulation of money (instead of the usual circulation of people) that determines the configuration of families and clans now. Being outside the money circuit often means being outside the family network.

For a while, *Elena* unfolds as a film about the separate existence of the two clans: one critic framed this social juxtaposition as 'snobs vs slobs' (*snoby i zhloby*) (Shakina 2011). Indeed, Zviagintsev analogizes the relative social autonomy and spatial non-coincidence of the two groups as two currents of money that do not intersect with each other: Elena supports Sergei and his family with her pension, while Vladimir provides Katerina with the necessary allowances.

This familiar narrative about 'poor' and 'rich' relatives acquires a tragic dimension in *Elena* when the precarious autonomy of the two financial flows – and two clans and two classes that these flows indicate – is threatened. Elena's older grandson, San'ka, faces mandatory army conscription, and there are only two ways to avoid it: either to become a student at the right university or to bribe the right official from the army conscription office. Given the grandson's attitude (he is a *gopnik*, a recent version of hooligan), money is paramount in either case. Elena's pension is clearly not enough, and it is up to Vladimir to save the grandson or let him go under. A potential conflation of money flows (and clans), however, does not happen. Vladimir rejects the unwanted chain of relatedness: the gift is not initiated.

This refusal to engage is interpreted by Elena not as a financial but a moral decision. Vladimir's reluctance to provide money for her grandson is seen as a form of social racism, as a judgement that is motivated not by personal qualities of the individual (Sergei and Katerina are losers, each in a different way) but by his/her origin. Some social failures are clearly better than others. The meaning of the individual's lack of competence or success is not stable; it varies, depending on the individual's social background. Differences in access to money turn out to be only a disguise for more fundamental, anthropological, innate differences.

Figure 10.1: Elena and her clan. A still from Andrei Zviagintsev's *Elena*.

Zviagintsev is careful in framing his essentialist message by skilfully displacing the social drama caused by money onto something else: in a classical move, he depicts relations among people as relations among things. Visually, *Elena* is not so much a drama of characters as it is a drama of objects. The conflict between people is always mediated by something material: be it a written note, a telephone or a game console. By minimizing direct interactions and introducing tangible mediators, Zviagintsev solidifies a *social* distance as a material one.[1]

It is hardly surprising, then, that in this world of things, the relations between Elena and Vladimir explode precisely at the attempt to objectify family ties in a legal document. Having barely survived a heart attack, Vladimir decides to compose his will. The drafting does not go well, and after several attempts Vladimir puts the draft off. However, he informs Elena about his intention. In a matter-of-fact tone, he explains his decision to leave all his property and money to his daughter, while providing Elena with monthly financial support for life. This attempt to short-circuit the flow of money within one clan/class becomes a final straw: Elena takes things under her own control. Adding a few Viagra pills to Vladimir's daily cocktail of medicine, she waits until Vladimir quietly dies in his bed from a heart attack.

Elena never gets caught; nor does she tell anybody about the real circumstances of Vladimir's death. Drafts of Vladimir's will are carefully burnt, and in the end her crime is rewarded: Vladimir's property is equally divided between Elena and Katerina. In the final scene, Elena reunites in her spacious apartment with her son, two grandsons and a pregnant daughter-in-law. Life goes on.

It is precisely this open-ended finale of a story about murder motivated by money that makes *Elena* so significant and symptomatic. By shifting his gaze to material objects and by relying on 3/4 shots in portraying people, Zviagintsev unsettles any form of affective identification with the film's characters, positioning the viewer as a remote witness above (or on the side of) the conflict instead. Neither endorsing nor condemning the killing and with cold and distanced precision, *Elena* presents a case of *samosud*, an act of punishment in the name of a personalized version of justice. Nobody deserves pity in the film. Yet nobody is blamed, either. *Samosud* emerges here as a technical tool of sorts, as a default mechanism that restores the natural balance.

When Woody Allen retold and reframed Dostoevsky's *Crime and Punishment* in his *Match Point* (2005), he got rid of Raskolnikov's original fascination with superhuman abilities to transcend moral limits, picturing instead a generally unfair life. Indifferent to issues of justice and ethics, Allen's life is mostly governed by chance that could save (undeserving) individuals from oblivion, poverty or punishment. For Woody Allen, crime without punishment serves as an example of a general lack of causality in the modern world. Like in a tennis match, one can direct the movement of the ball only to a point: the simultaneity of different processes initiated by different players makes it next to impossible to control or predict the outcome of the social game.

Zviagintsev's version of crime without punishment is not about the celebration of chance or the evacuation of responsibility, though they are a part of the story, too. Nor is *Elena* driven by the theme of passion or revenge. Instead, the quiet murder is a calculated action here, 'an asocial concept of justice' (Goscilo 2010: 141), an action that is rooted in some fundamental belief in a hierarchy of values. *Samosud*, as Zviagintsev shows us, is not reducible to exercises of violence only. As the etymology of the word suggests, *samosud* requires a mental evaluation of options; it involves a deliberate judgement, not a spontaneous reaction.

In numerous interviews that followed the premiere of *Elena* Zviagintsev made it clear that the film is not a story about Elena's temporary blackout that pushed her to an unreasonable action. Rather, this is a paradigmatic story about the clash of civilizations of sorts, with Vladimir, 'who seems to be firmly controlling the world', on the one side of the divide, and with 'Elena-Motherland [...] constantly producing the thread of matter, giving birth to the flesh with nobody to animate it, on the other (Maliukova 2011). Valerii Kichin, an outspoken film critic, pushed this line of the argument to its limits, (seriously) suggesting to perceive Vladimir as a contemporary incarnation of Russian aristocracy, as a perfected and civilized Lopakhin from Anton Chekhov's *The Cherry Orchard* (1904). This new Lopakhin is

pragmatic and hard-working; against the background of the cadavers who are only capable of drinking and guzzling, he appears like a spiritual nobleman [...] This is why it is so painful to see how the lifestyle that he so lovingly created would be so easily destroyed by the new barbarians, who would spit with gusto from the balcony [of his apartment]; just like they spat in 1917, having thrown Rachmaninoff's grand piano out of the window. […] We are in pain not only because these cadavers would turn a nicely furnished world in a pigsty, so familiar to them; we are also in pain because they are devoid of basic human qualities, and any society that is made up by them has no future.

(Kichin 2011)

Kichin would have liked the fact that one of the initial titles of the film was *The Invasion of Barbarians* (Borisova 2011). Unlike Kichin, Zviagintsev is reluctant to reduce the social to the biological, preferring to gloss over the main message of the film as a story about 'a personal apocalypses' (Bobrova 2011) that takes place against the backdrop of 'total metastasis' of social bonds in contemporary (Russian) society (Solntseva 2011). Elena's *samosud*, then, becomes a symptom, a metonym, a point of entry into a larger field of enquiry. The aesthetic distancing in *Elena* elevates a particular murder to the status of allegory, effectively reframing a criminal plotline as a story about the triumph of Evil in the world where nobody deserves pity.

Lonely avenger: Pointed strikes

Zviagintsev's *Elena* – with its distancing gaze and muted emotions – is a serious cultural evidence of the gradual transformation that the perception and representation of violence has gone through after the collapse of the USSR. Perhaps it would not be a mistake to suggest that the film reached a certain peak in tracing the process of privatization of violence in post-Soviet Russia. The epic tonality of *Elena's* 'quiet murder' presents a striking contrast with random exercises of power administered by 'violent entrepreneurs', which was so common for the Russian cinema of the 1990s.[2]

The domesticated nature of violence highlighted by Zviagintsev brought with it yet another important aspect: not only does violence become strategically deployed within the closed limits of the private space, but it is also seen as justifiable. Relativized and contextualized murder, in other words, lost its absolute negative quality. *Samosud*, as a self-performed act of justice, has emerged as a key outcome of this re-evaluation of acceptability of privately exercised force. Important here, though, is that these (aesthetic) representations of taking law (and punishment) in one's own hands are often construed as implicit or explicit performances of political disagreement with existing modes of social validation.[3]

The almost universal praise of *Elena* by Russian critics documents another important change: the film's conflict had a class-based dimension, which was not ignored by reviewers, but only a few decided to dwell on it. Following Zviagintsev's suggestion to see the film's characters as timeless 'archetypes' (Egiazarova 2011), most critics refrained from reading the film as a mirror reflection of on-going processes in the country. This aesthetic modality of reading is relatively new: until very recently rhetorical and tropological interpretations of cinematic characters were mostly overshadowed by much more reality-driven concerns with cinematic authenticity. The public perception of Govorukhin's *Voroshilov Sniper* is a good point in case. With poster-like boldness, Govorukhin's film articulates a message that was somewhat obscured by Zviagintsev's epic tonality, namely: 'frontier justice', as the English equivalent of *samosud* suggests, emerges when the state and law lose their regulatory power. *Samosud*, then, is not a consequence of a fundamentally flawed human nature but the result of concrete social conditions.

Despite their radical differences in visual aesthetics and narrative structures, *Voroshilov Sniper* and *Elena* focus on the same issue of the moral acceptability of violence. There is a significant difference, though. The dilemma of suspended or withdrawn judgement ('crime without punishment'), which is so crucial for Zviagintsev, manifests itself only in rudimentary terms in *Voroshilov Sniper*. Govorukhin's main question is not whether crime could or could not be punished. The main ethical issue of his film is whether crime could be punished by extrajudicial means. The crux of the drama in *Voroshilov Sniper*, therefore, has to do with the recognition of the radical non-correspondence of justice and law.

Voroshilov Sniper is, perhaps, the first post-Soviet cinematic production that expressed in an accessible visual language the idea that social humiliation, taken together with a lack of protection from the state, could be counterbalanced by self-executed acts of revenge aimed at restoring justice and punishing the offenders. True, to some extent this positivization of 'the man with a gun' already took place in Aleksei Balabanov's *Brother* (1997). Yet the point of Balabanov's film was not so much to demonstrate the collapse of legal system but rather to depict the process of self-organization, the process of self-structuring of the criminal milieu that emerged in the 1990s independently of the state. Mainly, *Brother* focused on the possibility of preserving the moral compass ('Truth') in the situation of political and ethical *bespredel*.[4] *Voroshilov Sniper* starts from a different premise and from a different historical location. The title of the film is indicative here, referring to the badge of honour with the same name that was introduced in 1932 by the Soviet government in order to reward and stimulate the mass movement of snipers. The Soviet past is evoked here as a spring board for a moral counterattack, but also as a last resource of social skills.

The plot of the film is an explosive mixture of melodramatic twists, detective themes, comic lines and action-movie clichés assembled against the backdrop of the corrupt post-Soviet state. In a small town not far away from Moscow there is an odd family. Ivan Afonin, a veteran of the Great Patriotic War with multiple awards and decorations, takes care of Katia, his 18-year-old granddaughter, a student at a local musical college. Katia's father is missing; her mother – Ivan's daughter – is hardly present, constantly shuttling between Russia and Turkey with textiles and coat furs for sale. Govorukhin depicts this break up of the generational chain and the fragmentation of the family structure as parallel to the decomposition of larger societal bonds. A compressed synopsis of the situation in the country delivered through Ivan's television creates the necessary political landscape – with miners on strike in Siberia, with the government paying off arrears of wages and with 'band-formations' getting active in Dagestan.

These social upheavals, however, are distant, entering Ivan's well-measured life only sporadically. By and large, the quiet provincial town seems to be mostly immune to the corrosive influence of post-Soviet capitalism: pensioners are still playing their chess games at the communal table in a leafy courtyard, just as they played them 20 or 30 years ago. From the point of view of its material world, *Voroshilov Sniper* is constructed as predominantly late-Soviet; changes are mostly episodic intrusions: they are perfunctory and odd rather than systemic and overwhelming. It is exactly this apparent singularity of (disturbing) changes that creates a structural and poetic possibility for Govorukhin's overall message: even a lonely avenger can protect his family and his dignity with pointed strikes. In *Voroshilov Sniper* wrong-doers are still localized in time and space; Zviagintsev's universal triumph of Evil has to wait for its hour.

The time capsule of the provincial idyll in *Voroshilov Sniper* is destroyed when one day Katia accepts an invitation of two male acquaintances from a high-rise next door to join 'a birthday party' of their friend, a young businessman. The birthday turns out to be a pretext: the 'party' quickly becomes a nasty gang-rape. The three young rapists present three social groups: a successful businessman – 'a huckster from the high-rise', as Ivan calls him in the film – a student of structural linguistics, and the son of the colonel who is in charge of the local police. The social division of the world presented by Govorukhin is indicative. The young *troika* of New Russian rapists symbolizes a peculiar mélange of money, intellect and state power, being juxtaposed to the group whose symbolic capital is nothing but a reminder of the vanished state, like the ribbons of the Soviet awards that Ivan continues to wear on his jacket. Explaining his ideas, Govorukhin pointed out in an interview, that the film was addressed first of all at the older generation, those 'robbed and humiliated' people whose 'biographies were undeservedly slandered, and who were presented to their own children as the object of hatred and contempt' (Iaropolov 1999).

In a sense, the rape becomes a trigger that turns the 'humiliated and insulted' Ivan into a lonely avenger, presenting him as a 'saviour' so predictable for the rape-avenge genre (see Makoveeva 2010: 149). This transformation does not happen right away, though. Govorukhin – himself a Duma deputy – is careful in showing how Ivan is actually pushed to take the law in his own hands by corrupt legal institutions, which rely on the mutual protection of their members. The beginning of the film even offers a promising, if false, lead. When Ivan turns for help to his friend and neighbour, a local policeman, the *troika* of rapists quickly gets arrested by a group of low-rank police officers who fully share Ivan's outrage and promise to punish the criminals 'according to law, and to justice'. Things get back on the predictable track very quickly, though. Justice cannot be restored. Family ties matter. The police chief of the town makes sure that his son and the two friends are immediately released, and the *troika* quickly resumes its flashy and loud parties in the high-rise.

Ivan's pleas to investigators and prosecutors for protection prove to be unsuccessful. Under the colonel's pressure, the criminal case is turned inside out; during an interview with Katia, a repulsive investigator explains to her that since there are no clues and evidence, he has all the reasons to suspect that Katia herself could have seduced young boys in order to marry one of them, or to claim the high-rise apartment (or at least some money) as compensation later. 'In the absence of crime in the act', the case is dismissed.

It is symptomatic that, just like in *Elena*, the fundamental structure of the dramatic conflict is conceived in *Voroshilov Sniper* as a modern-day confrontation of two family clans. It appears that the logic of blood relatedness in both cases is perceived as reason and motivation requiring no further explanation: social, economic, political or aesthetic networks are only super-structural phenomena that are rooted in and shaped by the family basis. The 'call of blood' seems to undermine any other forms of rationality.[5] Ivan, certainly, shares this logic, but with a twist. The opposite 'clan' is seen as an alien formation, as 'occupants', as he calls them. And the question that Ivan repeats in his conversations with state officials – 'Where have you all come from?' – reflects well this fundamental epistemological confusion about the origin of the new invaders.

The metaphor of occupation suggests a model for action: losing his hope, Ivan gradually realizes that he is in a state of war and therefore must act accordingly. Within a few days,

Figure 10.2: A lonely avenger. Still from Stanislav Govorukhin's *Voroshilov Sniper*.

he sells his small country house and buys a sophisticated rifle with a telescopic sight. The lonely avenger is finally born. However, Ivan's way of doing justice is carefully choreographed. He is not a typical murderer, his punishments are metered. Like in *Elena*, *samosud* here is a carefully constructed plan of action. Andrei Plakhov, a leading film critic in Russia, wrote in April 1999, right after the release of *Voroshilov Sniper*: 'Precision is important in the film – because Ivan is not just your average avenger; he is also a humanist. Just like NATO's pointed strikes on Yugoslavia, Ivan hits carefully. He does not kill the offenders; he just leaves them crippled for the rest of their lives' (Plakhov 1999). Thus, the student of structural linguistics is shot right in his groin at the moment when he tries to open a bottle of champagne. The huckster from the high-rise is punished even in a more sophisticated manner: with a detonating bullet, Ivan explodes the fuel tank of the businessman's BMW, severely scorching the businessman's buttocks. The last offender requires no external action: scared to death by the threat of this castrating vengeance, the son of the police chief loses his mind, and in a feat of paranoid self-defence shoots his own father (see Figure 10.3).

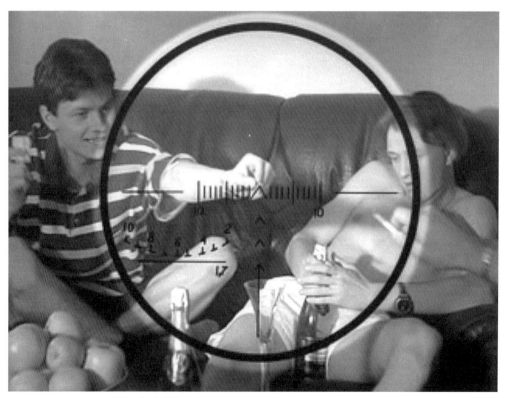

Figure 10.3: Targeting evil, locally. Still from Govorukhin's *Voroshilov Sniper*.

This series of punishments does not go unnoticed, but Ivan cleverly hides his traces and seemingly escapes public attention. In the end, justice seems to be restored, or at least the offenders are punished. Yet, the finale is framed in a melancholic tonality: Ivan's last question 'How should I live now?' is amplified by Katia's final song about a lonely accordion player who 'is searching for somebody in the darkness and is failing to find anyone.'

As a story about the lonely search for justice in the darkness, *Voroshilov Sniper* usefully articulates one of the major issues of Yeltsin's Russia. In a less than subtle way, the film raised questions about the emergence and exercise of frontier justice: the privatization of violence becomes a do-it-yourself protective tool in a situation of institutional corruption and legal collapse. Commenting on his performance as Ivan in the film, Mikhail Ul'ianov stressed in an interview the detrimental repercussions of the lack of structuring limits in Russia of the 1990s: 'When you travel outside Russia, you realize that life there is not that extraordinary; it is just another complicated life. But in that life, there are such things as logic, common sense, some legal barriers, which cannot be trespassed. We've managed to destroy all the barriers. But human beings are not perfect. Without a moral stopper, any person can go astray' (Kaushanskii 1999).

A lonely avenger who relies on his gun to pointedly administer justice is only a partial answer to this lack of moral stoppers. As Govorukhin shows in the very end of the film, Ivan's spectacular success would not have been possible without a tacit but indispensable solidarity of the weak formed behind his back, saving him from crucial failures. Annoyed with their powerful and corrupt bosses, low-rank policemen become Ivan's unexpected ally. What is interesting about this alliance (that would fade away by the time of *Elena*), is that the solidarity of the powerless is being built not around the promise of law or systemic changes. There is no illusion about a commonly shared symbolic order any more: as Ivan puts it in the film, 'every state office is staffed with a scoundrel'. Rather, it is Ivan's violent intervention; it is his act of *samosud* that serves as the ultimate form of social boding. Self-exercised punishments and acts of incursive justice are seen as a welcome corrective measure by those who are deprived of access to the law, but who still retain the will to do justice. Reflecting on this logic, one of the critics entitled (ironically) his film review 'A gun with ethics in sight' (Bogomolov 1999). *Samosud* emerges, then, as an effort to establish moral stoppers from below, as an attempt to prevent the complete 'going astray'. As Viktor Pronin, the author of the novel that served as the literary basis for *Voroshilov Sniper*, epitomized this self-regulating function of *samosud*, 'when law went sideways, people sorted it out themselves' (Kopulova 2008).

The initial title of the film would have pointed in a similar direction, too. Originally, the film was called *The Sicilian Defence* (Bakushinskaia 1999b), playing on two popular meanings of the term. First, the title drew attention to the chess opening that implies a very aggressive response to white's initial move, suggesting that a lack of initial advantage does not necessarily determine the outcome of the game. The second meaning evokes popular associations with the Sicilian Mafia and its code of honour, blood vengeance and clan feuds. Taken together, both meanings produce a peculiar post-Soviet version of the incalcitrant pushback from below spearheaded by the experience of humiliation and a desire for justice.

Govorukhin's romanticization of the lonely gunfighter and the ethical solidarity of the powerless encountered a mixed reaction. The broad audience loved it, and the film has been regularly shown on Russian television ever since. The reaction of critics and officials was less unanimous. The film's premier was an unusual event of sorts. For the first showing, Govorukhin invited only his colleagues, deputies from the Russian Duma, who apparently were enthusiastic about the film (Plakhov 1999). However, when in April 1999, the film festival 'Pravoporiadok i obshchestvo' (Law, Order and Society) decided to show *Voroshilov Sniper* at its opening ceremony in Moscow, the Ministry of the Interior that sponsored the festival vetoed the film as unacceptable (Bondarenko 1999).[6]

Critics were mostly negative. Some hated the film, describing it as 'glaringly undignified' (Medvedev 1999). Others saw in it a bleak copy of Hollywood films about 'dirty cops', with Ivan as a 'Stallone on pension' (Bakushinskaia 1999a). In their negative criticism, reviewers seemed to agree that the movie was nothing but a large-scale gesture of support for class hatred, violence, and *samosud*. Pointing out the logical flaws, some reviewers emphasized again and again that the film had nothing to do with 'real life'. Viktor Matizen, for instance, maintained that *Voroshilov Sniper* significantly 'lowered the bar of credibility' (Matizen 1999). Iurii Bogomolov went as far as to suggest that Govorukhin with his 'pathetic propagation of *samosud*' helped 'to raise further the revanchist sentiments among the Communists and the Fascists' (Bogomolov 1999).

More than a decade later, these charges look misplaced and myopic. Govorukhin's film was certainly far from being a masterpiece, and yet it did attract attention to the problem of social and legal vulnerability of those who were excluded from the circuits of power and money. In a sense, *Voroshilov Sniper* marked ground zero of the gradual privatization of violence in Russian cinema: from Ivan Afonin's 'pointed strikes' to Elena's 'quiet murder'. The range of exercises of judgement (augmented by self-executed punishments) mapped out by these two films demonstrates how violence 'trickles down'. Not unlike the transformation of power traced by Foucault, we see how spectacular explosions of vengeance in *Voroshilov Sniper* gradually evolved into a hardly noticeable microphysics of deadly violence in *Elena*.

The war of provocations

The normalization of *samosud*, the translation of violence from a language of public punishment into a language of domesticity, as I have been suggesting, is possible due to two main trends. The aestheticization and decontextualization of violence help to uncouple it from issues of morality and responsibility. Privatized and sanitized, violence becomes a technical tool and an artistic device; ethical concerns are saved for Dostoevsky. The second, important aspect is the increasing inability of Russian law in particular and Russia's political sphere in general to offer a usable and effective language for expressing social discontent and/or political disagreement. *Samosud*, a self-performed act of justice, is usually a forced recognition of the fact that the tools available for mediating social (or interpersonal) conflicts here and now are ineffective. 'Despair', as Zviagintsev observed recently, results from realizing that people in power 'have no conscience; in principle, they could have been restrained by law, but law is not working. [...] hence, there is nobody to appeal to' (Solntseva 2011). From a different perspective, Govorukhin pointed in a similar direction when he described his film as a 'political manifesto' (Kaushanskii 1999). Indeed, to make a political statement, one has to rely on non-political tools.

I want to finish my exploration of the aesthetic privatization of punishment with a brief discussion of one non-cinematic example: the recent activity of the art-group Voina (War). Presenting its social provocations within the tradition of street art and carnivalesque reversals of hierarchies, the group relies predominantly on aesthetic tools to make their political critique visible and heard. The type of *samosud* practiced by Voina is located between Govorukhin's lonely avenger with his pointed strikes and Zviagintsev's microphysics of everyday violence. Spectacular yet diffused, Voina's actions conflate 'crime without punishment' with 'punishment without crime'. What I find indicative about this version of *samosud*, though, is its deliberate manifestation of the group's right and ability to judge the authorities. The act of symbolic punishment in this case is directed against the very system that is supposed to guarantee the efficacy of law. To push it even further: it is the (assumed) illegality of the legal system that Voina draws attention to in its actions. And it is precisely this refusal to submit oneself to the corrupting effects of the existing legal system that allows Voina to impose its extrajudicial sentences.

The site of the group explains that Voina initially emerged as a 'family business' of sorts: the group was created in Moscow in 2005 by Oleg Vorotnikov and Natalia Sokol, a husband-and-wife couple.[7] A year later, Vorotnikov and Sokol met with Alexei Plutser-Sarno, an artist and a writer, who became Voina's main 'media-artist', chiefly responsible for generating the group's texts and for defining its conceptual tools (Plucer 2022 [sic]).

Perhaps like no other artistic group in Russia, Voina has been extremely effective in using new media for making itself known. In fact, the group's reputation is almost entirely based on its online self-presentation: very few art-actions performed by Voina were (meant to be) seen in real time. In a very idiosyncratic form, the group combines radical aesthetic gestures with an anti-establishment political critique. Since 2007, it has been staging what could be called artistic and political provocations in Moscow and St Petersburg, progressively getting more and more political. I want to draw attention only to a few provocations that attracted a lot of media attention in Russia.

On 29 May 2009, the group attended the final hearing of a controversial court case in Moscow: several religious organizations sued Andrei Erofeev, an art-curator from a major Moscow art-museum, for offending and disrespecting their religious feelings. As complainants claimed, Andrei Erofeev denigrated their religious identity by exhibiting caricatures of the Russian saints and distorted images of Russian icons at the show 'This is Religion: Be Cautious'. Voina had no particular connection with Erofeev, nor was it directly interested in the show that he organized. Yet Voina decided to use this celebrity trial as an opportunity to express its own political verdict. The group strategically occupied almost all the seats available in a small court room, and when the judge expressed surprise at seeing so many young people, she was informed that the young people were law students who had come to the court to watch law-making in real life and not in textbooks. While the judge was reading the 150-page long decision, the group unpacked their musical instruments in the back of the room and interrupted the hearing by a punk-song with a chorus line: 'All policemen are bastards: Don't forget it'. After performing the song, the group quickly left the building. The action was taped and made promptly available on the Internet (see Plucer 2009).

By the summer of 2010, the group had become well known among the readers of the Russian blogosphere, and two major actions solidified Voina's reputation as the most creative author of political critique in contemporary Russia. On 14 June 2010 (Che Guevara's birthday), several activists of Voina painted an oversized phallus on one of the draw bridges in St Petersburg. The performance started at 1.30 a.m., shortly before the bridge was scheduled to be raised. It took the group only 23 seconds to paint a phallus that was 65 metres long and 27 metres wide. When this part of the bridge was erected, the phallus faced directly the regional headquarters of the FSB (see Plucer 2010a).

In his interviews, Alexei Plutser-Sarno, the main ideologue of the group, suggested that this action was the first mature gesture of the art-group. And yet, he dismissed any attempts to read Voina's performances in political terms. As he explained, 'we are not going to become political. We will continue to paint the portrait of the gangsterism (*banditizm*) that surrounds us by using exclusively artistic tools. The erected picture on the bridge is not politics; it is art. It is a portraiture of the hierarchy of power (*vertikal vlasti*) that we have in our country today' (Anon. 2010).

Figure 10.4: Voina's 'portraiture of the hierarchy of power'. St. Petersburg, 14 June 2010.

Figure 10.5: Revolting the police-world: Voina's nine seconds of repentance and revenge. St. Petersburg, September 2010.

Another performance of the group took place on 16 September 2010, on the Day of Judgment (*Sudnyi Den'*), as Voina emphasized in its online postings. Called 'A Palace Revolt', it began near Mikhailov Palace in St Petersburg, the building where in 1801 Tsar Paul the First was killed during a palace revolution. The main (printable) slogan of the action, though, was 'Give us a place to stand on, and we will turn over the police-world'. And they did turn – if not the police-world, then, at least, some police cars. The performance had an elaborate scenario: a small child (Vorotnikov's and Sokol's son) would play with a ball near a police car; the ball would get under the car, and in order to pacify the crying kid, a group of men would turn the car upside down to release the ball (one of the slogans of the action was 'By Helping a Kid, You are Helping the Country'). Then the group would disappear with the ball. Over the course of several days, the group performed several actions around the city, each of which took only nine seconds.

The metaphors of revolt and turnover, as the group explained, were not entirely accidental: in Russian, the police are often known as 'werewolves [or shape-shifters] in uniform' (*oborotni v pogonakh*). Unlike its Russian equivalent, 'werewolf' lacks a crucial point – *oboroten'* means someone who turns inside out, someone who turns around. Most of the cars that the group turned upside down were the cars of the road police. As Plutser-Sarno explained, 'the road police are fond of robbing drivers on the roads of our huge motherland. Vehicles are a criminal tool that these werewolves in uniform use to achieve illegal goals. Therefore, these nine seconds were nine seconds of repentance and revenge' (Plucer 2010b).

Of course, Voina's attempts to present their actions exclusively in aesthetic terms are a ploy. Voina is not Christo. While being political, their actions are not politics, though. They are devoid of systemic effect, they are not institutionalized. But more importantly, they are not aimed at producing any alternative vision. Voina's 'protest art', the group's performative revolts, are a gesture of disagreement and judgement. They are an oversize prank aimed to demonstrate that suppression is not complete, that the authorities have no monopoly on exercising public judgement, and, perhaps more importantly, that the authorities, in fact, have no legitimate authority. Realized as guerrilla attacks, these exercises of incursive justice play on the margins of law.[8] Yet by turning political judgement into an aesthetic act, Voina points to a gaping non-correspondence between the existing legal practices and institutions of law on one hand, and the popular perception of justice on the other.

Despite their significant distinctions, the quiet murders, pointed strikes, and performative revolts that I have been exploring in this essay, are similar in their motivational structure and mode of self-validation. At their core lies the fundamental 'disrespect of the laws', to use Voina's own description.[9] It is not this legal nihilism that makes these cases interesting, though. Rather, in its own way, each case shows how this 'disrespect' becomes counterbalanced by do-it-yourself justice, with home-made evaluative judgements and privatized punishments. When law goes astray, people have to sort things out by themselves.

Works cited

Anon. (2006), 'Russian town hit by race violence', *BBC News* 4 September, http://news.bbc.co.uk/2/hi/europe/5312078.stm. Accessed 15 July 2012.

Anon. (2010), 'Art-gruppa Voina: "Bandity nas popytaiutsia sgnoit' na zone"', *Ves.lv* 18 June, http://www.ves.lv/article/128576. Accessed 15 July 2012.

Bakushinskaia, Ol'ga (1999a), 'V boi idut odni stariki', *Komsomol'skaia Pravda* 11 May.

——— (1999b), 'Voroshilovskii strelok', *Komsomol'skaia Pravda* 10 June.

Beumers, Birgit (1999), 'To Moscow! To Moscow? The Russian Hero and the Loss of the Centre', in Beumers (ed.), *Russia on Reels: The Russian Idea in Post-Soviet Cinema*, London: I.B. Tauris, pp. 81–83.

Beumers, Birgit and Mark Lipovetsky (2009), *Performing Violence: Literary and Theatrical Experiments of New Russian Drama*, Bristol: Intellect.

Bobrova, Natal'ia (2011), 'Elena – net povesti pechal'nee na svete', *Vecherniaia Moskva* 30 September.

Bogdanov, Vladimir (2009), 'Ostanovit' "voroshilovskogo strelka"', *Rossiiskaia gazeta*, 16 February.

Bogomolov, Iurii (1999), 'Ruzh'e s eticheskim pritselom', *Izvestiia* 22 April.

Bondarenko, Vladimir (1999), 'Krasno-korichnevyi Ul'ianov', *Zavtra* 7 May.

Borisova, Dar'ia (2011), 'Elena khoroshaia ili plokhaia', *Kul'tura* 8 September.

Egiazarova, Ilona (2011), '"Elena" Uzhasnaia pokorila ves' mir', *Vokrug TV*, 2 November, http://www.vokrug.tv/article/show/Elena_Uzhasnaya_pokorila_ves_mir_32440/. Accessed 15 July 2012.

Galitskaia, Ol'ga (2011), 'Vybor Eleny', *Trud* 30 September.

Gomzikova, Svetlana (2011), 'Pravosudie po lichnomu schetu', *Svobodnaia pressa*, 22 July. http://svpressa.ru/society/article/45617/. Accessed 15 July 2012.

Goscilo, Helena (2010), 'Between the sword and the scales, or celluloid justice', *Studies in Russian and Soviet Cinema* 4.2, pp.137–145.

Iaropolov, Iaroslav (1999), 'Pulia kak argument rossiiskogo pravosudiia', *Moskovskaia Pravda* 6 April.

Kaushanskii, Vladimir (1999), 'Razgovor za kadrom. Tak ne khvataet seichas kapitana Zheglova!', *Krasnaia zvezda* 30 April.

Kichin, Valerii (2011), 'Andrei+Elena+ Kann', *Rossiiskaia gazeta* 23 May.

Kopulova, Vera (2008), 'Voroshilovskii kurok', *Moskovskii komsomolets* 22 September.

Makoveeva, Irina (2010), 'The woman-avenger on the post-Soviet screen', *Studies in Russian and Soviet Cinema* 4.2, pp. 147–159.

Maliukova, Larisa (2011), 'Andrei Zviagintsev: Bogatye i bednye… Nevozmozhnost' vybora', *Novaya gazeta* 23 May.

Matizen, Viktor (1999), 'Osobennosti levoi okhoty', *Novye Izvestiia* 22 April.

Medvedev, Aleksei (1999), 'Nikto ne smeet obizhat' Katiu', *Vremia MN*, 22 April.

Oushakine, Serguei (2004), 'Mesto-imeni-ia: sem'ia kak sposob organizatsii zhizni', in Oushakine (ed.) *Semeinye uzy: Modeli dlia sborki*, vol.1, Moscow: NLO, pp. 7–54.

——— (2007), 'Aesthetics without Law: Cinematic Bandits in Post-Soviet Space', *Slavic and East European Journal* 51. 2, pp. 357–390.

——— (2009), 'Totality Decomposed: Objectalizing Late Socialism in Post-Soviet Biochronicles', *The Russian Review* (Special Issue on Documentary Trends in Contemporary Russian Culture ed. by Birgit Beumers and Mark Lipovetsky), 69.4, pp. 638–669.

Petrakova, Anastasiia (2011), 'Andrei Zviagintsev: Skhema "dobro pobezhdaet zlo" ustarela', *Rabochii put'*, 7 September.

Plakhov, Andrei (1999), 'Tochechnyi udar', *Kommerstant-Daily* 22 April.

Plucer (2009), 'Novaia aktsiia Voiny "Khui v Ochko". Pank-kontsert v zale Taganskogo suda: pensia "Vse menty – ubliudki!"', *LiveJournal* 29 May, http://plucer.livejournal.com/157798.html. Accessed 15 July 2012.

——— (2010a), 'Novaia aktsiia Voiny "Khui v PLENu u FSB!" i inauguratsiia Nashego Prezidenta Leni Ebnutogo', *LiveJournal* 24 June, http://plucer.livejournal.com/265584.html. Accessed 15 July 2012.

——— (2010b), 'Novaia aktsiia gruppy Voina "Dvortsovyi perevorot", ili "Khuevomu musoru – iaitsa meshaiut!"', *LiveJournal* 19 September, http://plucer.livejournal.com/297581.html. Accessed 15 July 2012.

——— (2022 [sic]), 'BLOG OF THE VOINA GROUP MEDIA ARTIST ALEX PLUTSER-SARNO. POST 1: LINKS, ACTIONS, INTERVIEW', *LiveJournal* 9 July, http://plucer.livejournal.com/193939.html. Accessed 15 July 2012.

Shakina, Ol'ga (2011), 'Elena: Sotsial'naia tragediia broneboinogo deistviia', *Vremia i den'gi* 7 October.

Solntseva, Alena (2011), 'Andrei Zviagintsev: "Prishlo vremia govorit' pravdu"', *Moskovskie novosti* 19 December.

Volkov, Vadim (2002), *Violent Entrepreneurs: The Use of Force in the Making of Russian Capitalism*, Ithaca: Cornell University Press.

Notes

1   This tendency of post-Soviet cinema to focus on objects as substitutes for people is described at length in Oushakine (2007) and Oushakine (2009).

2   See Volkov (2002). Aleksei Balabanov's *Zhmurki/Dead Man's Bluff* (2005) provides a perfect encyclopedia of visual clichés and narrative moves for representing random violence of the 1990s.

3   For a recent discussion of cinematic *samosud* see the cluster on the theme of retribution in contemporary Russian cinema edited by Vlad Strukov for *Studies in Russian and Soviet Cinema* 4.2 (2010).

4   For a discussion see Beumers (1999). Within a few years, this idea of 'the moral hero in immoral situations' was developed further in Balabanov's *Brat-2/Brother-2* (2000) and Sergei Bodrov Jr's *Sestry/Sisters* (2001).

5   This trend is discussed in more detail in Oushakine (2004).

6   In 2005 the festival changed its name to *Detectivefest*.

7   Different websites suggest somewhat different chronology of Voina's emergence and development. See http://free-voina.org/about. Accessed 15 July 2012.

8   Following the Palace Revolt, a criminal case was initiated against Voina. In November 2010, two members of the art group were arrested; they were released on bail in February 2011. See more details on http://free-voina.org/arrest. Accessed 15 July 2012.

9   See 'Kto takaia Voina?' http://free-voina.org/about. Accessed 15 July 2012.

Chapter 11

Freedom and Uncertainty: The Cinema of Slava Tsukerman

Peter Rollberg

Slava Tsukerman is arguably the most innovative and irreverent independent American film-maker of Soviet émigré background. Born in 1939, he grew up in Moscow, matured into a documentary film-maker during the Thaw, immigrated to Israel with the so-called Third Wave, and finally settled in the United States where his outrageous *Liquid Sky* (1983) became a cult hit to which his name is inextricably linked to this day. Tsukerman's Soviet origins sensitized him to the peculiarities of the West, but his relation towards Russia and her Communist past – particularly its cultural legacy – underwent a conspicuous transformation over the course of his career. Intelligentsia émigrés such as Tsukerman anticipated the process of passionate abandonment of the Soviet project two decades before it became a mass phenomenon. But earlier than many others this film-maker also confronted the painful uncertainty that resulted from suddenly gained freedom. This transformation is reflected in his films of the first decade of the new millennium, revealing a re-evaluation that resonates with the perceptions of many intellectuals who lived in both political systems. The return to his roots at a time when Russia had lost its Soviet straightjacket marks an intriguing artistic evolution that Tsukerman underwent with a fierce sense of independence and self-conscious inner freedom, regardless of which society he inhabited.

During the years following the release of *Liquid Sky*, the film's notoriety among connoisseurs turned into a problem for its creator: not only did it remain Tsukerman's best-known work over the following three decades, it also virtually overshadowed every other of his subsequent pictures. None of those films – neither the stylish *Poor Liza* (2000), nor the unusual historical documentary *Stalin's Wife* (2004) – were able to change the automatic association between Tsukerman and *Liquid Sky*. His latest feature film, *Perestroika* (2009), has not brought a turnaround either. This could indicate that Slava Tsukerman will be remembered as the creator of one masterpiece, groundbreaking and style-shaping but stand alone. There can be no doubt that he has tenaciously built his career as a self-conscious outsider to mainstream cinema, a principled auteur. The price for maintaining that status was high, which is evident from the small number of films he was able to complete. But it is this very auteur nature of his oeuvre in its entirety that deserves renewed critical attention. The cinema of Slava Tsukerman presents a fascinating case due to its peculiar evolution in three different cultural paradigms, a peculiarity shared by few independent filmmakers. Particularly intriguing is his idiosyncratic relationship with the Soviet culture from which he stems, which he abandoned, and to which he returned as a sovereign artist revisiting his past with a refined optic.

Tsukerman's artistic searching stands prototypical for the philosophical crisis and painful reorientation that has been dominating post-Soviet discourses since the turn of the twentieth to the twenty-first century. The Cold War paradigm that had shaped the worldview of generations of intellectuals suddenly revealed its moral convenience, which had been taken for granted. The disappearance of this paradigm and the need for new cultural, ethical and spiritual parameters was perceived by many intellectuals as a crisis of values. Observers from all facets of the political spectrum were unable to accept that the abolition of Communism meant the 'end of history', as suggested by Francis Fukuyama, and that free market capitalist democracy was the only option that fully responded to human nature. Tsukerman's *Perestroika* aims at capturing both the disturbing sense of global confusion and the urgent need for (re)orientation. It synthesizes insights and motifs that characterized the century of Stalinist tyranny, Brezhnevite stagnation, perestroika and the complete breakdown of the Soviet project, leaving them all behind with a look back in anger, ironic forgiveness and sincere despair over humanity's future outlook. *Perestroika* is remarkable for its vision of the late twentieth-century crisis of meaning, but also as a synthesis of Tsukerman's cinematic oeuvre of five decades.

Subverting the Soviet paradigm: *A Night for Reflections*

Slava Tsukerman's formation as an artist was shaped by the transition from high Stalinism to Thaw liberalization, however modest. At the age of 20, he made his first film as an amateur, immediately causing a minor sensation: his short *I Believe in Spring* (*Veriu vesne*, 1960) won the first prize at the Soviet Festival of Amateur Films and, as part of the reward, was released nationally. After studying for a year at the Moscow Institute for Construction, Tsukerman was admitted to the prestigious Soviet State Film School, VGIK. The institute, whose curriculum emphasized the development of broad cultural erudition far more than purely technical skills,[1] provided the aspiring director with a more clearly defined cultural self-consciousness. His literature teachers in particular – more so than the actual film experts – imbued in him a sense of awe for world literature. Upon graduation, Tsukerman was assigned a position at the Central Studio for Science Films (*Tsentrnauchfil'm*) in Moscow. He intended to make the most of that opportunity.

At first glance, working at a studio with a narrow pragmatic mission – the production of shorts that educate audiences about the sciences in a popular manner – may seem stifling for an ambitious young director who was dreaming of creating artistically innovative feature films. But already by the 1940s, Tsentrnauchfil'm had established for itself a niche with a surprisingly broad range of opportunities both in regards to genre and style and included occasional full-length feature film productions. There were two cinemas in Moscow specializing exclusively on popular science films (*nauchno-populiarnye fil'my*) that screened Tsentrnauchfil'm's entire output – roughly 300 shorts annually. But much more significant was the inclusion of these films as a regular part of the gigantic Soviet distribution network that showed them prior to the main feature film.[2] What some viewers eagerly waiting for the comedy or swashbuckler must have experienced as a frustrating inconvenience gave documentary film-makers a chance to reach the most intelligent strata of Soviet viewership, indeed a chance to convey an original idea and to set in motion thought processes that would last longer than the memory of the entertainment feature.

After directing a number of documentary shorts that revealed originality in visualizing scientific problems, *A Night for Reflections* (*Noch' na razmyshlenie*, 1972) became Tsukerman's first feature film in which the boundaries of what legitimately could be produced at Tsentrnauchfil'm were put to the test, in particular ideologically. It is a key film for this film-maker's entire oeuvre, concluding his first phase in a peculiar way – more personally revealing than any studio official could ever have suspected. Vladimir Matlin,[3] the author of the screenplay, had a long-standing creative partnership with Tsukerman that began with the short *Dima, the Robin, and Dad's Boots* (*Dima, Chizhik i papiny sapogi*, 1963) and continued with a popular science documentary, *The Heat of Cold Numbers* (*Zhar kholodnykh chisel*, 1967). *A Night for Reflections* was different from those shorts in that its central question – namely, what factors determine human decision making – was dramatized as a dialogue between two characters who, as it turns out at the end, give voice to a conflict within one and the same person.[4] *A Night for Reflections* was in tune with intellectual debates of the late 1960s and early 1970s when the still new field of cybernetics[5] was endorsed by influential Marxist-Leninist philosophers who hoped for its potential to synthesize data from the entire spectrum of hard sciences into one mathematically grounded super-discipline which, most importantly, was assumed to be compatible with the basic Soviet ideological doctrines. But in reality, the film's quasi-cybernetic surface was part of its cover-up, concealing a philosophically and politically deeply subversive concept.

The 20-minute black-and-white film features two characters, both of whom remain nameless. One is an intellectual faced with the necessity to make an important decision, the other an unexpected visitor who questions the assumptions upon which that decision will be based. The circumstances in which their debate unfolds can hardly be called realistic. When the first, the decision maker, comes home from work, he finds the other, the challenger, sitting in his apartment – an audacious, uninvited guest whom he had never seen before and who irreverently drags him into a dispute. The viewer quickly realizes that the displayed situation is intended as metaphorical and that the conflict is not so much between two human beings as between two worldviews.[6] The decision maker and his challenger represent two opposite poles within a discursive space in which the conditions of human decision making *per se* are debated. To retain this abstract level, the actual subject of the first character's decision is never explicitly stated, although it becomes clear that it must be vital and carrying existential risks, otherwise the emotionality of the dispute would be unmotivated. Magically, the challenger conjures a billiard table in the middle of the room and invites the decision maker to a game by which he illustrates his concept of determinacy. Accepting the challenge, the decision maker formulates a whole range of arguments in support of his innate freedom to make the decision that he considers right because it is based on ethical principles. In turn, the challenger uses examples from statistics and quantum physics to prove that freedom of decision making, regardless of ethical considerations, is merely an illusion. In the end, the outraged decision maker throws a billiard ball at the challenger – an act of despair when he has run out of arguments. But, rather than hitting his opponent, he destroys a mirror: the decision maker and the challenger are the same person.

Thus, what seemed like a heated, high-level intellectual debate was in fact a passionate inner monologue. The two 'opponents' personify voices within one man who is at a crossroad of his life and weighs the pros and cons of the decision he is about to make. Given the Soviet ideological context with its emphasis on objective laws and determinacy, the decision maker's arguments, pointing to the dignity of a reflecting individual who refuses to accept the status of a mere particle in a Brownian movement assigned to him by statistics, are particularly meaningful.

Although the challenger turns out to be an intrinsic part of the decision maker's persona, he is imbued with unmistakable Mephistophelian features resembling the chess-playing personification of 'Death' in Bergman's *The Seventh Seal* (1957) and the philosophical challenger Woland in Bulgakov's *Master and Margarita*. While such challengers can be interpreted as representations of a dialectical relationship consistent with the Marxist-Leninist dogma, Tsukerman's cinematic discourse on individual freedom was certainly treading on dangerous ground, notwithstanding the relative intellectual openness in Moscow's intellectual milieu at the time. To give *A Night for Reflections* conceptual support and thus a realistic chance for release, the prominent philosopher and historian of science, Bonifatii Kedrov,[7] came to the project's pre-emptive defence, lending it legitimacy with an endorsing introduction to the screenplay that was published in the journal *Znanie – Sila* (*Knowledge is Power*). Innokentii Smoktunovskii, Soviet cinema's emblematic intellectual of the 1960s,[8] agreed to play the Doppelgänger role, delivering an outstanding performance, charging abstract utterances with believable emotional energy and making the clash between cold determinism, on the one hand, and the humanistic revolt against it, on the other, psychologically plausible.

Tsukerman's direction reveals his experience in visualizing abstract ideas that he had gained over a decade of making science documentaries. An impressive example is the usage of rapid motion when showing anonymous masses of people walking the streets of Moscow, illustrating the challenger's claim that it is statistical laws guiding these people's movements, not their free individual decisions.[9] But it was precisely the brilliance of execution that rendered the film even more ideologically suspicious and subversive than the published screenplay already was. Indeed, Tsukerman's audacity in demonstrating a degree of intellectual freedom that Soviet citizens were not expected to possess in itself rendered *A Night for Reflections* dangerous in the eyes of ideological watchdogs. Thus, the decision of the studio administration to only award the film the fourth – i.e., the lowest – quality category was its way of neutralizing this subversive picture while at the same time avoiding a scandal. Surely, Tsukerman's film did not contain any explicit political statements. But the fact that, despite its seeming abstractness, it was prevented from official release shows Soviet officialdom's profound unease about *any* discourse on individual responsibility and freedom of decision making. In the end, Tsukerman's film was only screened a few times semi-officially in a number of scientific institutions. No review of the film ever appeared in the Soviet Union.

A Night for Reflections left one intriguing question unanswered: what exactly was the decision over which the protagonist agonized for an entire fateful night? And what did the decision maker conclude in the end as he was walking 'decisively toward the huge circle of the sun' (Matlin 1971: 23)? By the time the film was completed, both the author of the screenplay and the director had applied for emigration. Viewed with *that* decision in mind, the protagonist's inner debate acquires a much more concrete relevance, mirroring the vital dilemma that thousands of Soviet Jews were confronting at the time. When Slava Tsukerman got permission to leave the Soviet Union in the spring of 1973, he did so with a film in his luggage that had given unique artistic expression to the process leading up to this step. *A Night for Reflections* was an extraordinary artistic and intellectual document, and, on a more practical level, the director's *entrée billet* for the next phase of his career.[10]

Assaulting the Soviet paradigm: *Moscow Doesn't Answer*

Slava Tsukerman's decision to leave the USSR[11] surprised many of his colleagues: after all, his career to that point seemed enviably successful (Iudkin 2001). But for Tsukerman, an 'Aesopian' kind of film-making – artistically impressive though the results may be – did not represent an acceptable artistic path for his future: he needed the freedom to make the groundbreaking films he knew he was capable of. From early on, Tsukerman cultivated the self-image of a non-conformist, and compromises such as adopting a pseudonym in order to hide his Jewish origins or joining the Communist Party to improve his career chances were unthinkable to him (Dimamishenin 2009). Still, emigration turned out to be a difficult process (Anon. 2000: 2).[12]

After three months in the *ulpan* where Tsukerman and his wife needed to learn Hebrew, he was hired by Israeli television. The first film he made there was *Moscow Doesn't Answer* (*Moskva ne otvechaet*, 1973) about Jewish physicists who were denied the right to emigrate to Israel, so-called '*otkazniki*' ('refuseniks'). The ten-minute short, produced by Tsukerman's wife, Nina Kerova, deals with everyday anti-Semitism in the Soviet Union and its impact on the situation of Jewish intellectuals, among them the physicist Benjamin Levich who disappeared after expressing the wish to leave the USSR.[13] The film's title refers to telephone lines of Jews that are being cut off so that they can no longer communicate with their relatives and supporters.[14] The film was sold to many countries and alerted audiences to the plight of Jewish intellectuals in the USSR.

The creative freedom Tsukerman now enjoyed was enhanced by the new situation of Israeli cinema in that period. In the words of Anna Wexler Katsnelson, 'Emerging out of the early years of what Judd Ne'eman called 'Zionist Realism', when cinema served a distinct ideological purpose and was actively co-opted into state building, film-making in the 1960s saw a gradual shift towards the personal and the auteurist' (Katsnelson 2008: 128). The situation could not have been more inspiring for Tsukerman. Thematically, *Moscow Doesn't Answer* can be seen as an inverted continuation of his earlier films about scientists, only that the focus shifted towards an aspect of their lives that was taboo in the USSR. Tsukerman depicts the absurdities of the emigration process, its opaqueness and unpredictability, the psychological terror applied by Soviet authorities, as well as political activism, isolation and resolve.

The Moscow intellectuals he portrayed had indeed made their decision – it was no longer a question of if, but when. The film's peculiar imagery conveys the unbridgeable distance between Israel and the Soviet Union: while Jerusalem appears in live colour footage, Moscow is represented through black-and-white stills. Thus, *Moscow Doesn't Answer* brings out in the open everything that could only be implied in *A Night for Reflections*. But while the earlier film impresses with its stylistic and conceptual sophistication, the latter film engages the viewer with its openly polemical and emotional approach. Thus, on the one hand, Tsukerman's newly won freedom allowed him to directly address formerly taboo subjects, but, on the other, it also necessitated a simplification of his cinematic language in order to convey a clear message to a maximum number of viewers.

Another documentary made by Tsukerman in Israel, the prize-winning *Russians in Jerusalem* (the Russian version of which, with Tsukerman's own voice-over, was called *Zhili-byli russkie v Ierusalime*, 1974)[15] reveals Tsukerman's continued interest in historical subjects.[16] In this documentary, he reconstructs Russian religious traditions in the Holy City, familiarizing Israeli viewers with little-known facts, for example, that before World War I, more pilgrims hailed from Russia than from any other country – 15,000 Russians visited Jerusalem in 1913 alone. As in his previous film, photo documents are combined with contemporary footage. The director treats his subjects – for example, monks in an Orthodox monastery – with exemplary respect and tact. And yet, the national and international success of *Russians in Jerusalem* turned into a self-perceived 'psychological defeat' with regards to Tsukerman's long-term goal of making feature films. Tsukerman realized that in order to make successful documentaries, a director did not have to know a country and its culture deeply; however, a successful *feature* film could never be made without a profound knowledge of the country in which it was taking place (Anon. 2000: 1).[17]

Tsukerman later called the three years spent in Israel a 'dress rehearsal' for the next phase of his career, his immersion into American cinema (Anon. 2000: 1). Once again, despite success and recognition, he decided to leave, this time taking up residence in New York and taking his film-making to a new level.

Beyond the Soviet paradigm: *Liquid Sky*

After numerous shorts, *Liquid Sky* was Slava Tsukerman's first full-length feature film. It looked and sounded so distinctly American and was so infused with the atmosphere and spirit of New York that a viewer unaware of the film-maker's Soviet background would be

Figure 11.1: Still from *Liquid Sky*: Margaret/Jimmy (Anne Carlisle). Courtesy of Slava Tsukerman.

unable to suspect a recent émigré as its author. The documentaries made in Israel were solid professional work, but from the point of view of film aesthetic, they were largely in tune with mainstream standards and can hardly be called pioneering. Not so *Liquid Sky*. It would have been unacceptable to Soviet norms from any standpoint, thematically *and* stylistically: '*Liquid Sky* might look too shocking for puritanical Soviet tastes' (Batchan 1987: 49). Thus, making a film with the radical aesthetics of *Liquid Sky* was tantamount to burning the bridges with the past.

Tsukerman's screenplay cleverly picked up on trends in commercial cinema – the trivial fascination with aliens from outer space and the degradation of cinema to mere sensational spectacles – and subverted them in a provocative manner. *Liquid Sky's* principal characters are the fashion model Margaret; her roommate, the drug-selling singer Adrian; and the male model Jimmy, a homosexual drug addict. All three frequent the same New York night club. One night, Margaret's Manhattan penthouse is visited by a flying saucer carrying aliens who are interested in harvesting heroin which they need for sustenance. However, observing Margaret, they become aware of an even stronger pleasure-inducing chemical that is released during orgasm. The first time they watch a sex act is when Margaret is raped by an actor. The aliens kill the rapist exactly in the moment of his orgasm by sticking an arrow dagger in his neck. The next character to take an interest in Margaret's apartment is

Johann Hoffmann, an astronomer and UFO researcher from West Berlin who studies alien activities worldwide. Only Hoffmann understands the connection between the mysterious deaths of the people entering sexual relations with Margaret. However, he naïvely believes that Margaret herself needs to be saved, whereas she has begun to enjoy her role as a 'killer by aliens'. Thus, she kills Jimmy at a photo shooting by talking him into having oral sex. The unsuspecting Johann tries to warn Margaret, but she stabs him and calls for the aliens to take her with them, disappearing with the space ship.

Liquid Sky's appearance is dark and foreboding, featuring verbal and physical violence to a degree that was unusual even for an independent film in the early 1980s. And yet it contains an unmistakable undercurrent of irony. For example, the aliens arrive on a spaceship that literally has the size of a saucer; Johann Hoffmann features a thick German accent which sounds grotesque in the New York environment he is trying to alert; and, most importantly, Margaret and Jimmy, who constantly fight but are strangely bound to each other, are played by the same actress, Anne Carlisle – a curious variation of Smoktunovskii's performance as both the decision maker and adversary in *A Night for Reflections*. The film abounds in symbols that invite speculation: for example, the mask behind which Adrian hides her drugs resembles Margaret's face, but it could also be a reference to the mask in the orgiastic dance of *oprichniki* in Eisenstein's *Ivan the Terrible* (*Ivan Groznyi*). The scientist is the prototypical enlightener who tries to defend reason and order against anarchic chaos, but his knowledge ultimately proves useless: he dies together with the other inhabitants of this obsessively self-destructive culture.

Liquid Sky is groundbreaking both on the visual and on the acoustic level. In a number of scenes, we see the world from the viewpoint of aliens, through infrared lenses. The cause of the visual distortions remains obscure for some time and produces a sensation of disorientation in the viewer. Tsukerman, who has repeatedly mentioned his indebtedness to Brecht, also uses the soundtrack to create powerful estrangement effects. Courtenay Gallon, author of a detailed analysis of the film's score, points to the pioneering techniques used by Tsukerman: 'The main catalyst for the music in *Liquid Sky* was a synthesizer known as the Fairlight CMI. Although several synthesizers had preceded it, the Fairlight was the first digital model. The machine was specifically chosen by the film's director to manipulate real world sounds' (Gallon 2007: vii). The music has more than just a mood-setting function; it determines the film's entire choreography. Thus characters' movements resemble those of marionettes; the choices they make in this realm of unlimited freedom seem to be induced by a hypnotic, pounding musical rhythm that few can escape.

When *Liquid Sky* was released, it brought Tsukerman overnight fame. In August 1983, *USA Today* reported '*Liquid Sky* was snapped up by savvy American distributors who knew a new wave hit when they saw it. Now selling out each of five daily screenings at the 170-seat Waverly Theater […], *Liquid Sky* will be released in the rest of the USA shortly' (Story 1983). However, the film's interpreters were far from consensus. Vincent Canby (1983) wrote: 'More than anything else, 'Liquid Sky' is an alien's vision of American civilization light-years beyond all others in decadence, something the film accepts without comment'. For others, *Liquid Sky* became the 'favorite film of drug addicts, ufologists, and punks of all times and peoples' (Dimamishenin 2009). Tsukerman insisted that he himself never was a punk, nor did he pose as one. And yet, the underground cultural milieu consisting of people considerably younger than the director, accepted him, perhaps because he saw an aspect in their cultural revolt that was akin to his own perception. Tsukerman admitted that the punk world fascinated him because of its cultural dynamics (Batchan 1990: 33). 'In youth revolt there is always a kernel of truth, for revolt is the blossom that, once it opens, becomes the blossom of the future' (Iudkin 2001). The film does allow for a reading as a fundamental critique of western civilization, although it never preaches morality. Thus, Alexander Batchan's rather apodictic statement that *Liquid Sky* 'uses a new wave subject to make a broader (and heavily moralistic) statement on the precarious state of Western mass culture and society in general' (Batchan 1990: 17) is not supported by any element of the film. Rather, *Liquid Sky*, the 'hallucinatory cyberpunk freak-out' (Barker 2009), is permeated with the permissive spirit of Andy Warhol's Factory; as a matter of fact, Warhol was supposed to play a part in the film, with a monologue of his own (Mashkova 2002).

Figure 11.2: Still from *Liquid Sky*: Adrian (Paula Sheppard) and the Mysterious Mask. Courtesy of Slava Tsukerman.

But what, if anything, connects *Liquid Sky* to Tsukerman's origins? For one, the film was called the ultimate cult film that 'enriched the spectrum of American cinema with the visual language of the 1920s Russian avant-garde' (Anon. 2004). The director himself repeatedly pointed to his love for the 1920s Soviet avant-garde, which may have inspired *Liquid Sky*, but that argument still needs corroboration by concrete facts. On a political level, Jim Hoberman speculated that the alien attack on Manhattan might be a metaphor for a Soviet invasion, a notion to which the director reacted with amusement before suggesting yet another possible motivation. Referring to Hoberman's article in *The Village Voice*, he stated that '*Liquid Sky* contains everything I could not do in Russia […]. I can suggest the third unconscious motive: to make a film which would be impossible to show in Russia at the time and thus to strike out the past' (Batchan 1990: 17). The latter remark provides an important clue for understanding this artist's self-reinvention: by completely eliminating the past. While *A Night for Reflections* was an implicit assault on the fundament of Soviet society and *Moscow Doesn't Answer* its explicit counterpart, *Liquid Sky* marks a radical new beginning, intended to leave the past behind. In a remarkable way, *Liquid Sky*, precisely because of its moral ambiguity, appears not as a critique but a declaration of love for ultramodern western decadence, its insistence on unlimited freedom, its aggressive individualism and both the aesthetic brilliance and short-sighted self-destructiveness resulting from them. The film was made with such radical fervour as no other émigré film-maker had dared to bring to the screen. For Slava Tsukerman, it was an overdue act of self-liberation and self-rejuvenation. He had finally shown what he was capable of.

The success of *Liquid Sky* surpassed all expectations. It won prizes in Montreal, Sydney and Brussels, and ran for three years in art-house theatres in New York, Boston and Washington D.C. Tsukerman was invited to Hollywood to discuss possible projects with a number of luminaries but returned to New York a few months later without contract. The films that were suggested to him were all, in one way or another, variations of his independently produced masterpiece, only tamed and rendered acceptable for mainstream audiences, including the inevitable 'positive ending'. In the years to follow, despite periods of doubt, Tsukerman ultimately never made the transition from independent to mainstream cinema. He continued to explore the possibilities offered by various venues of independent film-making without ever settling for a convenient deal. He made a living through contract work, mostly commercials for New York businesses. When 17 years after *Liquid Sky*, he returned to the big screen with an adaptation of Nikolai Karamzin's *Poor Liza* (2000), the surprise about his choice could not have been bigger. This classical period piece features beautiful, funny and surprising digital effects, but it was by no means a modernization of the canonical text that some of Tsukerman's admirers had expected. The opposite is true: made with mostly American actors on original Russian locations, *Poor Liza* visibly strives for loyalty to the letter and spirit of the original – regardless of the fact that Pushkin already had parodied it! Tsukerman's respectful and visually elegant adaptation does point towards illusions and self-deceptions of the age of Enlightenment, but the director takes the story's feelings seriously and adds a touching portrait of the writer himself (a fine performance by Ben Gazzara) who acts as an erudite and compassionate narrator.

Admirers of *Liquid Sky* were flabbergasted both by the Tsukerman's thematic choice and stylistic execution – why did he refuse to continue the promising path begun with his New York cult picture? *Poor Liza* also signifies Tsukerman's unexpected return to Russian subject-matter. His bridges to the past were obviously not burnt completely, and the deeper layers of Russian culture attracted the film-maker with logic-defying intensity. But his return to Russia was that of a free man who now could confront the past as a sovereign artist and intellectual.

Poor Liza won the grand prix of the festival in Gatchina, but, critical recognition notwithstanding, its distribution remained in limbo. At this point, Tsukerman turned to a subject that continued to fascinate audiences in America and Russia and that was even closer to his own experience than eighteenth-century absolutist Russia: the Stalin epoch. Again, it is hard to imagine a sharper contrast between two pictures than the witty and picturesque *Poor Liza* and the provocative and dissonant *Stalin's Wife* (*Zhena Stalina – Nadezhda*, 2005) that followed it. *Stalin's Wife* is a feature-length documentary, some of whose stylistic peculiarities can be traced back to Tsukerman's early work at Tsentrnauchfil'm and Israeli television. But it also contributed something highly original to the discourses on Stalin and Stalinism that were so in vogue at the turn of the centuries: Tsukerman made an honest attempt to capture the dark fascination of its central figure without denying the dictator's psychopathologies or the bestialities he ordered. The historical footage assembled by the director and his crew, complemented by interviews with surviving eye-witnesses, form a narrative that does not follow the familiar norms of documentaries as popularized by the History Channel. Indeed, Tsukerman's montage is far from smooth, it prefers sharp visual and conceptual contrasts at the expense of easy fluidity, forcing the viewer to come up with his own judgement about what to believe. The soundtrack as a whole and the music in particular are so atypical for films of this genre that even reviewers who normally overlook film music took notice. It conveys an unsettling, nervous dynamic, as if the described historical processes were moving along with brutal unstoppability – similar to the masses moving along Moscow streets in *A Night for Reflections* and the punk crowds in *Liquid Sky* – and the human beings involved were hardly conscious of the part assigned to them by the rattling state machine.

In *Stalin's Wife*, the director conveys the reconstructed facts but leaves the viewers to themselves with their decisions and conclusions. Eye-witnesses contradict each other repeatedly, without Tsukerman's interference or comment; not even aesthetically does the film reveal a preference for either party. Such a viewing experience may be frustrating for those who crave certainty and truth; it certainly is an outrage for those who expect moral finger pointing. Tsukerman's Stalin film confronts the viewer with disturbing complexity but leaves it unresolved and unexplained, just like the enigma that its title character's death represents to this day. When *Stalin's Wife* was screened at the Montreal World Film Festival in August 2004, *Variety* aptly formulated the film's central questions: 'Did dictator Joseph Stalin's second wife, Nadezhda Alliluyeva, shoot herself in the head, or was she murdered? What could daily life have been like with the revolutionary-turned-tyrant?' (Cockrell 2004: 53). Without going into detail, the reviewer calls the film 'solid if stylistically unspectacular' (Cockrell 2004: 53). The latter statement only works if one measures *Stalin's Wife* against the provocative novelty of *Liquid Sky* – compared to the normative aesthetics of mainstream historical documentaries, it is quite unusual. But, more importantly, Tsukerman's motivation differed from that of other film-makers dealing with the Stalin phenomenon. For, rather than lecturing about historical horrors, *Stalin's Wife* deals with the unreliability of individual and collective memory.

'Striking out the past', possible motive for making the free-spirited *Liquid Sky*, had proved impossible. Both *Poor Liza* and *Stalin's Wife* betrayed Tsukerman's irresistible attraction to the Russian past, slowly but consequently approaching a point at which its different dimensions could be synthesized into one picture.

Reconsidering past and future: *Perestroika*

Tsukerman's move to the West was motivated by an irrepressible drive to establish himself as an auteur to whom artistic freedom is the highest gift. As *A Night for Reflections* is a clear document of non-conformism, a credo film for Tsukerman's entire oeuvre, *Perestroika*, made four decades later, marks the film-maker's return to his beginnings. The film is an ironic look back at Soviet communism in its various periods, focusing on the Cold War and the aftermath of Soviet self-abolition. But those who expected a pathos-filled perestroika-cum-liberation tale could not but feel frustrated. Tsukerman's point of reflection is one of a far greater distance – after all, perestroika as an idealistic and failed political attempt to reform the Soviet system had itself become history. The title points only in part to the historical period of 1985–91; the term perestroika in the sense of 'transformation' is also used in the broader sense of a large-scale and even global whose outcome is yet to be understood.

Remaining truthful to his principle of auteur independence, Tsukerman returned to his Russian and Soviet roots when it was least expected and least commercially advantageous. *Perestroika* is a film whose blend of radical individualism and global scope make it a stylistic and thematic tour de force – not a political feature, as the title seemed to indicate, but a playful philosophical treatise. *Variety*'s Andrew Barker perceptively observed that in *Perestroika*, the director 'fuses both halves of his filmmaking persona, turning the semi-autobiographical story of a returning Russian refugee into a deeply strange, breezily existential cocktail of Milan Kundera and Federico Fellini' (Barker 2009). While the film does have certain marks of an autobiography, only in a few scenes does it literally reconstruct events from the director's life. Rather, *Perestroika* attempts a reflection on the major factors that shaped Tsukerman's path, bringing together Stalinist schooling and western modernity, Soviet intelligentsia illusions and post-Soviet misery. It is also testimony to Tsukerman's

Figure 11.3: Still from *Perestroika*: Sasha and Helen in a Moscow Cafe (Sam Robards and Ally Sheedy).
Courtesy of REF Productions.

fascination with two mega-metropolises: Moscow and New York. The powerful aura of these two cities forms the film's visual core, the two centres of gravity between which the main character meanders. Moscow's gigantic pseudo-classicist palaces stand in sharp contrast to New York's geometrically outlined vastness; the former conveying imperial hubris which reduces humans to dispensable ants, the latter presenting a void whose arbitrariness challenges individuals to fill it with whatever content they like (see Figure 11.3).

The film's story is comparatively simple, yet its narrative structure is sufficiently involved. In 1992, astrophysicist and former émigré Sasha Greenberg undertakes a trip to Moscow. Invited to give the keynote address at a cosmology congress, he hopes for nostalgia but instead finds chaos, both in people's lives and society as a whole. Greenberg's initial intention was to get a deeper understanding of the decisions he had made in the past, instead his personal confusion takes on existential dimensions. His desire as a scientist to find order and coherence in the universe echoes his need to establish coherence in his own life, which is marked by a tempestuous, hurtful love and alcoholism. Sasha's loyal wife Helen, who helped him leave the Soviet Union in the mid-1970s by marrying him and campaigning in the United States for his release, has long become disillusioned in him, soberly understanding his psychological instability, his never-ending search for answers and his dissatisfaction with life. His lover, a young documentary film-maker with an interest in ecological topics, is more independent than Helen and pursues her own goals exploring post-communist Russia. Among numerous former colleagues and friends, Greenberg reconnects with his erstwhile love interest, Natasha, who once wanted him to father her child before emigrating to the United States. The fourth woman in this uneasy constellation is Elena, Natasha's daughter, who attracts Sasha with her angelic beauty – an attraction that is clearly erotic, despite the realistic possibility of him being her father – and who in turn is attracted to him.

But love, too, is just another facet of the new general world disorder, leading to the film's central question: is there a way out of the chaos that seems to reign supreme in both Sasha Greenberg's life, in late-perestroika Moscow and in the world overall? Or, formulated within the context of Tsukerman's oeuvre, has the desired freedom of decision making declared in *A Night for Reflections* and the hedonistic freedom celebrated in *Liquid Sky* ultimately led to the disintegration of all meaningful human order? In the finale, Elena and Sasha together ring an ancient church bell. While this ending may appear like a symbolic, moralistic gesture, Tsukerman's film as a whole is far from a call to action. For activism is but one facet of an entire spectrum of life models, no more consequential than any other. After the disappearance of the world's East-West bipolarity that had assigned every person exact trajectories in its Cold War paradigm, the ability to freely choose from an endless variety of worldviews and life patterns throws the film's characters into a dilemma.

Perestroika was made 20 years after the phenomenon that gave it its title. In 2009, no longer did the word perestroika carry the salvation promise of the late 1980s. Looking back with irony rather than anger, Tsukerman composes a non-chronological string of episodes in which characters encountered by Greenberg in the tumultuous, confused and angst-ridden post-perestroika years trigger associations with their respective roles in the past. The irony at times is forgiving, at times bitter, for example, when the film exposes faux friendship rituals such as collective singing to the guitar around the kitchen table. In *Perestroika*, Tsukerman's engagement with the world is still wild and unruly but not in the anarchic fashion that shocked in *Liquid Sky*. Indeed, Sasha Greenberg's quest for universal order may reflect the director's own desire for positive evolutionary patterns that would help determine meaningful individual lives.

The film's most intriguing character is that of physicist Aleksandr Gross, who in the 1940s betrayed the United States and defected to the USSR to help the Soviet military build a nuclear bomb, ostensibly to establish parity between the emerging superpowers. F. Murray Abraham portrays Gross – a Mephisto not unlike the challenger in *A Night for Reflections* – as a dangerous genius who engages his former mentee Greenberg in a principled philosophical debate about science and ethics. The fact that both characters are physicists is significant – they represent the field that explores the structure both of the cosmos and of the particle, as well as the discipline that has the means to approach the innermost enigmas of the world but also provides the means to destroy it. In a disturbing way, Greenberg's and Gross's biographies mirror each other: the former left the Soviet Union to live and work in America, while the latter left the United States to live and work in the USSR. Both have strong arguments to support their decision. This unsettling symmetry is new in Tsukerman's world, considering the clear moral choices presented in *Moscow Doesn't Answer*. Ethically, Greenberg's superiority seems to lie at hand: he left a despicable, illiberal system stifling human dignity and creativity, whereas Gross made his choice at a time when the Soviet Union was a Stalinist monstrosity. But, looking back at his life, Greenberg is far from triumphant: his freedom has not relieved

Figure 11.4: Still from *Perestroika*: Memories of a Soviet Childhood. Courtesy of REF Productions.

him from the tormenting dissatisfaction with his role both as a man and as a scientist, whereas Gross can claim to have helped secure world peace and brought several people happiness. And, ironically, more than anybody it is Gross who can relate to Greenberg's inner torments. At the end, Gross reveals that the beautiful Elena is his daughter, not Sasha's.

The distinction between the episodes taking place in Moscow in 1992, in 1952, and in the early 1970s is marked aesthetically, mostly by shot composition and manipulations of colour. While 'present-day' Moscow is shot in quasi-documentary fashion, with a nervously moving hand-held camera and glitzy light effects, the Stalinist and Brezhnevite past are shown in unappealing, bleak greenish and brownish tones: 'Adding to the overstuffed ambiance is a blithely experimental way with form that will keep you busy separating past from present' (Taylor 2009). This stylization in *Perestroika* carries an aesthetic indictment of the society in which Tsukerman and his protagonist grew up.

Perestroika's quasi-autobiographical nature was hard to miss – the *New York Times* critic called it 'a pseudo-memoir' (Lee 2009), featuring, among other episodes, the unconditionally faithful young pioneer pledging allegiance in front of a huge Stalin portrait and the mockeries from other kids who are calling him 'kike' and make him 'beg for a beating'. But the film also represents a synthesis of Tsukerman's oeuvre in its entirety, including the first decade of science documentaries. In *Perestroika*, problems of physics are discussed for their philosophical relevance, leading to peculiar cosmological speculation about the chances for universal order or disorder. It is a film nourished by the experiences of the twentieth century and energized by the keen sense of disorientation that characterized Russia at the century's end. More than that, it captures aspects of today's zeitgeist that are of global relevance – perestroika viewed as the prelude to a profound transformation of humanity beyond comfortable ideological paradigms.

Works cited

Anon. (2000), 'Slava Tsukerman: Kul'turnye plasty interesnee otdel'nykh sudeb', *Russkii bazar* 27 (5 July).

Anon. (2004), 'Slava Tsukerman', *Reiting personal'nykh stranits*, 31 March, http://www.viperson. ru/wind.php?ID=203048). Accessed 15 May 2010.

Barker, Andrew (2009), 'Perestroika', *Variety*, 23 March.

Batchan, Alexander (1987), 'Mad Russian', *Film Comment*, June, p. 49.

—— (1990), 'The "Alienation" of Slava Tsukerman', in Petrie, Graham and Ruth Dwyer (eds), *Before the Wall Came Down: Soviet and East European Filmmakers Working in the West*, Lanham NY and London: University Press of America.

Canby, Vincent (1983), 'Independent Movies Take a Turn for the Better', *The New York Times*, 31 July.

Cockrell, Eddie (2004), 'Stalin's Wife', *Variety* 22–28 (November).

Dimamishenin [username], (2009), 'Tsennye bumagi. Tverdaia zemlia i Zhidkoe nebo Slavy Tsukermana', *Peremeny* http://www.peremeny.ru/column/view/919. Accessed 31 May 2012.

Gallon, Courtenay (2007), *Liquid Sky: Cult Cinema, Film Scoring, and the Fairlight CMI*, Thesis submitted to the Florida State University College of Music.

Iudkin, Viktorii (2001), 'Slava, kotoryi snimaet sam po sebe', *Chaika* 28 December.

Katsnelson, Anna Wexler (2008), 'Belated Zionism: The Cinematographic Exiles of Mikhail Kalik', *Jewish Social Studies: History, Culture, Society* 14.3, pp. 126–49.

Lee, Nathan (2009), 'Social and Political Transformations', *The New York Times*, 17 April.

Mashkova, Anastasiia (2002), 'Slava Tsukerman: "Menia nazyvaiut chempionom otkazov"', *Kul'tura*, 8 (21–27 February), http://www.kultura-portal.ru/tree_new/cultpaper/article.jsp?number= 352& crubric_id=100443&rubric_id=208&pub_id=192358. Accessed 15 May 2010.

Matlin, Vladimir (1971), 'Chelovek – reshai!, ili Dialog o prichinakh', *Znanie – sila* 11, pp. 22–23.

Story, Richard David (1983), 'In New York. Movies: A new cult classic', *USA Today*, 30 August.

Taylor, Ella (2009), 'Go Perestroika', *Los Angeles Times*, 20 March.

Notes

1 The central components of the VGIK curriculum for film directors were developed by Sergei Eisenstein in the early 1930s.

2 This arrangement had been suggested by Lenin himself who wanted to establish cinema as a cultural force by removing commercial priorities and making newsreels and educational shorts compulsory for each screening.

3 Matlin, Vladimir (b. 1931), writer and journalist; began to work at Tsentrnauchfil'm studio in 1955; immigrated to the United States in 1973.

4 The screenplay was published under the title 'Chelovek – reshai!, ili Dialog o prichinakh' (Matlin 1971: 22–23).

5 One of Matlin's previous screenplays, *I Search for the Laws of Creativity* (*Ishchu zakony tvorchestva*, 1966, directed by Aleksandr Burimskii), dealt with questions of cybernetics.

6 The unrealistic framework needs to be accepted by the viewer as the external pretext for the thought experiment.

7 Kedrov, Bonifatii Mikhailovich (1903–85), Russian chemist, philosopher, and historian of science, member of the Academy of Sciences of the USSR (1966). In his surprisingly non-dogmatic introduction, Kedrov commends the author of the screenplay for only minimally simplifying the complexity of the problem; Kedrov himself invokes God and argues in favour of a complex synthesis of determinism and freedom of decision making.

8 Smoktunovskii, Innokentii Mikhailovich (1925–94). Casting him for the difficult part of decision maker and challenger was based on his performance as physicist Gusev in Mikhail Romm's groundbreaking *Nine Days of a Year* (*Deviat' dnei odnogo goda*, 1964); this information was provided during my interview with Vladimir Matlin, 23 May 2010. Given the highly dialogic nature of Romm's film as well as its confluence of scientific and ethical questions, it seems safe to assume that it impacted *A Night for Reflections*.

9 The published screenplay contains several precisely described visual elements: stop-motion, reverse shots, rapid shot from bird's eye view, slow motion as visual quasi-reactions to the verbal debate. See Matlin (1971: 22–23).

10 Tsukerman showed the film to another émigré, Edward Ettler, who invited him to work for Israeli television (telephone interview with Slava Tsukerman, 22 April 2010).

11 The first famous film-maker to leave the USSR and make *aliyah* in Israel was Mikhail Kalik in 1971. He directed the controversial full-length feature *The Three and the One* (Shloshah ve-ahat, 1973) which became a critical and financial disaster; see Katsnelson (2008: 126–49).

12 In this interview, Tsukerman mentions that prior to *Liquid Sky* he had considered four screenplays whose production failed for lack of financing. However, the exploratory phase brought him in contact with punks whose perception of the world he found similar to his own, including their admiration for Vladimir Maiakovskii.

13 In *Perestroika*, Tsukerman tells a similar story: the main character is a physicist who falls in love with an American and tries to leave the country with her.

14 In the end, there is another visual effect reminiscent of *Liquid Sky*, an infrared surreal camera spectrum.

15 The film won the prizes for Best Documentary and Best Directing at the 10th Hollywood Festival of World Television in 1974.

16 In 1964, he made the feature-length documentary *Architecture of Ancient Moscow* (*Arkhitektura drevnei Moskvy*), and in 1968, the ten-minute *Pushkin's Moscow* (*Pushkinskaia Moskva*), among others.

17 'Tsukerman attributed the sensational flop of Mikhail Kalik's first Israeli film precisely to that shortcoming: it was made before the director had sufficiently experienced life in Israel. This view largely coincides with Anna Katsnelson (2008: 126–49).

Chapter 12

Muratova's Cinema before and after Perestroika: Deconstructing and Rebuilding Film Aesthetics

Eugénie Zvonkine

The emergence of Kira Muratova's oeuvre has been marked by a tumultuous historical period. Her career has traversed turbulent political epochs, such as the end of the Thaw, the stagnation period, perestroika and, more recently, the political and economic conflicts between Russia and Ukraine.

Historically, Muratova's filmography can be divided into two periods: the Soviet and the post-Soviet one. I consider it more appropriate to characterize the second half as post-Soviet rather than Ukrainian, since Muratova's unique position is possible only in the post-imperial context, where strong cultural links between the countries are still intact. Until 1991 Muratova was obviously a Soviet film director (her Romanian origins notwithstanding). But after the collapse of the Soviet Union, the situation changed: Muratova was now officially a Ukrainian film-maker. Her cinema also presents some specifically Odessite characteristics. However, the Russian Ministry of Culture continues to support her films, thus demonstrating a continuity of the ties between her films and Russian culture. Her Ukrainian producer Oleg Kohan fights for her recognition as a Ukrainian film-maker while admitting that she is not completely so: 'I consider that neither [Roman] Balayan[1] nor Muratova made properly Ukrainian films, but since they live in this country, we must finance them and see it as an honour'.[2] The former head of the cinema sector in the Ukrainian Ministry of Culture, Anna Chmil, explains that the ambiguous status of the director has been a problem more than once when she was to receive financial help for her films from the State:

> A great artist is able to reproduce the reality of this country, and even the specificity of the town of Odessa. [When I financed her films], I was accused of financing a director with no connection to national cinema. I used to give an unequivocal answer to this comment: tell me, please, what kind of reality and what characters does Kira reproduce in her films? My opponents would start to give contradictory arguments. [...] every real-life detail in a film is determined, among other things, by the geographic location where it takes place.[3]

Muratova makes her films in Russian. She says that her 'first language is Russian, and [her] first beloved country is Russia' (Bollag and Ciment 1988); the films are nourished by Russian, but also Soviet cultural references. But she cannot be considered as a Russian film director: born in Moldavia, she studied in Moscow and since 1964 lives in Odessa. Finally, the mere fact that a director with such a life story lives and works in contemporary Ukraine is a result of the Soviet past and of the ties preserved since the Soviet era.[4] Therefore, the only concept that applies to Muratova's recent work is that of post-Soviet cinema.

In terms of film production and distribution, her cinematic oeuvre can be divided into three periods. She has worked at least in three different systems of film production and distribution: the Soviet system, the transitional period of perestroika and the present-day commercial system.

During the first period, the frame that defines Muratova's work is that of the Soviet film industry. As Birgit Beumers reminds us, 'the film industry was a full-fledged sector of the Soviet economy and administration' (Beumers 2009: 149). What we now call censorship was actually a part of a global financing, production and distribution system. The situation changed during perestroika, when the financing, production and distribution system were still Soviet, but the constraints had diminished. During the first years after rehabilitation, the directors whose destiny has suddenly changed are praised as 'survivors', as the living proof of the effectiveness of perestroika:

> Yesterday they told me: 'You are stupid and blind, get out of here!' Now suddenly: 'You are a genius! Everything you do is great!' Black became white. 'Start working immediately, film anything you want.' They started to use me in their own interests: 'Look how well things turned for her, and all those who think that everything is as it was before, can go to hell.'
>
> (Taubman 1991)

However, even during this relatively calm period, Muratova managed to unsettle and even shock the censors and to jam the system that had become much more pliable. Aleksei German

Figure 12.1: Still from *Asthenic Syndrome*.

wrote that the director 'who managed to make a "shelf-movie" in 1990 should have a monument erected in his name. Muratova succeeded' (in Bykov 1997) – with *Astenicheskii sindrom/Asthenic Syndrome* (1989) (see Figure 12.1). François Albéra is right when he notes that Muratova 'remains once again in the margin, during the short "reprieve" in cinema between the end of the Soviet regime and the "wild" capitalism that followed' (Albéra 2005: 618).

After the collapse of the Soviet Union, Muratova suddenly found herself, as all former Soviet film-makers, in the context of a liberal economy and destroyed film industry. This collapse sealed the end of Soviet censorship as well as of Soviet film institutions. These changes were brutal in some instances, and less so in others (like the privatization of the studios). Finances had to be found through private funds or state institutions, but the latter did not function for several years because of the economic instability of the post-Soviet era. However, Muratova considered these difficulties as more acceptable: 'What happens now is the dependence on money, on the audience. But I believe these difficulties are more natural, whereas the ideological difficulties were not' (Taboulay 1991: 60). Muratova entered a new era, where difficulties with the censorship had been replaced by financial ones, and these should be expected for such an eclectic and sometimes hermetic film director as Muratova.

These extremely diverse conditions give Muratova's films an even more eclectic and heterogeneous appearance, going from an openly auteur narrative such as *Dolgie provody/Long Farewells* (1971) to a genre film (*Tri istorii/Three Stories*, 1997) or a fairy tale (*Chuvstvitel'nyi militsioner/The Sentimental Policeman*, 1992). It is then quite understandable that in the 1990s even her most determined supporters, like Viktor Bozhovich,[5] consider her work to have lost coherence. A few years later several scholars, including Zara Abdullaeva (2008) and Jane Taubman (2005), uncovered recurrent motives in her films and wrote in-depth studies of certain aspects of her aesthetics, as did Irina Sandomirskaia (2008) in her analysis of sound in *Asthenic Syndrome*. But the body of her films seems to resist, giving rise to the question about how we can apprehend this oeuvre in its diversity. How can we understand the logic of its aesthetic evolution? If we take a film directed at the end of the Soviet era and a film made in contemporary Ukraine, how would these films connect to each other and how can we trace coherent aesthetic choices between works produced in such different contexts and so different in their narrative and formal choices?

In my book *Kira Muratova, a Cinema of Dissonance* (2012), I argue that the answer resides in the aesthetical organization of her oeuvre. Its aesthetics seem to have undergone drastic transformations after the end of the Soviet period, as though the exterior constraints of censorship (and the entire film industry) had been replaced by an interior constraint of narrative structures and the introduction of mythological and archetypal figures. This way Muratova's films preserve an internal tension between deconstructing elements (dissonances) and regulating procedures. Moreover, I argue that dissonance is the architectonic form of Muratova's oeuvre. For Bakhtin, 'drama is a compositional form' (dialogue, acts), but 'tragic and comic are the architectonic forms of its realisation' (Bakhtin [1924] 2006: 35). Muratova's films would then be 'fiction' by their compositional form and 'dissonant' by architectonic form. Thus, even when the compositional form of the films undergoes changes (sentimental drama, comedy, fairy tale), their architectonic form (dissonance) remains the same.

Thus, Muratova uses the same aesthetic logic of fictional construction and we can trace an obvious continuity between two films, the first made in the Soviet period and the second in the post-Soviet era: first, *Asthenic Syndrome*, an apocalyptic film about the end of the Soviet era, directed during the transitional period when Soviet film production was still in place but the censorship was much less present. The project was financed by the Soviet system but struggled to finally obtain the licence for distribution. Second, *Melodiia dlia sharmanki/ Melody for a Barrel Organ* (2008), a sad Christmas tale about two children, was financed by the private Ukrainian production company Sota Cinema Group, but mainly (70 per cent) through the Ukrainian state funds.[6] In both cases, the films were mainly state funded, but in the first case the whole production system was organized and controlled by the state, while for the second film the situation resembled that of western film industries where so-called auteur films are partially financed by the state. At first sight the films seem very different: a pointedly eclectic film about the end of Soviet era, made in two parts (one black and white and the other in colour); and a film about two children lost in the big city of Kiev on Christmas Eve. And yet, in these two films Muratova still makes use of the same aesthetic devices and the same architectonic form by simply adapting it to the universe she wants to depict.

Albéra justly observed that the 'gaps that interest Muratova are to be found not only on the political and ideological level, but also on a private, personal one. A social neurosis that is reflected in the interiority of an individual or an individual neurosis that spreads to the whole society' (Albéra 2005: 619). We shall analyse here how the director staged the entire society of a certain period through her representation of social space.

Asthenic Syndrome is a film in two parts that depicts the itinerary of two characters suffering from depression. The first is woman who has recently been widowed and who is unable to deal with everyday life and communicate with others without violence. The second character is Nikolai, a school teacher who dreams of being a writer and presents the opposite symptom: he falls asleep everywhere, in his own way unable to connect with others and with the world around. In this feature, the image of the collapsing country is rendered through a disorderly narrative structure. In the second part, where Nikolai is the main character, the plot line often abandons him to wander off and follow episodic characters. In one such episode the seemingly chaotic sequence of events eventually forms a recognizable pattern and transforms the episode into a metaphor for the Soviet Union: a young man, Serioga, has just found out about the death of his friend Kolia and goes around telling everybody about it. Serioga comes to the door of an apartment, because he wants to warn his friend Misha about Kolia's death. The door is opened not by his friend, but by a mannered old lady (supposedly Misha's mother). Their dialogue seems almost nonsensical:

Serioga: Is Misha here? I'm asking you if Misha is here! Is Misha here?
Silence.
Mother: First of all: how do you do?

Serioga: How do you do! How do you do! How do you do! Is Misha here?
He collapses on the floor.
Mother: Oh, Seriozha, why are you so pale?
Serioga: Is Misha here?
Mother: Misha's gone to someone's name day party.
Serioga: Goodbye.
Mother: Goodbye.
Nobody moves.
Mother: Seriozha, Misha told me that Kolya had been stabbed to death. How did this
     happen?
Serioga: So he knows already?
Mother: He told me himself. But I … (*she rolls her eyes*) didn't understand a thing!

What at first appears to be the core of the episode is the impossible dialogue between generations. Serioga and the old lady exchange words that show their inability to communicate: her words and manners are from the literature of the nineteenth century (such as *imeniny*, the name day) and her expressions typical for a parent-child relationship such as 'First of all, how do you do'. Social conventions dominate the dialogue.

But what happens before this apparently central dialogue reveals even more about the real intention of the sequence. While approaching the apartment door, the young man passes by an old lady singing a *chastushka* as she faces the camera, thus disrupting the diegetic illusion. The refusal to create a fictional context for the song (no audience, no plot necessity, and the singer facing the camera) makes this element stand out as heterogeneous and underlines its semantic importance. Moreover, contradicting the local vector of the action (following the young man), Muratova has the song start before the beginning of the shot and continue after the young man has left the frame. The camera lingers on the singing woman to let her finish the second verse:

I will uncover a mystery for you
And will tell you a secret.
My life on earth is hard
But I hope for nothing in life.
Our life was great
When Stalin was still alive.
He made the life of the working people
Much easier to live.

The woman sings her nostalgia for the Stalinist period in the form of a Russian folk rhyme, a *chastushka*, which has obviously been created during the Soviet period. Muratova intentionally chooses this specific 'minor form'. A lot has been written on the link between certain forms of folklore and the Stalinist era. Natal'ia Skradol' (2011) has pointed out

Figure 12.2: Still from *Asthenic Syndrome*.

that these texts 'existed not only in parallel with the major forms, but were necessary for the support of the latter, and played an important part in the construction of the language and the conception of the specific world of the Soviet era'. Moreover, she considers that these minor forms prospered during Stalinism: 'one can assume that there is a direct link between Stalinist politics and the peak of popularity' of the *chastushka* during the first part of the twentieth century. Skradol' explains this popularity by the will to create a pseudo-authentic popular foundation for Soviet ideology: 'Their brevity and their stylistic lack of inventiveness, the fact that they were easy to remember and thematically omnivorous, made the *chastushka* lyrics especially attractive for ideologues, who saw in the creation of new, Soviet folklore an endless field of possibilities to legitimize the popular status of the new power and of the national character as the main feature of the art of the masses.' The old woman singing this pseudo-popular folk song brilliantly sums up in only a few seconds the complete infiltration of ideology in the spirit and everyday life of Soviet people.

The next frame shows the young man in a close-up, making Gorbachev's portrait on his hat stand out. This feature of his attire puts him in immediate opposition to the old lady. Nikolai, the main character of the second part of the film, a middle-aged man absent from this episode, has been analysed by the scriptwriter and actor who played him in the following way: 'Because of his age, he is at the juncture between Stalinists and Gorbachevites. And this rift crosses his soul' (Popov 1989).

Here these two incompatible embodiments of Soviet history cross paths in a corridor leading to a communal flat. Indeed, the doorway where the mannered old lady is standing leads to a communal apartment that remains out of the field of vision, when several new characters exit the flat and initiate a new plot line.

An aging couple follows two men while complaining about their living conditions. Their expressions suggest that they are talking to some civil servants on a routine inspection. 'You come and you go', they call out to them. The couple cries out standard reproaches, such as 'Why did I go to the war? I shed my blood!'. But the standard lines sound absurd because the couple is clearly addressing the wrong people. One man has long hair, the other one is black, which means both of them clearly belong to the student and intellectual milieu (during the 1980s the only black people one could see in Moscow were students from African countries studying in the People's Friendship University founded in 1960 and named after Patrice Lumumba).

Their dialogue also identifies them as intellectuals, since it is an abstract philosophical discussion about the 'human desire of universal love'. Then the couple turns to Serioga, asking him if he comes from the 'town hall' or 'town council'. It then appears that there are no civil servants, that the couple has invented them out of sheer despair, because of their unbearable living conditions and the perpetual feeling of injustice.

The woman (the wife in the ageing couple) comes out of the same door where the extravagant old lady is standing, but she looks quite different from her: she wears no jewellery, no make-up and has a complexion and clothes that hint at a much lower social status. We may recall Lev Rubinstein's description of the inhabitants of the communal apartment, among them always an old lady from the former nobility side by side with proletarian families (Rubinstein 2000). The description of the apartment that is out of sight and thus left to the spectator's imagination is given by this second woman as appalling: 'Everything is broken, ruined. Both cookers are broken; there is no gas cooker, nothing. There's no running water, nothing. The ceilings are collapsing'. The old lady, who looks like a retired diva, and the working-class woman seem to share this living space which has been abandoned by the state.

All generations and social classes are thus crammed into this short and apparently chaotic episode. The model of the collapsing Soviet society as represented by Muratova is the communal flat. While the characters are leaving the building, they pass by a huge letter K, standing in either for *kommunizm* or for *kommunalka*.

Muratova is far from being the only one to suggest the communal apartment as a microcosm of Soviet society. In 1994 Yuri Slezkine took the model of the communal apartment to analyse the Soviet ideology of the cohabitation of nationalities (Slezkine 1994: 414–52). In his essay on communal apartments and their specific mythology, Lev Rubinstein ascertains that 'The communal apartment is not only the space of real life (or half-real life as it starts to appear in the historic perspective) for real people, but a permanently functioning model of something. [...] The communal apartment, even before the kolkhoz and the Gulag, appeared as a universal representation of how utopia rapidly mutates into anti-utopia' (Rubinstein 2000). Moreover, Rubinstein thinks that 'the communal being determined the communal consciousness'. Iakusheva (2007) also considers that the 'kommunalka was transformed from a lodging and social problem into an ethical and communication problem, since it determined not only specific relationships, but also influenced views, characters, the way of thinking and living of its inhabitants'.

The communal apartment appears in Soviet art very early on. Rubinstein notes that 'kommunalka and art is a theme which is almost inexhaustible' (Rubinstein 2000). He argues that in films communal apartments appear as late as the 1960s, 'never to disappear again'. But in reality one can find many examples of communal living in Stalinist cinema, always with a positive connotation.

Thus, Muratova's sequence has to be set into the context and continuity of a long history of representation of communal living. But her image is particularly bleak: a space in which all generations and classes are crammed together, with no social or material infrastructure and no care from the state.

Muratova's *Melody for a Barrel Organ* is set in contemporary Ukraine and tells the story of two little orphans, Alena and Nikita. After their mother's death, the social services intend to separate them, so they run away in the search of their fathers (their mother conceived them from different men), whom they barely know. Throughout the film, the fathers remain out of reach. The children's itinerary makes *Melody* an 'encyclopaedic film' (in the words

Figure 12.3: Still from *Melody for a Barrel Organ*.

224

used by Muratova to describe *Asthenic Syndrome*). Thus *Melody* visits all the key spaces of contemporary Ukraine: a train station, a casino and a supermarket. At first sight, these spaces appear to stand in total contrast to the spaces crossed by the characters of *Asthenic Syndrome*: where the latter shows shabby places deserted by the State, the first shows glossy halls, shiny lights and a profusion of technology, expensive items and consumable goods.

The last part of the film is set in a supermarket, which is filmed by Muratova in a manner as to transform it into a vision of contemporary society. In this space, the most tragic events unravel, even though the place is first presented as an ideal fantasy of contemporary capitalist society, where one of the main activities on Christmas Eve is to shop for gifts. When the character played by Renata Litvinova and dressed up as a fairy godmother arrives at the supermarket to fetch the little boy Nikita and save him, she comes too late, but instead of trying to find him, she finally decides to shop for gifts.

In his analysis of Muratova's films of the Soviet period, Viktor Bozhovich called the emerging words of the chaotic dialogues *nad-tekst*, an 'over-text' that discloses the core meaning of the events going on. For instance, during his argument with his wife and mother-in-law in *Asthenic Syndrome*, Nikolai suddenly bursts out 'Incommunicability!', and this word covers in the soundtrack his wife's and his mother-in-law's lamentations – and sums up the situation. Thus, the words which remain audible in the overwhelming soundtrack become keys to possible explanations or an analysis of fictional situations.[7]

However, in *Melody*, the over-text – even though it is present in the soundtrack – accomplishes the reverse function. In the supermarket the cushioned, disembodied voice in the loudspeakers functions as a voice-over and resembles a fairy-tale storyteller, but it misleads the audience.

Figure 12.4: Still from *Melody for a Barrel Organ*.

Throughout the film, the children struggle to move from one space to another in the desperate search for their fathers. They are at best forgotten by compassionate grown-ups and at worst deceived or rejected by others. In this warm and shiny space of the supermarket the voice suddenly promises that all the dreams will come true, giving the spectator a new spark of hope for what the future holds for the main characters. This hope is strengthened as the spectator witnesses an encounter between the little boy Nikita and an older man, played by the famous actor Oleg Tabakov – a star who appears late in the film and is immediately identified as a possible saviour for the children. When he sees Nikita, the spectator hears these words:

> Dear clients! On the second floor, there is a recreation room for children. During your shopping, you may leave your children in the care of experienced and qualified teachers and instructors who will keep them busy with educational games. […] Christmas. The happiest and most beloved holiday. On this day, all our parents and relatives, young and old, wait with pounding hearts for their Christmas gifts, the most wanted, surprising and ravishing gifts. On this day we all become kids again and hope to find under the Christmas tree the most secretly wished-for gifts that we had already lost hope to receive.

The older man leaves the supermarket and goes to his car, but then decides to return to the supermarket and help Nikita. The second part of the text is repeated by the announcer as the man makes his way back to the supermarket – but the message is only an advertisement. The announcement is misleading: the boy will not be magically rescued; the supermarket will not be the place where secret hopes become true, but the place where the children are definitely doomed: Alena is arrested and Nikita is robbed and thrown out into the cold.

The supermarket is by definition a space of post-Soviet society that did not exist before. Muratova thus emphasizes the drastic historical changes by inserting a sentence from a previous film in the soundtrack of the supermarket sequence: 'Cashier, don't check out the mutton' (*Kassa, baraninu ne vybivat'!*). It is a very specific and historically dated sentence: one could hear this kind of exclamation in Soviet stores, where each product first had to be paid for at the cashier, and then it could be collected after queuing at the corresponding counter. This sentence was intended to warn the cashier not to take money for an item already out of stock. In the supermarket of *Melody for Barrel Organ* this sentence is a playful allusion from the director, underlining its incongruity in this new space.[8]

And yet, in *Melody for a Barrel Organ*, the supermarket is the place of permanent disruption of social links. A group of 'nouveau riches' arrives there to play a thrilling game: the best thief wins. Later we discover that the game organizer pays for everything that they steal. But over five minutes, the spectator sees almost all the customers shoplifting with delectation and without any restraint. The impulse to hoard is represented by a woman who hides some of the stolen goods in her panties. This image of wild consumerism as a feature of post-Soviet society seems quite accurate, even in such an excessive representation.

When the editing brings us to the surveillance room, we discover that the store's detectives are asleep in front of the CCTV display. Even the institutionalized gaze through the surveillance cameras does not seem to form a link between social agents. Society as composed of separate blocks is the image that appears on the fragmented screen where several video displays appear in the same frame.

The sequence in the supermarket presents three different gazes: the images of static surveillance camera contrast with the constantly moving camera of the film itself; the director's gaze is filmed from a high angle, squashing the motley characters into the multicolour and multiform products of the setting. And later in the sequence a third gaze is introduced, when a surveillance specialist advertises to the supermarket manager a new surveillance method: 'There are cameras put up for show that give the visitor the impression of safety. He's under the impression that only a narrow strip is under surveillance, while the real points of surveillance remain thoroughly hidden. And we literally control all the space'. He then shows an example of the new appliance and this time the images appear much more cinematic than in the previous surveillance shots. The camera moves around and the editing brings us closer to the consumers' faces. The camera is thus on the level of Alena's starved face while she is eating stolen bread. The only one of the three gazes that can change the unravelling narration has serves to trap the heroine.

The two spaces of kommunalka and supermarket are much more than simple settings: they are symbolic spaces, producing a synthetic picture of society at a given period. The supermarket in *Melody* is much more significant than merely as a place of consumption. It becomes the space where the final disruption of the social contract takes place. The only possible interaction is competition or theft, attitudes that divide and take away. The only glances that are exchanged aim at surveillance. In this fairy-tale supermarket the children's tragic destiny will be sealed: the girl is arrested and the boy is thrown out and freezes to death.

The kommunalka described by Muratova reminds us of the definition given by Iakusheva (2007): '"Kommunalka" is associated with the market fair (*bazar*), the public bath, the railway station, thus becoming a synonym of generalized indifference and estrangement (despite the outward resemblance to a community), and also of shameless intrusion in private life'. While the spaces chosen by Muratova are historically typical of the given periods, the director's conclusion is almost the same: the conditions have changed from extreme dilapidation to excessive consumerism, but people are just as abandoned, disconnected and left to their own fate (no higher power, earthly or divine, to rescue them) as ever. A sense of decadence and an era coming to an end is present in both films.

In these two films the compositional and architectonic forms are interrelated: the compositional form is the choice of a diegetic space into which the film director crams characters from different social contexts and generations. The architectonic form is defined by a choice of space that gives a synthetic image of society.

Moreover, in both films Muratova comments on the relationship of this society with art. Significantly, there is a film theatre on the second floor of the supermarket. The fairy-tale voice invites the shoppers to make the most of the Christmas sale and attend the film *Two in One* by Kira Muratova that is screened on the second floor. The boy stands in front of a

Figure 12.5: Still from *Melody for a Barrel Organ*.

huge poster of the film. But none of the diegetic characters respond to the invitation; neither the poster nor the announcement captures their attention – and nothing will change in the children's fate. Muratova slips in here a bitter observation about the role of art in society, or rather about its total lack of impact.

In *Asthenic Syndrome*, a film screening also forms part of the plot: here the cinema is full, even though when the lights are back up, it transpires that nobody really watched the film. The theatre is emptied instantly while the presenter vainly tries to initiate a discussion about 'serious movies', quoting Muratova among other directors. In *Melody*, the situation is even more radical: the theatre and the film have been eliminated from the frame and exist only as a hint in the visual field and the soundtrack.

Muratova concludes that art has no power over society: it is like a passer-by, reflecting life in its own way. And vice versa, we could conclude that – while the social and economical changes influenced Muratova's films compositional form – they never really altered the architectonic form of her oeuvre and her uncompromising gaze on society around.

Works cited

Abdullaeva, Zara (2008), *Kira Muratova : iskusstvo kino*, Moscow: NLO.
Albéra, François (2005) 'Kira Muratova', in Piero Brunetta (ed), *Dizionario dei registi del cinema mondiale*, vol.2, Turin: Einaudi.

Bakhtin Mikhail (1924), 'Problema soderzhaniia, materiala i formy v slovesnom khudozhestvennom tvorchestve', quoted from the French translation 'Le problème du contenu, du matériau et de la forme dans l'œuvre littéraire (2006), in *Esthétique et théorie du roman*, Paris: Gallimard, pp. 23–39.

Beumers, Birgit (2009), *A History of Russian Cinema*, Oxford, New York: Berg.

Bollag Brenda and Ciment Michel (1988), 'Entretien avec Kira Mouratova', *Positif* (324).

Bozhovich Viktor (1988), *Kira Muratova, khudozhestvennyi portret*, Moscow: Gosudarstvennyi komitet SSSR po kinematografu, Soiuzinformkino.

—— (1992), 'Iz zhizni fantomov', *Iskusstvo kino* 7, pp. 14–17.

Bykov Dmitrii (1997), 'Ia ne koshka, chtoby liubit' liudei voobshche', interview with Kira Muratova, *Nedelia* 12. Cited from Bykov's page on *LiveJournal*, 9 April 2011, http://ru-bykov. livejournal.com/980096.html. Accessed 1 August 2012.

Iakusheva, Liudmila (2007), 'Ot real'nosti k znaku: kommunal'ka kak khudozhestvennyi obraz', in G. Sudakov (ed.), *Russkaia kul'tura novogo stoletia: Problemy izuchenia, sokhranenia i ispolzovania istoriko-kul'turnogo nasledia*, Vologda: Knizhnoe nasledie, pp. 676–682. Cited from http://www.booksite.ru/fulltext/suda/kov/7_07.htm. Accessed 1 August 2012.

Popov, Sergei (1989), 'Tupik?', interview with G. Riazanov and T. Khoroshilova, *Komsomol'skaia Pravda*, 12 October.

Rubinstein Lev (2000), 'Kommunal'noe chtivo', in *Domashnee muzitsirovanie*, Moscow: NLO, pp.135–142. http://www.kommunalka.spbru/cfm/bilingual_view.cfm?ClipID=731&TourID =0&Format=fromBooks. Accessed 27 August 2012.

Sandomirskaia, Irina (2008), 'A Glossolalic Glasnost and the Re-Tuning of the Soviet Subject: Sound Performance in Kira Muratova's *Asthenic Syndrome*, The Second Funeral of Stalin, Glasnost and Asthenia', *Studies in Russian and Soviet Cinema* 2.1, pp. 63–83.

Skradol', Natal'ia. (2011) "'Zhit' stalo veselee", stalinskaia chastushka i proizvodstvo "ideal'nogo sovetskogo sub"ekta"', *NLO* 108. http://magazines.russ.ru/nlo/2011/108/s14.html. Accessed 1 August 2012.

Slezkine Yuri (1994), 'The USSR as a Communal Apartment, or How a Socialist State Promoted Ethnic Particularism', *Slavic Review* 53.2, pp. 414–52.

Taboulay, Camille (1991), 'Entretien avec Kira Muratova', interview with Kira Muratova, *Cahiers du Cinéma* 442, p. 60.

Taubman Jane (1991), 'Kinematograf Kiry Muratovoi', interview with Kira Muratova, *Literaturovedcheskie teksty*, http://www.az.ru/women_cd1/html/preobrazh_2_1994_ge.htm# note4. Accessed 1 August 2010.

Taubman, Jane (2005), *Kira Muratova*, New York: IB Tauris.

Zvonkine, Eugenie (2012), *Kira Mouratova, un cinéma de la dissonance*, Lausanne: Age d'Homme.

Notes

1   Roman Balayan, born 15 April 1941 in Azerbaidjan, is a director of Armenian origin. His most famous film, *Polety vo sne i naiavu/Dream Flights* (1982), was produced at the Dovzhenko Studio in Kiev where Balayan has been working since 1969. Oleg Kohan produced his film

Raiskie ptitsy/Birds of Paradise (2009), so it is quite natural for him to group Balayan and Muratova together. Like Muratova, Balayan has worked in Ukraine, although he is not an ethnic Ukrainian.

2 Oleg Kohan, interview with the author, Kiev, 7 April 2009.

3 Anna Chmil, interview with the author, Kiev, 9 April 2009.

4 Many of Muratova's recent films have been co-produced by Russia and Ukraine.

5 Bozhovich was the first to write a book on Muratova (1988); however, he soon distanced himself from the new turn in her aesthetics (Bozhovich 1992: 14–17).

6 Oleg Kohan, the director of Sota Cinema Group, underlines that this percentage does not take into account publicity, festival promotion, distribution, etc. Interview with the author, Kiev, 7 April 2009.

7 Irina Sandomirskaia (2008) describes Muratova's infamously overwhelming soundtracks as a place of opposition between what the spectator is prepared to hear and what s/he really hears. The voices are then assimilated to the rest of the soundtrack that explores the contrast between the habit of the listener and the re-learning of listening.

8 This sentence is first pronounced in a completely different situation by a character of *Three Stories*, and Muratova also inserts it in the soundtrack of a supermarket sequence in *Nastroishchik/The Tuner* (2004).

Chapter 13

The Place of Action Must Not be Changed: Aleksei Balabanov's St Petersburg

Birgit Beumers

Peter the Great built the city on the marshland of the Neva as a 'window on Europe': a window for Russia to look upon Europe. Like a window that consists of a glass pane and a frame, the city is a plain surface and of little attraction as an object for the camera. Instead, it offers a view – onto the city through its glass pane. The camera thus forms a double lens: it captures the separating glass and thus distances the city from the spectator, while at the same time offering a superior, perfect view.

When Leningrad/St Petersburg makes one of its rare appearances in Soviet/Russian film, it is often an artificial, artistically created and framed image. It may be an identical copy or a mirror image of Moscow, as in El'dar Riazanov's *Ironiia sud'by/Irony of Fate* (1975); a city of drawn and painted monuments that has a stifling effect on its inhabitants, as in Nikita Mikhalkov's *Oblomov* (1980); a city with empty streets and a lifeless society made up of cardboard façades, as in Mikhalkov's *Oci cernye/Dark Eyes* (1987). Petersburg is an object for painting, a city of exquisite beauty too subtle to be photographed or filmed. It has never been shown as a bustling, lively place, but always as a façade, a window, a surface with no original content; such a message was brought home in a more profound sense in Aleksandr Sokurov's *Russkii kovcheg/Russian Ark* (2002), debating the originality of Russian art and culture. Exceptions are a some films from the early 1990s[1] and a few recent films, such as Aleksei Uchitel''s *Progulka/The Stroll* (2003) and Oksana Bychkova's *Piter FM* (2006) which show a city with a fast pace of life, not unlike Moscow, making it palatable to youth culture; or Igor' Voloshin's *Nirvana* (2008), uncovering the city's sub-culture. Despite a more frequent screen appearance of St Petersburg in the new millennium, even here the images refer to the past and re-create a city of the pre-Revolutionary era, as is the case in Aleksei German Jr's *Garpastum* (2005), or the phantasmagorical city of Joseph Brodsky's childhood in Andrei Khrzhanovskii's *Poltory komnaty/A Room and a Half* (2008). Playing both with the concept of Petersburg's role as a point of transition from one culture to another (Russia and Europe, Asia and Europe) and with the phantasmagorical aspects of the city is Iurii Mamin's *Okno v Parizh/Window on Paris* (1993), a late perestroika comedy about a schoolteacher who discovers a secret window in a communal apartment that offers at certain times access to a magic place: Paris. Once again, the image of St Petersburg serves as a template against which the ideal city – Paris – is drawn.

With its prominence and descriptions in nineteenth-century literary, especially Fedor Dostoevsky and Nikolai Gogol, however, St Petersburg carries another 'image': of a place between the real and unreal. With its extreme beauty and fine architecture, with its criminal backyards and courtyards, St Petersburg may have been a favoured location of writers, but not for film-makers; apart from the above films it has hardly featured as a contemporary location; instead, it has been shown as a city of an imagined past.

Against this backdrop, it is curious that most of Aleksei Balabanov's films are set in St Petersburg or contain at least an episode set in his adopted home town. Balabanov, originally from Sverdlovsk (Ekaterinburg), consistently returns St Petersburg to the screen. His films *Schastlivye dni/Happy Days* (1991), *Brat/Brother* (1997) and *Pro urodov i liudei/Of Freaks and Men* (1998) are not only set in Petersburg, but the city plays an active part in these films.[2] Yet instead of showing Petersburg as a live and real city, Balabanov favours settings in cemeteries and empty streets – uninhabited or uninhabitable spaces: 'Balabanov's Petersburg is typically unpopulated' (Day 2005: 613). Moreover, his view of Petersburg deprives the city of its monumentality, although he never strips it of its picturesque qualities; nor does it become 'humanized'. Where Jennifer Day has demonstrated the '*museumness*' aspect of the city (Day 2005: 623), I argue that Balabanov shows Petersburg in a way that neither elevates the city to an art object nor makes it a lively, bustling, inhabitable city: it appears like a chimera.

A characteristic feature that stretches across Balabanov's oeuvre is his concern with performativity. In each of his films he creates a world that is the opposite of the real: it is invented and fictional, it is the space for a performance, a playground for magic and imagined journeys, where locations only appear to be authentic, but follow in fact entirely the laws of the imagination: they are phantasmagorical, or playgrounds of the imagination. According to the Dutch scholar Johan Huizinga, play has no aim (unless it is a competition); thus play is infinite. The rules of the game allow for repetitions with alterations, like a chorus with a refrain. Play is based on the imagination and thereby offers a way to explore the unknown by turning reality into a play-world (not unlike the function of the fairy tale) with its own rules, which create order that is absent from the real world ruled by imperfection. By pretending finiteness (each game has a beginning and an end, yet repetitions are infinite), play pretends that a segment of reality (which is chaotic and infinite) is ordered and harmonious for a limited period within the rigid structures of play and within a limited and defined space. In the chaos of infinity, play allows the appropriation of the unknown by downsizing it: 'play is a voluntary activity or occupation executed within certain fixed limits of time and place, according to rules freely accepted but absolutely binding, having its aim in itself and accompanied by a feeling of tension, joy and the consciousness that it is "different" from "ordinary life"' (Huizinga 1949: 28).

For Balabanov, St Petersburg is a place that is unreal: a 'deserted stage set' (Day 2005: 620), it offers a ground for the creation of a second, alternative reality:[3] often a world of the dead, an unreal space, or what might be interpreted as a ninth-thrice state and the tenth-thrice land (the land of the dead) whence the fairy-tale hero travels to gain experience and mature. Indeed, a reference to fairy-tale structures is useful in reading the composition of Balabanov's films: the city then becomes the space for a journey of discovery, a playing field that allows the protagonist to create another reality that draws on literary and cultural traditions of the nineteenth century, which is most obvious in *Of Freaks and Men*, but also in the decadent world of *Happy Days*, and the criminal world of *Brother*.

I suggest here that Balabanov does not represent St Petersburg as a city, but a space that is like a ghost of the past, that bears traces of the dead, giving those who are willing to 'play' the freedom to create a new order. I demonstrate that Balabanov's use of the location St Petersburg never changes and propose that there is continuity in the diversity of Balabanov's films, made in the early post-Soviet years and towards the end of the twentieth century, and ranging from auteur to mainstream cinema and covering a range of genres, from action thriller to melodrama, as he explores the performative aspect of the location in his films.

Happy Days is loosely based on Samuel Beckett's play (1961) and follows a nameless man (played by Viktor Sukhorukov), who is given different names by different characters: Sergei Sergeevich, Peter or Boris. He cannot remember his name, having recently been discharged from hospital after a head injury, which seems to have caused his memory loss. He wanders around Petersburg in search of a room, and of his galoshes. He rents a room, but is kicked out by the landlord once he has paid the woman who appeared to be the landlady; then he stays with a blind man and his father in a basement; finally he follows the prostitute Anna and stays in her house. However, in all these cases he sooner or later abandons his accommodation to rest on a bench in the cemetery. Balabanov's Petersburg is a Gogolian city, where façades and staircases mask the poverty of its inhabitants. It is a city of ghosts, of the dead; a chimera.

In *Happy Days* the shots of Petersburg form a triple structural circle to the film. The first frame opens and closes the film: at the beginning and the end of the film a tram with open windows runs through a narrow street. This tram is a dysfunctional means of transport: as there is no life in the city, there are no passengers to transport. In the finale the tram stands as if drowning in a flooded street that has turned into a canal, alluding to the constant danger to which the city is exposed, which envisions a return of the city to the element of water (see Figure 13.1). Both sequences begin with real shots of the tram, freeze the image and turn it into a drawing, inverting the process of animation that we encounter for example in *Oblomov*, where the artistic image is animated. For Balabanov, Petersburg is a real city in the first instance, which he then depicts in an artistic medium, rather than – as for Mikhalkov – an artistic impression that is filled with life.

From this opening follows an aerial view onto a square and a street (at the end it precedes this sequence): the second frame offers an aerial view of the city almost as if it had been drawn, pointing at the artificial quality of the real space (both in terms of camera perspective – the crane shot – and in terms of the time when the film is set), like in Baz Luhrman's images of Paris in *Moulin Rouge!* (2001). Balabanov thus comments in the first instance on the nature of the city as a living organism, before pointing at its picturesque, almost artificial qualities. These sequences are underlined by jazz music.

The third frame is formed by a scene of the tram passing through an empty street. In the beginning the landlady of the first flat (the 'tatarka') sees Viktor in the tram, runs after the tram

Figure 13.1: Still from *Happy Days.*

and collapses in the street; at the end Sergei Sergeevich sees her in the tram and the scene is repeated with the roles reversed. Once human beings are entrapped in the narrow and empty streets, the atmosphere becomes tragic and a Wagnerian score accompanies the scenes.

The tram possesses connectivity, but it has neither a destination nor the potential for circularity in its movement: it never returns characters to their point of departure. The tram follows, it seems, an open-ended line. The tram is dysfunctional, the streets empty. The city alienates its inhabitants: the façades bear no human features, the streets offer no perspective, and the panning and aerial shots are reserved for the artificial eye (the camera) and therefore present the city as if it were 'drawn'. Finally, the tram alienates characters and separates them from each other; it symbolizes for Balabanov the concepts of isolation and separation. The tram runs through the empty streets of St Petersburg in a ghost-like fashion, offering merely another frame (with its wide window frame) through which the streets can be viewed: 'the frame of the car mimics a strip of film, and we see the unrolling cityscape in the process of being encoded as art' (Day 2005: 617).

Indeed, the view through the window is crucial in a number of scenes. Often the empty streets are viewed through windows. Sergei Sergeevich looks several times onto people's domestic life through a window. Inside the houses with their pompous staircases reigns sexual exploitation (the woman in the transparent blouse with her little husband; Anna's prostitution; the man, who is also Sergei Sergeevich, beating the 'tatarka'). The façades disguise the perversion and vulgarity of city life.

Windows are far from offering a view onto a pleasant location. Instead, they are separators that exclude characters from domestic life, that protect Sergei Sergeevich from the items thrown at his window when Anna refuses to receive her 'clients', that tear apart those who wish to communicate (the tram). The window is thus an obstructive/protective pane of glass, a frame for perversities better hidden behind walls. The camera hardly ever offers a perspective of the streets, but mostly views the buildings on eye-level. Instead, it captures the arches to courtyards, windows and doorways which shows glimpses of a different space and a different life. One such view through a window offers a crystal image of Sergei's hopes: he sees a man conducting the Wagner tune that accompanies all sequences featuring Petersburg, while a tall statuette of a ballerina turns round (the little figurine of Sergei's music box). This image is an external and enlarged realization of the dream contained in the music box: the tune originates from a visible source, the figurine represents the longing for beauty, and the room is brightly lit (as opposed to streets).

A second important space in Balabanov's Petersburg is the cemetery: a place where the dead are buried and remembered by monuments and tombs. Anna visits her ancestors' remains in a little private chapel; other graves are encircled by fences as if they were 'homes'. Balabanov's focus on the monuments for the dead is contrasted with the architectural monuments of Petersburg that overwhelm the frame from the background and twice feature in aerial shots. The city itself is a monument to history, not a living space. The railings protect architectural treasures as well as monuments to the dead. Balabanov draws a direct parallel between the historical monuments of the city and the gravestones on the cemetery: he creates 'a necropolis-museum of empty streets, half-ruined buildings, and cold cemeteries' (Day 2005: 615). He differentiates, though, between monuments that bear a connection to life (the graves on the cemetery) and the ghost-like spaces of the inner city, as well as the monuments designed to make the city and its rulers immortal.

Sergei often visits the cemetery, as this seems to be a livelier place than the streets: here he meets the blind man with the donkey and the prostitute Anna, who both offer temporary shelter. Anna lives in a derelict music hall with an apartment for which she cannot pay electricity. A former aristocrat of German lineage (von Storch), she earns her living as a prostitute. The outcasts of the city find 'common ground' on the cemetery, where they are all equal, a feature that Balabanov would also use in *Brother*.

Petersburg is also a city full of beggars and criminals: Sergei Sergeevich roams the streets in search of shelter and galoshes (his were stolen by Sergei Sergeevich). He abducts the donkey from the blind man and abuses it as a carrier; then he tries to rob a drunkard of his galoshes. The crime theme would be developed, of course, in *Brother*.

With his shots of the city Balabanov creates frames, both structurally (the triple frame at beginning and end) and visually (window, frame and camera). These frames are void of content. Instead of creating a 'window' with a view or a frame to be filled with content, Balabanov empties the frame and removes even its glass pane (its ability to reflect). The façades cover – rather feebly – the vulgarity and *poshlost'* of Petersburg life, which itself is a farce. There are numerous illogicalities and inconsistencies in the narrative (if indeed there is one), and the film contains elements of slapstick and grotesque. Life is void of content, and all arrangements are temporary: rest can only be found in the cemetery, which is Sergei's favourite place. It corresponds most to the absence of content and meaning in 'real' life. Not unlike Sokurov, Balabanov offers the frame as a device that allows the creation of new, artificial images: 'the frame [at the end of *Russian Ark*] remains empty, reflecting the murky grey waters of the Neva (in a digitally mastered image, not a nature shot). This is Sokurov's own empty frame, in which the images of the past can be re-hung and reinstated: they can be returned to the frames from which they were removed during the war' (Beumers 2011: 176–87).

Where Day has argued that 'the glass of the museum case becomes the lens of the camera, and the gaze of the museum visitor becomes an act of voyeurism (Day 2005: 621), I would suggest a slightly different reading: if for Balabanov Petersburg is a frame containing no meaning, then the window becomes not a device for viewing, but a means of disguise and disclosure simultaneously: it pretends to hide a hideous reality, and to make a statement about emptiness in the absence of the glass pane. The empty frame implies that the canvas with the picturesque component has been removed, and there is nothing to be seen.

Brother is Balabanov's next film set in Petersburg, moving to the contemporary city. Yet Balabanov sticks with his favourite locations: the streets, courtyards, trams, bridges and the cemetery. Danila Bagrov arrives from the provinces in the city on a train, in a scene quite reminiscent of Balabanov's short film 'Trofim' for *Pribytie poezda/Arrival of a Train* (1996). Danila leaves the station and walks around the city, looking at the sights: the streets, the canals, the Bronze Horseman, the rostrums, the Isaak's Cathedral. Again, Balabanov's (rather than cameraman Sergei Astakhov's) camera never reaches above the eye-level, so we never see the roofs of buildings, the spires or the sky (see Figure 13.2). Balabanov's Petersburg is a place that denies overview; it is never seen from above, from the air.

Figure 13.2: Danila Bagrov 'visits' Kazan Cathedral in St Petersburg. Still from *Brother.*

The 'German' Hoffman takes Danila to his 'home', the Lutheran cemetery: the cemetery is Hoffman's 'rodina', where his ancestors rest. The German workforce that was drawn to Petersburg during the reigns of Peter the Great and Catherine the Great is no longer needed in the contemporary city: these great-great-grand-children of German origin are orphaned, isolated, lonely and deprived of social status. Bagrov has a lot of compassion for those on the margins of society. Danila listens to Hoffman's deliberations, and joins the 'inhabitants' of the cemetery who later help him bury the bodies of the men he shot, and whom he provides with food and drink. Hoffman comments that the city is a 'huge force' that takes energy away from the weak (like himself), but it strengthens those who are strong, like Danila.

The centre of Petersburg is depicted as a bustling shopping centre with McDonalds restaurants, Littlewoods and other western shops, as well as clubs. The street markets, both the *veshchevoi rynok* (selling things) in the street where Hoffman trades and the vegetable and fruit market where the Chechen is shot, are controlled by the mafia, and both form a contrast to these western shopping centres. People live not in the centre, but in the Primorsk region with its 1970's blocks of flats on the shore to the Baltic Sea. It is here that Danila rents an apartment; that the murder of some 'gangsters' takes place; that Danila meets Slava Butusov; and that he himself is shot at, but protected by the CD player.

The tram features for the first time as a means of transport when Danila collects a fine from a Caucasian 'black-assed worm' (*gnida chernozhopaia*): the space of the tram is taken up by people who have no right to it. Another tram, not an ordinary one, but an empty car which serves only to transport cargo or check the tracks, rescues Danila when he is on the run after having been shot in the stomach. The tram is driven by Svetlana, who protects Danila by not disclosing his whereabouts. Later a man stands on the rails with the tram approaching (not leaving, as in *Happy Days*) so that Krugly can enter the tram and quiz Svetlana over Danila's disappearance. Before his departure from Petersburg, Danila catches a final glimpse of the bridges over the Neva and watches a tram run over the bridge, offering a frame for the view on Petersburg and St Isaak's Cathedral (see Figure 13.3). It is his farewell to the city, and the end of his love affair with the tram driver. Trams run through the city with no apparent function or destination; they seem to run because the tracks are there. They provide an aperture, a window on to the city's artificial skyline, making it an object rather than a living organic conglomerate.

The fairy-tale structure applies to both *Brother* films (1997, 2000), where an Ivan-the-Fool figure (Danila) ventures into an unknown space: Danila comes to Petersburg, passes the various tests he is set and as a reward returns not back home, but to the capital; in the sequel he gets his princess (Dasha) as a reward, and returns again not home, but to Moscow. In both *Brother* films a connection is made to the fantasy genre, yet here no ghosts from the past are resurrected: unlike in post-Soviet culture where reference is made to the past that is different and 'Other' and from which the present needs to be cut off (see Beumers 2012, Nemchenko 2009), the present appears to be protected by the past and cemeteries are places of refuge.

Figure 13.3: The tram in St Petersburg. Still from *Brother*.

Pro urodov i liudei/Of Freaks and Men (1998) follows a similar structure as *Happy Days*: the film begins and ends with a sequence of Johann looking upon the Neva. At the beginning this sequence is shot in black and white, at the end in sepia tones. The locations of the film are houses with elaborately decorated staircases, a park and a cemetery. Yet the focus is more on three means of transport: the train, the tram and the boat, which all serve to conquer the city. The representation of the city in sepia shades, along with costumes and interiors, has clearly influenced the visual representation of the decadent Petersburg life of the pre-Revolutionary era in Aleksei German's *Garpastum* (2006), similarly dwelling on the eroticism hidden beneath the surface and suppressed under the elegance and décor of the period.

A train's steam engines are recharged outside Radlov's house and it features several times throughout the film, usually seen from the window of Radlov's study. The charging with steam represents the release of (sexual) energy, but the train is also acknowledged as a means of transport to escape from this world. The first time the train is seen Radlov promises Liza that they will travel to the West; this promise never comes true. The train is a novelty, a symbol, but never a means of transport, and as such it continues the (dys)function of the tram in Balabanov's earlier films.

The boat features twice as a means of transport: first when Johann triumphantly travels to Radlov to ask for Liza's hand – and is refused. The journey takes him through the canals onto the Neva, standing in the front of the boat with a bouquet of white lillies, as if travelling to a funeral. Ultimately, this is what his trip becomes: the 'funeral' of his aspirations to marry into a well-off and reputable family. Second, the excursion is repeated in exactly the same sequence, but with Viktor Ivanovich at the head of the formation in the boat as he is on his way to seduce Katerina Stasova. His aspirations are not disappointed, and he seems to carry the flowers to place on Katerina's 'coffin' (if we see his seduction as her ultimate death). The journey on the boat never offers a glimpse of the buildings above the eyeline until it enters the Neva, when the camera opens up for a panning shot of the cityscape. The tram features in a similar fashion to the boat, when the photographer Putinov, Viktor and Johann travel to Radlov's house to inaugurate the movie camera, forcing, on this occasion, Liza to pose for the lens. All three triumphant journeys are thus wonderfully arranged and choreographed processions that end in seduction, accompanied by the – parodically – triumphant music of Prokofiev's *Romeo and Juliet*. The streets and courtyards and canals are narrow and suffocate; only the river offers a perspective and a wider view with air and space. The final shot repeats the arrival sequence of Johann in the city: he departs by stepping onto an ice-floe that floats from Lake Ladoga down the Neva into the Baltic Sea in the late spring (see Figure 13.4): Johann too travels to the 'West'.

Petersburg in *Of Freaks and Men* is ghostlike and dead, with empty streets. There are hardly ever any people around when characters run along the streets. The city is beautiful when void of life, and therefore its beauty lies in life frozen, in other words death. Hence also Balabanov's preoccupation with cemeteries as a space of individual memory, and therefore life.

Freaks also explores the medium of the camera for exploitation and the creation of pornographic films rather than for artistic purposes. It thus dismantles the illusion of the medium of film as an artistic invention and underlines its commercial aspect. St Petersburg here features as a filter rather than an object of film and the camera. However, only this beautiful filter is capable of covering the underlying vulgarity and decadence. Petersburg

Figure 13.4: Johann on the ice floe. Still from *Of Freaks and Men*.

241

is a place where the drawing rooms form the setting for pornographic and sadomasochistic activities. The journey of Putilov, Johann and Viktor to their respective seductions by tram and boat is aesthetic and stylish in its performance, but vulgar in content. In this sense, Balabanov uses the camera to beautify the vulgar content behind the neutral façades. The fact that *Brother 2* and *War* are not set in Petersburg may serve partly as an explanation for their more commercial and less artistic value.

Balabanov's Petersburg is a city seen through a frame and a lens; it is an object void of living features, a beautiful façade that covers absences, vulgarity and crime. It is a frame without the canvas. Surprisingly, Balabanov's view tallies in a way with that presented in Sokurov's recent film, *Russian Ark*. The door or window that opens onto the Petersburg of the present at the end of *Russian Ark* offers a view from the past that makes the present look dull and uninteresting, void of colour and content. The lens of Sokurov's camera may be able to capture and glorify the past, but it is unable to extract any meaning from the city of St Petersburg today. Sokurov's Petersburg is thus an empty frame, like that of Balabanov's. Both film-makers refrain from bright colours in their depiction of the contemporary city, using largely grey shades (if they use colour at all). Thus, Balabanov's image of St Petersburg is an empty, grey frame, the colourful canvas of which has been lost. For Balabanov, the canvas is missing because of the artificiality of the city; for Sokurov, it is lost with European traditions.

The numerous monuments make Petersburg attractive for the tourist, but the city appears as an alien place to its inhabitants. The cemetery and the flat near Primorskaya are filled with life, but both are spaces on the outskirts of the centre. Correspondingly, Viktor's flat in the centre is a place where people die, Svetlana's centre flat is a place of violence and racketeering, and the flat where Danila rents a room to hide and prepare for the killing is inhabited by a drunkard. Life is not in the centre, but on the periphery; it is not in the apartments but on the cemetery, while it is in living spaces that people get shot. The cemetery contains human history, not that of officialdom and rule.

Thus, Balabanov's image of St Petersburg is an empty, grey frame, the colourful canvas of which has been lost. For Balabanov, the canvas is missing because of the artificiality of the city: the city is not portrayed or painted, but shown as 'undressed'. Balabanov challenges the centrality of St Petersburg and shows an empty centre, focusing instead on outskirts and emptied streets in an attempt to suggest a move from centre to periphery, and with it the increasing marginalisation of social groups formerly belonging to the centre. Balabanov's oeuvre thus offers a diagnosis of social, political and artistic developments of Russian cinema at the end of the twentieth century.

St Petersburg is a ghost city, a chimera, as is evident from the final frames of Sokurov's *Russian Ark*: shadows, decadence and decay lie behind decorum and ornaments. Like Audrey Beardsley, Balabanov's beautiful façades and streets hide shocking crimes. Balabanov has no nostalgia for that turn of the nineteenth to the twentieth century: he makes no attempt to revive the past, but declares dead that Petersburg of the past and opens the empty frame for new interpretations, meanings and images – of the present.

Works cited

Beumers, Birgit (1999), 'To Moscow! To Moscow? The Russian Hero and the Loss of the Centre' in Beumers (ed.), *Russia on Reels: The Russian Idea in Post-Soviet Cinema*, London: I.B. Tauris, pp. 76–87.

—— (2011), 'And the Ark Sails on…', in Beumers and Condee (eds), *The Cinema of Alexander Sokurov*, London: I.B. Tauris, pp. 176–187.

—— (2012), 'National Identities through Visions of the Past: Contemporary Russian Cinema', in Mark Bassin and Catriona Kelly (eds), *Soviet and Post-Soviet Identities*, Cambridge: Cambridge University Press, pp. 120–153.

Condee, Nancy (2011), 'Stoker' *Kinokultura* 32 (2011), http://www.kinokultura.com/2011/32r-kochegar.shtml. Accessed 10 January 2012.

Day, Jennifer J. (2005), 'Strange Spaces: Balabanov and the Petersburg Text', *Slavic and East European Journal* 49.4, pp. 612–624.

Graham, Seth (ed.) (2001), *Necrorealism: Contexts, History and Interpretations*, Pittsburgh: Russian Film Symposium.

Huizinga, Johan (1949), *Homo Ludens*, London: Routledge and Kegan.

Nemchenko, Liliia (2009), 'Traditsii sovetskogo poeticheskogo kinematografa v postsovetskom kino', in N. Kupina and O. Mikhailova (eds), *Sovetskoe proshloe i kul'tura nastoiashchego*, 2 vols, Ekaterinburg: Izdatel'stvo Ural'skogo universiteta, vol. 1, pp. 87–100.

Notes

1   Igor' Alimpiev's *Pantsir'/Shell* (1990), Iurii Mamin's *Okno v Parizh/Window on Paris* (1993), Dmitrii Meskhiev's *Nad temnoi vodoi/Over Dark Waters* (1993), Ivan Dykhovichnyi's *Muzyka dlia dekabria/Music for December* (1995), Dmitrii Svetozarov's *14 tsvetov radugi/Fourteen Colours of the Rainbow* (2000), Andrei Nekrasov's *Liubov' i drugie koshmary/Love and Other Nightmares* (2001), Andrei Razenkov's *Severnoe siianie/Aurora Borealis* (2001); also (partly) set in St Petersburg are Balabanov's *Mne ne bol'no/It doesn't Hurt* (2006), *Kochegar/The Stoker* (2010), and *Ia tozhe khochu/Me Too* (2012).

2   For a discussion of the Petersburg text in these films, see Day (2005).

3   Balabanov adopts a similar approach to music, which functions as a permanent counterpoint to the film's narrative. See, for example, Condee 2011; Beumers 1999.

Index

Bold page numbers indicate illustrations. References in endnotes are marked with 'n'. Titles are followed by author, or in the case of films, directors (dir.)

12 (dir. Mikhalkov), 167
12 Angry Men (dir. Lumet), 167
17 Moments of Spring, see Seventeen Moments of Spring
1962 (Arkhangelskii), 20
23,000 (Sorokin), 33
55 (dir. Mikhalkov), **168**

A
abject, 5, 50, 54–58
Abraham, F. Murray, 210
Abrikosov, Aleksei, 121, 127
Afghan War, 139
Afrika, see Bugaev
Akhmatova, Anna, 33, 77n
Akunin, Boris, 6, 67, 70
Akvarium, 97n
Alexander II, 19
Alexander III, 19
Alimpiev, Igor', 243n
Allen, Woody, 181
Alliluyeva, Nadezhda, 208
Andropov, Iurii, 161, 164, 165, 166
Anufriev, Sergei, 91
Apollo, Apollonian, 104, 106, 109, 110, 112
Arkhangelskii, Aleksandr, 20
Arrival of a Train, The (film almanac), 238
ASSA (dir. Solov'ev), 83, 84
Astakhov, Sergei, 238
Asthenic Syndrome (dir. Muratova), 218–25, (**218, 222**), 228

Asystole (Pavlov), 20
avant-garde, avant-gardist, 31, 32, 34, 85, 86, 87, 89, 92, 96, 98n, 102, 103, 106, 115, 125, 128, 206

B
Babaev Factory, 121, 123, 125–28, 130n
Babylon, see Generation 'P'
Bakhtin, Mikhail, 39, 54, 55, 57, 62n, 63n, 219
Bakuradze, Bakur, 44n
Balabanov, Aleksei, 8, 32, 194n, 234–42, 243n
Balayan, Roman, 217, 229n
Bambochada (Vaginov), 122
Barbey d'Aurevilly, Jules Amédée, 110
Baudelaire, Charles, 108
Baudrillard, Jean, 53
Beardsley, Audrey, 5, 242
Beckett, Samuel, 235
Beliaev-Gintovt, Aleksei, 7, 103–15 (**105, 108, 111, 113**)
Belle Epoque, 129
Benigsen, Vsevolod, 20
Berezovskii, Boris, 38, 68, 69, 71
Beuys, Joseph, 98n
Bildungsroman, 41
Blizzard (Sorokin), 37, 39
Blue Lard (Sorokin), 33
Blue Nights (TV serial), 16
Blue Noses, 39
Bolotnaia Square, 5
Bolshevik, 122, 169

Bond, James, 166
Bourdieu, Pierre, 144
Boym, Svetlana, 86, 87, 88
Brecht, Bertolt, 204
Brezhnev, Leonid, 15, 49, 68, 75n, 135, 161,
  162, 164, 165, 166, 198, 211
Bro (Sorokin), 33
Brodsky, Joseph, 33, 38, 233
Brother (dir. Balabanov), 183, 234, 235,
  238–9 (**238, 240**)
Brother 2 (dir. Balabanov), 32, 242
Brothers Karamazov, The (Dostoevsky), 122
Buddha's Little Finger, see *Chapaev and Voyd*
Bugaev, Sergei (aka Afrika), 4, 7, 83–92, (**84, 85,**
  89), 94, 95, 96, 97n,
Bulgakov, Mikhail, 17
Bummer (dir. Buslov), 178
Buslov, Petr, 36, 178
Butusov, Slava, 239
Bychkova, Oksana, 233
Bykov, Dmitrii, 6, 17, 19, 26n, 33, 67, 70, 72,
  75n, 76n

C
Cage, John, **84, 85**
carnival, canivalesque, 50, 54–58, 62n,
  63n, 103
Cartoons (Elizarov), 20
Cathedral of Christ the Saviour, 5
Catherine the Great (Catherine II), 83, 94,
  144, 239
Chapaev and Voyd (Pelevin), 40, 49, 50, 54,
  58–60,
Chaplin, Charlie, 83
chastushka, 221, 222
Chekhov, Anton, 17, 50, 122, 181
Cherry Orchard, The (Chekhov), 181
Children of the Arbat (dir. Eshpai,
  TV serial), 16
Chizhova, Elena, 26n
Chmil, Anna, 217
Christened with Crosses (Kochergin), 20
Christo, 192

Civil War, 15, 35, 86, 121
Cizevsky, Dmitry, 31
Clay Machine Gun, The,, see *Chapaev
  and Voyd*
Cold War, 198, 208, 210
collectivization, 15, 121
commemoration, 7, 133–47
communal flat (*kommunalka*), 223, 224,
  227, 233
communism, 3, 49, 56, 89, 91, 92, 112, 157,
  198, 208
conceptualism, conceptualist, 39, 53, 101
cosmism, 5, 27n, 101–118
Crime and Punishment (Dostoevsky), 181
Crush (film almanac), 36
Curtis, Tony, 93

D
dandyism, 7, 102–15
Dark Eyes (dir. Mikhalkov), 233
Day of the Oprichnik (Sorokin), 39
decadence, decadent, 3–6, 109, 110, 205, 206,
  227, 235, 240, 241, 242
Derrida, Jacques, 84, 88, 89
de-Stalinization, 37
Dima, the Robin, and Dad's Boots
  (dir. Tsukerman), 199
Dionysus, Dionysian, 106, 109, 112
dissidence, dissident, 16, 20, 22, 166
Donald Duck, 89, 90
Dorenko, Sergei, 70, 76n
Dostoevsky, Fedor, 122, 178, 181, 188, 233
Dovlatov, Sergei, 41
Drawing Lessons (Kantor), 21
Dugin, Aleksandr 103, 109
Duma, 70, 184, 188
Dykhovichnyi, Ivan, 243n

E
Einem, Ferdinand Theo von, 121, 124
Eisenstein, Sergei, 32, 39, 204
Elena (dir. Zviagintsev), 7, 177–82, (**180**),
  183, 185–88

Elizarov, Mikhail, 20

Eltang, Lena, 37

empire, 21, 22, 24, 85, 88, 102–5, 117n, 118n, 140

    Soviet Empire, 3, 85, 88

    Eurasian Empire, 112–3

    imperial, 3, 4, 7, 15, 19, 20, 21, 23, 27n, 70, 102–14, 123, 209, 217

Empire Style, 102, 126

Empire V (Pelevin), 60

Erenburg, Ilya, 38

Ernst, Konstantin, 70

Erofeev, Andrei, 189

Erofeev, Venedikt, 39, 45n

Etkind, Alexander, 17

Eurasianism, Eurasian, 7, 101–18

Evola, Julius, 102, 109

Evtushenko, Evgenii, 34

F

fairy tale, 157, 164, 219, 220, 225, 227, 234, 239

Fedorchenko, Aleksei, 33, 42, 44n

Fedorov, Nikolai, 114

Fellini, Federico, 208

First Channel (Channel One), 36, 70, 160

First Commando (Shprits, Klimov), 20

First Commando, The Truth (Starobinets), 20

First on the Moon (dir. Fedorchenko), 33

Flaubert, Gustave, 122

Fomin, Oleg, 164, 165

Fortress of Doubt (Utkin), 21

Foundation Pit (Platonov), 34

FSB (Federal Security Bureau), 22, 117n, 164, 190

FSB (Front of Quiet Prosperity), 104, 106

Fukuyama, Francis, 198

G

Gaidai, Leonid, 34

Gai-Germanika, Valeriia, 44n

Garpastum (dir. German), 233, 240

Gasparov, Boris, 31

Gazzara, Ben, 207

GenAcide (Benigsen), 20

Generation 'P' (Pelevin), 7, 33, 49, 50–58, 59, 61, 67, 68

Genis, Alexander, 53

George, Stefan, 110

German, Aleksei Jr, 36, 233, 240

German, Aleksei Sr , 40, 41, 218

Gesamtkunstwerk, 38

glamorization, 4, 16

Gogol', Nikolai, 122, 233, 235

Gol'dshtein, Aleksandr, 44n

Gorbachev, Mikhail, 164, 223

Govorukhin, Stanislav, 162, 163, 177, 182–88, 189

Grand Style, 103, 104

Great Patriotic War (see also WWII), 90, 139, 141, 183

Grebenshchikov, Boris, 97n

Griazev, Andrei, 5

Grishkovets, Evgenii, 33

Gromovs, The (dir. Baranov, TV serial), 16

Guattari, Felix, 84, 87

Gudkov, Lev, 3

Guevara, Che, 56, 190

Gulag , 17, 38, 40, 41, 224

Gumilev, Nikolai, 109

Gusinskii, Vladimir, 69

H

Happy Days (dir. Balabanov), 234–38 (**236**), 239

Happy Moscow (Platonov), 34

Hard-Hearted, The (dir. Mizgirev), 41

Hartley, Marsden, 110

Heat of Cold Numbers, The (dir. Tsukerman), 199

Help Gone Mad (dir. Khlebnikov), 41

Hero of Our Time, A (Lermontov), 160

Hipsters (dir. V. Todorovskii), 17

Hollywood, 160, 169, 188, 206

homo zapiens, 51, 52, 67–74

How I Ended this Summer (dir. Popogrebskii), 37, 41
Huizinga, Johan, 234
Huysmans, Joris-Karl, 110

I

I Believe in Spring (dir. Tsukerman), 198
Ice (Sorokin), 33
Ice Trilogy (Sorokin), 33, 39
Il'f, Il'ia and Petrov, Evgenii, 38
imper-art , 7, 102–115
In the First Circle (dir. Panfilov, TV serial), 16
intelligentsia, 5, 39, 56, 197, 208
Internet , 15, 17, 34, 75n, 190
Iron Curtain, 84
Irony of Fate (dir. Riazanov), 233
Isaev (dir. Ursuliak) , 36
Iskander, Fazil', 38, 45n
Ivan the Terrible (dir. Eisenstein), 39, 204

J

Jünger, Ernst, 104, 105, 109, 110, 113

K

Kabakov, Ilya, 53
Kalik, Mikhail, 213n
Kantor, Maksim, 21
Karamzin, Nikolai , 206
Kedrov, Bonifatii, 200, 213n
KGB (Committee for State Security), 157–71
KGB in Dinner Jackets, The (dir. Fomin, TV serial), 164, **165**, 166
Khamatova, Chulpan, 4
Kharitonov, Evgenii, 40, 45n
Khlebnikov, Boris, 36, 41, 44n
Kholin, Igor', 45n
Khrushchev, Nikita, 15
Khrustalev, My Car! (dir. German), 40
Khrzhanovskii, Andrei, 33, 233
Kino, 85
Kiss Not for the Press, A (dir. Zhulina), 7, 157–71 (**158, 170**)
Klimov, Aleksei, 20

Knabe, Georgii, 32
Kochergin, Eduard, 20, 26n
Kohan, Oleg, 217, 229n, 230n
Kolyma Tales (Shalamov), 40
Komar, Vitalii, 62n, 85, 86
Komsomol , 142, 164
Konfael' (chocolate), 124
Korkunov (chocolate), 124
Kosorukov, Gleb, 104
Kott, Aleksandr, 160, 161
Krasnyi Oktiabr' (factory), 121, 123, 127, 128, 130n
Kristeva, Julia, 5, 54, 55, 57
Kulik, Oleg, 38
Kundera, Milan, 208
Kurekhin, Sergei, 85

L

LaCapra, Dominique, 35–37
Larionov, Mikhail, 84
Lemmon, Jack, 93
Lenin, Vladimir, 15, 55, 83, 88, 89, 90, 94, 112, 114, 139, 212n
Lenov. G. and E. , 121, 128
Leonov, Leonid, 17
Leont'ev, Konstantin, 109
Lermontov, Mikhail, 160
Letter-Book (Shishkin), 34
Levine, Sherrie, 85, 95
Levkin, Andrei, 44n
Librarian, The (Elizarov), 20
Life of Insects, The (Pelevin), 60
Likhachev, Dmitrii, 32
Line-by-line Translation (Lungina), 20
Liquid Sky (dir. Tsukerman), 197, 202–8, (**203, 205**), 210
Liquidation (dir. Ursuliak, TV serial), **163**, 164
Lissitzky, El, 85–87, 89, 96
Litvinova, Renata, 225
Live Souls (Bykov), 33
Long Farewells (dir. Muratova), 219
Loznitsa, Sergei, 37, 44n
Luhrman, Baz, 235

Lumet, Sidney, 167
Lungina, Liliana, 20
Luzhkov, Iurii, 70

M
Maiakovskii, Vladimir, 86, 213n
Malevich, Kazimir, 86, 87
Mamin, Iurii, 233, 243n
Mamyshev-Monroe, Vladislav, 7, 39, 83,
    92–96 (**93**), 97n, 98n
Mann, Otto, 110
Marxist-Leninist, 199, 200
Mashkov, Vladimir, 163, 164
Master and Margarita, The (Bulgakov), 200
Match Point (dir. Allen), 181
Matlin, Vladimir, 199, 212n, 213n
Mazin, Viktor, 88
Media Sapiens (Minaev), 67, 71
Medvedev, Roy, 159, 160
Medvedkin, Aleksandr, 112
Meeting Place Cannot be Changed (dir.
    Govorukhin), 162, 163, 164
Melamid, Aleksandr, 62n, 85, 86
Melody for a Barrel Organ (dir. Muratova),
    220, 224–27 (**224, 225, 228**),
memorabilia, 83, 88
Menippea, Menippean, 39, 40, 45n
Meskhiev, Dmitrii, 243n
Mikhalkov, Nikita, 4, 33, 159, 167, 168, 169,
    171, 233, 235
Mikoyan, Anastas, 121, 125
Minaev, Sergei, 4, 6, 67, 71, 74
minimalism, 4, 40, 51, 52, 58,
Mironov, Evgenii, 4
Mit'kova, Tat'iana, 77n
Mizgirev, Aleksei, 41, 44n
Miziano, Victor, 101
modernism, modernist, 31, 32, 33, 34, 87,
    95, 96
Mokritskii, Sergei, 5
Molodkin, Andrei, 104, **105**
Monroe, Marilyn, 7, 93, 94, 95
Morimura, Yasumasa, 98n

Moscow Doesn't Answer (dir. Tsukerman),
    201, 202, 206, 210
Moscow Saga (dir. Barshchevskii, TV serial),
    16
Moscow to the End of the Line (Erofeev), 39
Moulin Rouge! (dir. Luhrman), 235
Mr Hexogen (Prokhanov), 67, 69, 114
Mukhina, Vera, **91**
Muratova, Kira, 8, 34, 40, 217–28
Museum of Applied Arts (MAK), Vienna, 83,
    88, 90
Museum of Architecture, Moscow, 3, 9n
My Joy (dir. Loznitsa), 37

N
Nabokov, Vladimir, 34
Nekrasov, Andrei, 243n
Neo-Academicians, 105, 109
Nestlé, 124, 125
New Drama, 4, 32, 34, 35, 36, 37, 41
New Economic Policy (NEP), 121, 123
Neznaika, 90, 98n
Nietzsche, Friedrich, 109
Night for Reflections, A (dir. Tsukerman),
    199, 200, 201, 202, 204, 206, 207,
    208, 210
Nirvana (dir. Voloshin), 233
NKVD (People's Commissariat of Internal
    Affairs), 166, 174n
non-conformism, non-conformist, 37, 42, 84,
    89, 101, 201, 208
nostalgia, 4, 6, 16, 18, 19, 20, 26n, 27n, 61, 86,
    87, 96, 101, 107, 166, 209, 221, 242,
Novikov, Timur, 84, 94, 98n, 103
NTV (television channel), 69, 73, 76n, 77n

O
Oblomov (dir. Mikhalkov), 233, 235
Of Freaks and Men (dir. Balabanov), 234,
    235, 240–42 (**241**)
Okudzhava, Bulat, 17, 34
Old Songs about the Main Thing
    (TV show), 35

Omon Ra (Pelevin), 60
Orlova, Liubov', 7, 83, 95
orthodox, 6, 101, 118n, 138, 168, 202
Ostankino, 72, 77n

P
Palace of Soviets, 112
Parfenov, Leonid, 18, 26n
Parshchikov, Aleksei, 38
Pasternak, Boris, 17, 33, 63n, 77n
patriotism, 16, 101, 110, 161, 162, 166,
    169, 171
Pavlov, Oleg, 20
Pavlovskii, Gleb, 71
Pelevin, Victor, 6, 7, 33, 39, 49–63, 67, 68, 69,
    70, 74
Peppershtein, Pavel, 45n
Pepsi, 49, 56, 57
perestroika, 18, 34, 36, 38, 75n, 87, 198, 208,
    210, 211, 217–30, 233
Perestroika (dir. Tsukerman), 197, 198,
    208–11 (**209, 211**)
Peter I (Peter the Great), 94, 233, 239
Petrenko, Igor', 160
Petrushevskaia, Liudmila, 40, 41, 45n
Pineapple Water for a Beautiful Lady
    (Pelevin), 40
Piter FM (dir. Bychkova), 233
Platonov, Andrei, 34
Playing the Victim (dir. Serebrennikov), 36, 37
Plutser-Sarno, Alexei, 189, 190, 191
Pomerantsev, Vladimir, 33
Poor Liza (dir. Tsukerman), 197, 207, 208
Poor Liza (Karamzin), 206
Pop Mekhanika, 85
Popogrebskii, Aleksei, 37, 41, 44n
Poppy Appeal, 144
Porechenkov, Mikhail, 164
postmodernism, postmodernist, 31, 32, 33,
    34, 52, 53, 61, 95, 96, 98n, 102, 106
post-Soviet, 3, 6, 7, 8, 15–27, 31, 32, 35, 38,
    39, 40, 41, 42, 49, 50, 51, 52, 54–58,
    60, 69, 73, 83–98, 106, 121–30,

    133–41, 143, 145, 147, 167, 178, 182,
    183, 184, 187, 194n, 198, 208, 217,
    219, 220, 226, 235, 239
pre-Revolutionary, 123, 124, 127, 233, 240
Prigogine, Ilya, 98n
Prigov, Dmitrii, 38
Prilepin, Zakhar, 17
Prishvin, Mikhail, 17
Prokhanov, Aleksandr, 6, 67, 69, 70, 77n, 114
Prokofiev, Sergei, 241
Pronin, Viktor, 187
Proskurina, Svetlana, 37, 44n
protest , 4, 5. 136, 139, 169, 192
Protest Day (dir. Mokritskii), 5
Pushkin, Aleksandr, 31, 41, 69, 77n, 206
Pussy Riot, 5, 39
Putin, Vladimir, 4, 7, 38, 49, 67, 69, 70, 71,
    72, 73, 75n, 76n, 101, 106, 157–71,
    174n

R
Raduev, Salman, 68
Raikin, Arkadii, 157
Razenkov, Andrei, 243n
Reagan, Ronald, 69
Red Square, 112, 139
Red Square (dir. Kubaev, TV serial), 165
refusenik, 201
Revolution (October), 27, 35, 123, 139
revolution, revolutionary, 22, 35, 104, 109,
    113, 143, 164, 191, 208
Riazanov, El'dar, 233
Robskii, Oksana, 4
Rodchenko, Alexander, 85
Romeo and Juliet (Prokofiev), 241
Room and a Half, A (dir. Khrzhanovskii),
    33, 233
Rossiia (chocolate factory), 123
Rot Front (chocolate factory), 121, 123, 127,
    128, 130n
Rozanov, Vasilii, 107
Rubinstein, Lev, 223, 224
Russia Channel, 165

Russian Ark (dir. Sokurov), 233, 238, 242
Russians in Jerusalem (dir. Tsukerman), 202

S
Sacred Book of the Werewolf (Pelevin), 40, 49, 50, 54, 58–60
Salammbô (Flaubert), 122
samosud, 7, 177, 181–88, 189
School (dir. Gai-Germanika, TV serial), 36
School for Fools (Sokolov), 38
Semenev, Iurii, 161
Sentimental Policeman, The (dir. Muratova), 219
Serebrennikov, Kirill, 36, 44n
Seventeen Moments of Spring (dir. Lioznova), 36, 161, 162, 164
Seventh Seal, The (dir. Bergman), 200
Shalamov, Varlam, 40, 41
Sharov, Vladimir, 45n
Shchusev, Aleksei, 9n,
Sherman, Cindy, 94, 95
Shishkin, Mikhail, 34, 44n
Shishkin, Ivan, 124
Shnurov, Sergei, 41
Shprits, Mikhail, 20
Shukshin, Vasilii, 45n,
Shvarts, Elena, 38
Sigarev, Vasilii, 44n
Silent Souls (dir. Fedorchenko), 42
Silver Age, 3, 33, 34, 123
Sinyavsky [Siniavskii], Andrei, 38, 45n
Smirnov, Igor', 32
Smoktunovskii, Innokentii, 200, 213n
Sobchak, Kseniia, 4, 38
Socialist Realism, Socialist Realist, 6, 32, 33, 34, 35, 39, 53, 62n, 85, 87, 92, 96, 121
Sokol, Natalia, 189, 191
Sokolov, Sasha, 38, 45n
Sokurov, Aleksandr, 34, 38, 233, 238, 242
Solov'ev, Sergei, 83, 84
Solzhenitsyn, Aleksandr, 45n
Some Like it Hot (dir. Billy Wilder), 93
Sorokin, Vladimir, 33, 37, 39

sots-art, 53, 62n, 102, 103
Soviet identity, 3, 4, 7, 92, 95, 98n
Soviet past, 3, 4, 6, 7, 15, 16, 17, 18, 19, 20, 24, 26n, 83, 88, 92, 96, 101, 127, 129, 135, 139, 141, 145, 183, 217
St George Ribbon, 144–47
stagnation, 5, 18, 19, 198, 217
Stalin, Joseph (Iosif), 15, 26n, 83, 88, 89, 95, 112, 135, 139, 145, 174n, 207, 208, 211, 221
Stalin's Wife (dir. Tsukerman), 197, 207, 208
Stalinism, Stalinist, 3, 7, 17, 26n, 35, 37, 42, 106, 159, 166, 198, 207, 208, 210, 211, 221, 222, 223, 224
Starobinets, Anna, 20
Statue of Liberty, 113
Stirlitz, 36, 161, 162, 164, 166, 167, 174n,
Stone Bridge (Terekhov), 22
Stone Maples (Eltang), 37
Stroll, The (dir. Uchitel'), 233
Strugatsky, Arkadi and Boris, 45n
Sugar Kremlin, The (Sorokin), 39
Sukhorukov, Viktor, 235
Suprematism, Suprematist, 86
Svetozarov, Dmitrii, 243n
Sword and the Shield, The (dir. Basov), 161, 162

T
t (Pelevin), 40
Tabakov, Oleg, 226
Tales for Idiots (Akunin), 70
Tarkovsky, Andrei, 38, 45n
television, 6, 15, 16, 19, 22, 26n, 27n, 44n, 51, 52, 55, 56, 58, 67, 68, 69, 70, 72, 73, 74, 75n, 77n, 92, 138, 140, 161, 162, 163, 164, 168, 183, 188, 201, 207
Terekhov, Aleksandr, 22, 26n, 27n
Tereshkova, Valentina, 124
Tertz, Abram , see Sinyavsky
Thaw, 34, 35, 85, 197, 198, 217
These Were Our Years (TV show), 16
Three Stories (dir. Muratova), 219

Tikhonov, Viacheslav, 161
Todorovskii, Valerii, 17
Tolstoi, Aleksei, 17, 38
Tolstoy, Lev, 122
Tomb of the Unknown Soldier, 135, 139
Tomorrow (dir. Griazev), 5
totalitarianism, 101, 103
Tretyakov Gallery, 3
Trifonov, Iurii, 45n
Triumphal Arch, 3, 9n
Truce (dir. Proskurina), 37, 41
tsarist, 15, 124, 129, 159
Tsereteli, Zurab, 4
Tsoi, Viktor, 85
Tsukerman, Slava, 7, 197–211, 213n
Tuner, The (dir. Muratova), 40
Tvardovskii, Aleksandr, 38
Two in One (dir. Muratova), 40, 227

U
Uchitel', Aleksei, 233
Ul'ianov, Mikhail, 187
Ursuliak, Sergei, 36, 163
Utkin,Anton, 21
Utopia, utopian, 5, 8, 23, 38, 89, 101, 103, 104, 105, 224

V
Vaginov, Konstantin, 122
Varlamov, Aleksei, 17
Velvet Revolution, 18
VGIK (Film Institute), 198, 212n
Victory, 15, 26n, 89, 104, 108, 111–15, 131–52
    over Napoleon, 3, 9n, 122

VITCh (Benigsen), 20
Voina (art group), 5, 7, 39, 189–92 **(190, 191)**, 194n
Volga-Volga (dir. G. Aleksandrov), 83, 95
Volodin, Aleksandr, 34
Voloshin, Igor', 233
Voropaev, Anatolii, 157, 169
Voroshilov Sniper (dir. Govorukhin), 7, 177, 182–188 **(185, 186)**
Vorotnikov, Oleg, 189, 191
Voznesenskii, Andrei, 34, 67
Vyrypaev, Ivan, 36, 44n, 45n
Vysotsky, Vladimir, 162

W
War (dir. Balabanov), 242
Warhol, Andy, 53, 84, 94, 98n, 205
Wilde, Oscar, 5
Window on Paris (dir. Mamin), 233
Wölfflin, Heinrich, 31
World War, First, 110, 121, 129, 144, 202
World War, Second (see also Great Patriotic War), 15, 26n, 94, 110, 124, 133, 135, 138, 139, 140, 141, 143, 144, 145, 147

Y
Yeltsin, Boris, 4, 55, 67, 68, 70, 75n, 76n, 139, 159, 169, 187

Z
Zamiatin, Evgenii, 34
Zhirinovskii, Vladimir, 38
Zhulina, Olga, 157
Žižek, Slavoj, 18, 102
Zviagintsev, Andrei, 177–82, 183, 184